"The Clean Sample©"
Charcoal drawing by Mark Sisson

A Nation of Meddlers

Charles Edgley
Dennis Brissett

Westview Press
A Member of the Perseus Books Group

For Den
Who always cared, but rarely meddled
Good-bye, dear friend

Copyright © 1999 by Westview Press, A Member of the Perseus Books Group

Published in 1999 in the United States of America by Westview Press, 5500 Central Avenue, Boulder, Colorado 80301-2877, and in the United Kingdom by Westview Press, 12 Hid's Copse Road, Cumnor Hill, Oxford OX2 9JJ

Library of Congress Cataloging-in-Publication Data
Edgley, Charles.
   A nation of meddlers / by Charles Edgley & Dennis Brissett.
      p.   cm.
   Includes bibliographical references and index.
   ISBN 0-8133-3307-5
   1. United States—Social policy.   2. Social control—United
States.   3. Social reformers—United States.   4. Privacy—United
States.   5. Liberty.   I. Brissett, Dennis.   II. Title.
HN59.2.E25   1999
361.6'1'0973—dc21   98-45152
                                                                              CIP

The paper used in this publication meets the requirements of the American National Standard for Permanence of Paper for Printed Library Materials Z39.48-1984.

10   9   8   7   6   5   4   3   2   1

Contents

Preface

This book is a continuation of themes we began analyzing in the mid-1980s. During that period we were observing the rapid and, in some respects, curious changes that were taking place in the way Americans related to one another around the ubiquitous and problematic notion of "health." These observations were assisted by the fact that we both taught medical topics at the university level—Brissett in the medical school at the University of Minnesota in Duluth (UMD), and Edgley in the sociology department at Oklahoma State University. In 1990, we published a piece titled "Health Nazis and the Cult of the Perfect Body" in the journal *Symbolic Interaction*. That article focused on the increasing incidence of what seemed to us nothing short of political fascism in the name of health—an ethic of shape-up-or-else. Later, after our examination of this emerging social phenomenon had been completed, it occurred to us that what we were calling health fascism was in fact merely a subtype of a broader social and cultural phenomenon—meddling. Thus the idea for this book was born.

Having written books and articles together before, we proceeded in our usual fashion, sending ideas and sources back and forth, meeting when we could, and tying up the phone lines between Minnesota and Oklahoma. This strategy was routinely interrupted by our respective professorial duties—which we had learned over a lifetime of collaboration to live with—but little did we know that tragic and fateful events would intervene to alter forever the nature of this project.

In February 1996, Dennis Brissett was diagnosed with multiple-site carcinoma. This gentle and honorable man, gifted thinker, influential teacher, and keen observer of everyday life was dying. Yet in spite of operations, chemotherapy, and days and weeks of pain, alleviated only partially by a pharmacopoeia that more often than not made him only sicker, his one wish, other than his hope for courage and acceptance in the face of the inevitable, was to work on this project as much as possible until the end. We did just that.

What we wanted to accomplish was to steer a subtle course between the politicized rhetoric of the right and the left—between what James Slaughter calls the "forces of order" and the "forces of liberty"—in order to produce a reasoned and textured analysis of what we believe to be one of the most significant cultural trends in contemporary America: the increasing tendency of Americans to meddle into each other's lives. It became apparent that this would be a very difficult task, for the same forces that have set off so much meddling in American culture also constitute the bipolar culture of postmodernism, whose center has become a black hole that seemingly sucks away all attempts at middle ground. Yet Denny insisted that we persevere, and I believe that the subtle distinctions he created between connection and privacy, along with his insistence on a sense of humility in conducting our relationships with others, allowed us to do exactly that. The argument in this book is therefore not an appeal to conservatives, liberals, libertarians, or any other political ideology. Indeed, there is much in it to offend all of these groups. Social scientists, whose own contribution to the increase in the sum total of meddlesome interventions is occasionally pointed out, may be particularly outraged. Yet our appeal for a less meddlesome society is both moral and practical. It is moral in the sense that it appeals to community and fraternity—traditional common grounds for both liberals and conservatives. And it is practical because, as is becoming ever more obvious, meddling simply engenders more meddling, and things get worse. But whereas the left abandoned much of this discourse in favor of a rhetoric of rights during the 1960s, the right (especially at its extremes) produced virtucrats like William Bennett and totalitarians like Patrick Buchanan for whom community and fraternity were little more than buzzwords for racism, fascism, and repression—for a "police state with cable TV." We believe that the reasoned middle ground we have forged, especially in the conclusion, is both sensible and workable. Most of the thinking here is Den's.

Denny worked on this project until the end. But that end came much too soon, and the call I knew would come was delivered by a close mutual friend on August 11, 1996, shortly after 8 P.M. He died at home in the company of his wife of thirty-four years and two of his four children. He was fifty-six years old. His notes about this work were on top of his desk—he had worked on them last just a few days before he died. This book is therefore a final written testimony to a life filled with accomplishment, loyalty, friendship, laughter, and love. Generations of medical students are better doctors because they knew him. Sociology graduate students could not have had a better mentor and friend. No matter how young you were when he took you on, you were never just a student but a priceless colleague. Students were drawn to him not simply because of his warmth and humanity, but because intellectually he was a giant. He was better at approaching the ideal set out by Georg Lichtenberg than anyone I have ever known: "to split an idea that everyone views as simple into seven others, just as a prism refracts light into different rays, one more beautiful than the next, and then again to collect an array of these and produce clarity where others see nothing but a dazzling confusion." Also one of the most modest, self-effacing, and almost shy men I have ever known, Den would blush at being compared to Georg Simmel or Erving Goffman, and yet he belongs in their company. Like them, he was a master of the art of insight and understanding.

Working with Denny was a genuine pleasure, and if you ever worked with him, he never let you go. If lives and careers momentarily took you in different directions, he would always see to it that they cycled back. He was a master of constructively criticizing his colleagues' work without in any way criticizing them. He never thought that any of us had it "right," and his work was never elitist but always inclusive. He managed to avoid all the silliness of intellectual fads and fashions in both his personal and professional life. He had steady convictions by which he lived, and passions for his work, but at the same time he believed, along with Kenneth Burke, that all academic systems are games—to be played seriously, but without the commitment of faith. Denny was never dogmatic; he recognized the multiplicity of possible perspectives with which to make sense of life. To the extent that this book reflects a sense of humility, it is because of Den. To the extent that it does not, it is because of my passions and excesses, which went untempered in the last stages of the development of a manuscript that needed his deft editorial touch more than ever as it neared completion. But in spite of his ability to see and give credence to the views of almost everyone, Den was never lost; he always knew who he was and what was important, both intellectually and personally. Even though his body failed him, he was, in the most genuine and historically accurate sense of the term, the healthiest person I have ever known.

This is not the book we would have completed had he lived, for after thirty years of collaboration we had become right and left arms to each other. Writing from a small room on the third floor of his home in Duluth, Minnesota, he tempered my intellectual excesses with his down-to-earth good sense. Lofty abstractions and attempts to engage in what P. M. Strong calls the kind of "intergalactic paradigm-mongering that frequently passes for really serious sociology" were always met by his good-humored reminder that we should confine ourselves as simply as possible to a description, analysis, and interpretation of the interpersonal features of the culture of everyday life. Hardly a Luddite, he nevertheless distrusted all attempts to reduce the study of humankind to technical formulas. He never mistook mere information for communication. His writing was always in longhand on plain paper, and his frequent letters usually ended cheerily with a comment about the weather in northern

Minnesota, a place he dearly loved. His own sense of community, fraternity, and fellowship can be seen throughout this book. Denny loved people—all kinds of people—and many of them who knew him in his everyday life probably didn't know he was a full professor in a medical school; his humanity and decency transcended work titles and the trappings of role that so many people take so seriously. He was the least pretentious person you could ever meet. Being his best friend was easy, for when you were in his presence, he made you feel like the most important person in his life. But you knew, too, that you were one among many, for he had countless best friends—Bob Snow at Arizona State, Ray Oldenburg at the University of West Florida, Kent Sandstrom at Northern Iowa, Mary Zimmerman at the University of Kansas, and Ramona Asher, Gary Davis, Bob Gibson, Larry Witmers, and Janelle Wilson at UMD, to mention just a few. Those of us who had the honor of knowing him were blessed with a friend whose intellect was tempered by a sensitivity to the often discouraging demands of life. Those who didn't had only to visit the Pickwick Tavern on the shores of Lake Superior, where he often stopped after work to keep in touch with his fellow man through the simple art of conversation. His spirit will undoubtedly meet you there and bid you welcome.

Charles Edgley

Acknowledgments

The major person to acknowledge upon completion of this book is not a colleague, a critic, an editor, or a spouse; it is my friend and coauthor, Dennis Brissett. Denny's death in August 1996 left an enormous void, but also created a driving desire to see the manuscript to completion. Nothing has been more difficult, or more rewarding, than to finally complete the last project that will carry his name. His presence was over my shoulder at all times.

Many friends and colleagues have also helped along the way. I should like to thank Ray Oldenburg and Robert Snow, two of our best mutual friends, who provided intellectual and personal companionship, inspiration, and guidance at time when such support was dearly needed. The same was done by others, some of whom you met in the book's Preface.

Several people at Westview Press have enthusiastically supported this project from the beginning, and were extraordinarily gracious and understanding when Denny's death left the project behind schedule. Lisa Wigutoff, the project editor, played a number of key roles in keeping the book on track. I should also especially like to thank Christine Arden, Westview's copy editor, who did the most competent and conscientious editing job one could have imagined. Intuitively grasping the point of the argument, she not only edited but pointed out inconsistencies and suggested additions of her own. She proved to be a colleague as much as an editor. The book would have been infinitely poorer without her deft touch. Thank you, Christine.

Some personal indebtednesses also need to be acknowledged. The members of Denny's family—wife Kareen and children Mark, Steve, Mara, and Sarah—have always treated me like family, opening both their home and their hearts for years before and certainly after Den died. I hope that in some way the completion of this book partially repays a debt I could never fully acknowledge or return to these special people.

The colleagues with whom Denny worked most closely at the Duluth campus were always in the background and, whenever I was in town, looked after me like the close friends they are. Janelle Wilson, Gary Davis, Larry Witmers, Bill Fleishman, Bob Gibson, and the elusive "Irishman" (the only name Den ever called him) contributed to this book in numerous ways unknown to them. Tracy Kemp, on the staff of the UMD Behavioral Science Division of the Medical School, played a special part in deciphering Denny's handwriting during the many years of correspondence required to get this project in order.

My own colleagues at Oklahoma State University were a constant source of support. Ed Lawry, Maureen Nemecek, and Wen-Song Hwu—my luncheon companions on the first Monday of every month for the past five years—heard every line of this book's argument at one time or another. Their patience and enthusiastic support in the face of my intellectual obsessions about the subject are especially appreciated. Michael Taylor helped me to understand the relationship between many of these ideas and the ethical framework of Emmanuel Levinas—an understanding that led to a sharper and more focused conclusion. Patricia Bell of the Department of Sociology contributed more to this project than she will ever know, both by participating in numerous discussions with me about the triumph of the meddlers, about which she has keen insights, and, perhaps even more important, as my department head, by keeping the university bureaucracy at bay so that I would have the time I needed to complete the manuscript. My friend and colleague Ken Kiser's intellectual and personal support have been a part of my life for twenty-five years. Many of the themes in this book were inspired by lively and insightful conversations with him about changes in contemporary culture. Mark Sisson of OSU's art department provided us with the charcoal drawing "The Clean Sample," which forms the frontispiece for the book, at just the right time. Christina Myers deserves special thanks for working through several nights to help meet the deadline for the index.

And, finally, this book is for Sally—for reasons too numerous and personal to be mentioned here.

C. E.

1

America:
A Nation of Meddlers

*Every third American devotes himself to improving and uplifting his fellow-citizen,
usually by force.*
—**H. L. Mencken**

There was a time long ago when the phrase "it's none of your business"
meant something. Not anymore. A boorish and persistent army of meddlers, equipped with righteous indignation and a formidable array of the-
ories and technologies, has made almost everyone's business its own.
Meddling in the lives of others is now the republic's most visible obsession. Examples are everywhere—from national crusades against bad
habits such as drinking, smoking, and gambling to the efforts of a group
in Woodbury, Minnesota, to create a "fragrance-free" work environment
where workers are insulated not only from the disgusting stench of tobacco smoke but also from the aroma of perfumes, shampoos, and after-
shave lotion. In Phoenix, Arizona, the city council passes a law requiring
that the installation of a swimming pool be accompanied by the child-
proofing of any access from the house to the pool, even if no children reside in the house. A company markets an instant urine cleaning kit so that
purchasers can tidy up their chemistry before going to work. In Floss-
moor, Illinois, the town council invokes an ancient ordinance outlawing
pickup trucks because their image is "inconsistent with residential living." In Tacoma Park, Maryland, a group of "concerned citizens" tries to
ban outdoor grills and lawn mowers, spawning a countermovement that
calls itself "pro-choice" on the question of charcoal and Toros. Twelve employees of Safeway file grievances after the supermarket chain mandates
that they smile and make eye-contact. Employees who fail to present an
appropriately friendly front are nabbed by company spies posing as customers and sent to a day-long remedial class that the employees dub
"smile school." A California entrepreneur has a new idea that he is certain
will sell: drug-sniffing dogs for the private sector. Parents, he said, could

rent them to sniff out their kids' rooms to see if they're hiding drugs. And big business could use them to sniff out the desks of employees they suspect of using drugs. That would avoid all those constitutional questions about urine testing and lie detector tests. Surveillance efforts by employers such as electronically monitoring the number of keystrokes per minute executed by computer operators, videotaping production lines, and timing employee visits to the bathroom seem all too commonplace.

Whereas a certain amount of meddling seems endemic to human association, the historical record indicates that, in earlier times, meddling was perpetrated almost exclusively in terms of widely agreed-upon precepts of public morality and civic duty. Such moral and civic meddling, though often resented, was at least expected, and was confined primarily to legitimate authorities and institutions. Other persons who meddled, such as gossips, snoops, and assorted amateur practitioners of the meddling trade, have always been high on the list of public nuisances.[1] But the quantum leap in meddling came in the last half-century when the roster was extended to include full-time practitioners who actually made a living meddling into other people's lives. As Philip Rieff (1991) has described it, this "triumph of the therapeutic" resulted in a proliferation of professional meddlers. Even H. L. Mencken, that dogged critic of the meddlesome impulse, might be surprised if he were still around to see how much more that impulse rules the country now than it did at the turn of the century. We meddle in the name of almost everything: health, safety, efficiency, the bottom line, God, "the children"—you name it, and there will most likely be someone there to meddle on its behalf. We meddle with virtually anyone who crosses either our path or our vested interests. And we meddle with just about anything people do as long as it happens to be something we ourselves do not do. We have become a nation of meddlers.

Just what is meddling? Many people don't know, and most find the word obscure and amusingly quaint. For in late-twentieth-century America the term—which still carries with it (properly, we think) a multitude of negative connotations—has been euphemized through a wide variety of double-talk. As a result, much meddling appears in the guise of altruistic service supplied by helpful benefactors. At its barest minimum, *to meddle* means to mix, mingle, combine, blend, or intersperse. This all sounds fairly neutral; but, in actual historical use, the term *meddling* has customarily carried with it strongly adverse sentiment, suggesting the unwelcome and usually annoying attention that another is directing to one's affairs.

In what appears to be its earliest usage, the term dates back to Herodotus (c. 445 B.C.), for whom meddling was "stirring something that should not be stirred." That description still strikes us as both apt and contemporary, although there is always plenty of disagreement about what should and should not be stirred. The word appears again in Watson's

(1602) *Decacordon*, which contains the phrase: "The priests found more favour at the hands of the civil magistrates than the Jesuits could find because they had cleared themself of all state meddles." In 1864, the remark was made that "the foreign policy of the noble Earl [of Darby] may be summed up in two short, homely but expensive words–'meddle' and 'muddle.'" And the tombstone of Captain Archibald Campbell, laid to rest in an island cemetery near Venice in 1891, says simply: "The heart knoweth its own bitterness and the stranger intermeddleth not therewith."

Meddlers, of course, are people who meddle; and although a somewhat favorable connotation for *"meddling* can occasionally be salvaged through a definitional twist, meddlers are almost universally despised. According to Earle Miscrosm, "A meddling man is one that has nothing to do with his business, and yet no man is busier than hee." In an essay written in 1850, Thomas Macaulay warned of "a meddling government, a government which tells them what to read, and say, and eat, and drink, and wear." Thomas Fuller in 1792 told us that meddlers are "the Devil's body-lice, they fetch the blood from those that feed them." Jane Taylor's (1801/1976) *Original Poems for the Infant Mind* feature the infamous character "Meddlesome Matty," who made everyone else's business her own. And a Scottish proverb urges that we "Come not to council unbidden." The hazards resident to the meddler are also well known, as attested by the English proverb that reminds us to "never put your hand between the bark and the tree."

Meddling Transformed:
The Euphemisms of Meddling

During a time when people spoke more plainly, there were countless words that suggested meddling. People complained about meddlers in no uncertain terms: *Bother, butt in, fiddle, horn in, impose upon, mess* or *monkey with, prattle, pry, tamper, tinker, trespass*, and *violate* were all used to describe meddlesome behavior. Informally we may still hear an occasional reference to such colorful complaints, but the terrain has changed. In an age where the skills of public-relations merchants transform anything into something else, one almost never hears the word *meddling* except in a jocular context. Since we seem to have forgotten that some aspects of a person's life ought to be preserved beyond the reach of the meddlesome impulse, the term *meddling* has also had to be transformed.

Workers and bureaucrats in the helping professions are among the more visible representatives of meddling by euphemism. Social workers, for instance, never meddle; they engage in "professional intervention strategies." They and their colleagues don't butt in or tamper with other people's lives; they practice "crisis intervention," especially with drinkers, poor people, addicts, and the mentally ill. They don't intrude or tinker; they "empower" or "treat." They have a "professional involvement" with a "client," "patient," or "case." Meddling itself is transformed into assessment, negotiation, and case management. Encroachment and invasion into the life of another is converted through the fustian language of psychotherapy into a "professional confrontation" and is simply part of what skillful "therapy" is all about. Should the client happen to believe that the intervener is actually meddling, and have the temerity to say so, the client, of course, is charged with being in "denial." By postulating the psychological reality of denial in their clients, meddlers can force unwilling ones to do their bidding and at the same time feel justified and even noble in doing so. By casting the object of one's meddling as a person who is variously impaired, disabled, ignorant, wrong-headed, or sick, the professional meddler is able to discount the meddlee's version of reality as a distortion emerging from whatever underlying condition is alleged to be the cause of the meddlee's problem.

There are also a growing number of meddlers, professional and otherwise, who engage in education and public-awareness programs. Health promotion experts who regale against the horrors of obesity, alcohol, fat, and sugar would have us believe that they are not meddling but simply educating an ignorant public.[2] Busybodies and crybabies are mystically transformed into "concerned" citizens and "social action" groups engaged in improving the commonweal. Members of Mothers Against Drunk Driving (MADD) who intrude in the court proceedings of intoxicated drivers by mau-mauing judges and lawyers are not meddling; they are "friends of the court" educating the judiciary about the reality of drunken driving. The hordes of sincere migrants who travel from city to city confronting each other on right-to-life issues are not meddling but simply demonstrating their deep moral convictions in an effort to make a better world. Nowadays, those who would bother other people, impose their values, and interfere with their fellow citizens' lives are rarely denounced as loathsome meddlers and seldom admonished to mind their own business. Instead, they are more likely to be regarded as altruistic people demonstrating an honest and benevolent concern for their fellow citizens.[3]

Toward a Definition of Meddling

A century ago it would have been unnecessary to define meddling—everyone knew what it was and denounced it roundly. As the term has since fallen into disuse, however, a fresh definition is in order. To wit: Meddling involves a thrusting of oneself, often boldly, into the affairs of others. Meddlesome acts are those which impertinently and promiscuously tamper with that which, under usual and ordinary circumstances, would not be considered within the domain of the meddler. Meddling, then, can range from simple nosiness or eavesdropping to the offering of services or attention, to outright, direct interference in other people's lives. Meddlesome acts are intrusions, or obtrusions, that invade what is ordinarily considered to be another's private world. It is the very power of the meddler to convert the usual into the unusual, and the ordinary into the extraordinary, that allows the private realm of the meddlee to be viewed as a public arena susceptible to—indeed, requiring—meddlesome intervention. So, in a fundamental sense, meddling involves an appropriation of and a proprietorship over the heretofore private matters of another, whether these be matters of word, deed, or thought. Whatever the subject of the meddling, or the manner in which it is done, meddling implies that the meddlee is not comporting him- or herself as he or she might. Nevertheless, from the standpoint of the meddlee, most meddling is seen (at least initially) as unwelcome, if not downright improper, and certainly unnecessary, annoying, or offensive.[4]

There are, of course, instances (and these are multiplying rapidly in this therapeutic state) in which people actually volunteer to be meddled with. These individuals willingly, if not eagerly, visit any one of the growing legions of professional meddlers who bill themselves as ready to deal with those tortured souls overwhelmed by their problems and victimized by their circumstances. Soul-baring has become a national obsession. Turn on any talk show and you are likely to encounter an increasingly diverse array of pitiful wretches divulging the dirty secrets of their lives to a national audience. Self-help groups abound, all predicated on the idea that baring one's soul—not merely to a friend, clergyman, or confidant but to as wide a group of witnesses as possible—is therapeutic. These venues at least have the saving grace of being more or less voluntary. But there are many more instances in which people seek out professional meddlers as the least unfavorable option among a number of diminishing and less attractive alternatives. The benevolent coercion often used to "encourage" drinkers to "voluntarily" submit to the meddling of alcoholism treatment is a prime example. Under these circumstances, which now apply to a much wider range of personal problems than drinking, the incipient meddlee opts for the lesser of a number of evils. The alcoholic is offered treatment instead of jail time; the schizophrenic, therapy instead of mental hospitalization; the drug addict, counseling instead of a court appearance. The offering of such Faustian deals defines a situation that may be technically "voluntary" but hardly free. It is an offering that one refuses at one's own peril.[5] Unfortunately, most meddling goes well beyond even this dubious measure of assent and involves actions that are clearly against the objections of the person or persons being meddled with–a kind of interpersonal rape. Whereas involuntary incarceration and rehabilitation are perhaps the most easily discernible of these, most everyday, nonprofessional meddling also involves the unsolicited and often unwelcome sticking of the meddler's nose into someone else's business.

Obviously, not all this meddling is bad. In fact, the consequences of meddling, at least in terms of what the meddler wishes to accomplish, may be quite positive. But whether meddlesome interventions succeed or not (and there is always a way to make them seem successful), a deeper concern is the *attitude* of meddling that has become so prevalent in our society. Increasingly, it seems, people are stampeded into believing, with very little reflection and much headstrong arrogance about the matter, that meddling and being meddled with are cultural virtues—indeed, that they are the hallmark of what good people do for each other. In fact, the alternative to meddling is now often seen as an apathetic, uncaring, isolated disregard for others, symbolized by those tragic instances in which cries for help go unheard or unanswered. Meddling presumably alters this apathetic scenario by demonstrating one's "concern." Still, although apathy and isolation may well be problems in themselves, it seems to us that the solution to them does not reside in the meddlesome acts that now pass for community spirit and social involvement.[6]

An even more pernicious aspect of meddling, however, is the fact that meddling is done so impertinently. It is the impudent arrogance, effrontery, and audacious presumptions of the meddler that make meddling so different from most other forms of human association. Meddlers neither approve nor indulge the meddlee's behavior. At the same time, they presume to understand—or at least claim to be in possession of an understanding of how to understand–not just the behavior but the self, relationships, and entire life of the meddlee.[7] In short, it is the meddlers wholesale, know-it-all arrogation of the meddlee that makes meddling the bane of modern civilization. In the process, differences between the meddler and meddlee become inequalities, establishing the moral, intellectual, and psychological superiority of the meddler. As Alida Brill (1990: 74) has observed, "[P]rivacy invasions are virtually always justified for a higher moral purpose or public good or for a nobler motivation than privacy protection." So it is little wonder that people take such pride in being meddlers. Indeed, meddling may well be the last bastion of socially sanctioned snobbery in an egalitarian society.

The Circumstances of Meddling

An understanding of the circumstances in which people meddle tells us much about this pestilence abroad in the land. Unlike more noble attempts to mediate disrupted relationships such as apologies and excuses, those time-honored techniques with which we bind up relationships gone awry, meddling is rarely a response to those who have somehow directly interrupted or interfered with the meddler's own behavior. Rather, meddling involves the "disinterested tendency," of which Svend Ranulf (1937) spoke earlier in this century, to inflict punishment or control over others whenever the meddler's rights, or those of his or her agent or constituents, have allegedly been violated. In a nation besieged by "rights talk," agents and constituents are important players in the meddling situation because so much meddling is done in the name of someone or something else. These claimed rights may range from such mundane ambitions as a "decent night's sleep" or "peace and quiet" to the more sublime privileges of living in a safe, moral, and healthy world, free of everything from sidestream smoke to the disturbing knowledge that Arctic seal pups are being dispatched by lucripetous Danes. Meddling serves to reaffirm these rights by intruding into the lives of those who violate them.[8]

Having one's rights violated unfortunately carries with it these days the insistent counterright, or even obligation, to meddle with the violator. In a nation devoted to converting every privilege, need, aspiration, and interest into a right, it becomes more and more difficult to escape the wrath of someone's meddlesome behavior. As the epidemic of potential victims alleging sexual and other harassments so clearly illustrates, somebody's rights may be violated by almost anything one says or does. It is therefore not the least bit surprising that the protection of such claimed rights has occasioned a burgeoning number of vigilantes, snoops, and tattletales. For example, it would stretch the bounds of credulity to claim that the consumption of fatty foods violates the rights of others. Yet in the postmodern[9] sense of things, such brazen dietary misconduct is often an occasion for meddlesome intrusions that question the miscreant's intelligence, moral fitness, or addictive personality. Eating with others these days is often less a celebration of food and friendship than an opportunity for critical assessments of the amount and kind of food on our neighbors' plates. In a nation of meddlers there is always someone watching. As Henry Fairlie (1989: 43), writing in *The New Republic*, observes: "We used to raise our hands in horror at the Cultural Revolution in China, when friends and even family informed on women who used cosmetics. But America too is becoming a nation of informers. We are encouraged to go around checking on everyone's eating, drinking, smoking, sexual proclivities, and general hygiene."

Situations in which people meddle may also involve a violation of the meddlers' sense of truth or belief; that is, meddlers simply believe they know what people should and should not be doing. Whether the source of this belief is divine inspiration, scientific observation, "special knowledge," or life experience, meddlers, as a group, envision themselves to be inside dopesters. They not only know the right thing to do but also presume to know the connections of people's actions to their bodies, psyches, and souls, as well as to society and the world at large. Meddlers are comfortable generalizing from the specific, limited, and usually physical consequences of certain behaviors to the yet largely uncharted realms of character, personality, and social fabric. There is little doubt, for example, that smoking, drinking, and unsafe sex may be bad for people's bodies. But it is an arrogant act of meddlesome faith to then claim that such indulgences are necessarily bad for their minds, selves, psyches, and souls. Meddlers are true believers who confuse the frequent validity of their particularistically derived views with a proprietary right to impose their generalizations full-bloom on others. In a nation of puritanical meddlers, *should* is the predominant word and the consequences of those things that one *should not do* are regularly generalized far beyond any reasonable evidentiary standard.

Moreover, meddling often arises when the meddlee's behavior is construed by the meddler to be of evil or unsavory portent. Meddlers fancy themselves as seers, divining the long-term consequences of what could just as well be construed as situationally contained behaviors. Meddlers seldom see acts as discrete, viewing them instead as slippery slopes. Certain bad behaviors lead ineluctably to other worse behaviors. Smoking leads to drinking. Drinking leads to alcoholism. Alcoholism leads to child abuse, broken marriages, co-dependency, violence, and highway carnage. Better to nip such behaviors in the bud. Meddlers are quintessential bud-nippers. In their view, life is a series of progressive or regressive diseases for which early intervention is the only antidote. So, part of the circumstance under which people meddle involves the imperial sense that the direction of the meddlee's life is wrong and can only lead to rack and ruin.[10] Stopping things in their tracks is the only way to avoid the banefully inevitable catastrophes that lie ahead. We are all only a drink, a cigarette, or a one-night stand away from utter devastation.

Meddling also occurs when there is a violation of the meddler's sense of self-conviction. Meddlers seem to meddle most when the behavior of the meddlee challenges, discredits, or undermines the self of the meddler. In a nation where selfhood is becoming more and more defined by what people *don't* do than by what they do, defending oneself becomes a matter of attacking and controlling what others do. The meddlee's own self-denial becomes the justification for denying others the opportunity to do whatever it is that the meddler is not doing. In this sense, people meddle because their very selves are threatened. Deviance, from whatever standard is asserted or presumed, challenges the life of the meddler—not by threatening to sweep him into the abyss of inequity implicit in the meddlee's dissolute behavior but merely by existing. Deviants undermine the meddler's self-assurance by demonstrating and living the obverse. As the politics of postmodern society becomes more and more a matter of someone's preferred way of living being imposed on everyone else, it is almost as if much meddling is done not because the meddler really cares about the person in whose life he is intruding but, rather, because he fears that if people are allowed to live that way, pretty soon he'll be forced to live that way too.

These days, however, people are known not only by what they don't *do* but also by what they don't *tolerate.* "I don't drink, smoke, use drugs, or eat the wrong foods" is not enough. Now self is preserved by adding emphatically: "and I don't tolerate those who do!" If the meddlee seems to be happy, interesting, fun-loving, and perhaps even healthy, satisfied, and fulfilled, this fact only increases the grim-faced challenge offered the meddler. A colleague of ours recently acceded to the nagging of family and friends by making an appointment at the university's "Wellness" Center to have a complete medical workup. After passing all the physical tests with flying colors, he was instructed to fill out a questionnaire about his life. He confessed that he drinks quite a bit, smokes cigarettes, doesn't exercise, and eats unapproved foods. Because of his excellent physical condition, the practitioners at first accused him of lying; and when he convinced them he had been truthful, they insisted that he was of a rare type who, though in perfectly good health, dies suddenly with no warning. Such responses are increasingly common among meddlers who don't get their way.

In a society where character may always be on trial, people now establish who they are by making clear, often in a meddlesome way, what they do not approve of. This aspect of situations in which people meddle is reminiscent of Eric Hoffer's (1966) observation in *The True Believer:* "The burning conviction that we have a holy duty toward others is often a way of attaching our drowning selves to a passing raft. What looks like a hand is often a holding on for dear life. Take away our holy duties and you leave our lives puny and meaningless" (p. 23). Moreover:

> A man is likely to mind his own business when it is worth minding. When it is not, he takes his mind off his own meaningless affairs by minding other people's business.
>
> This minding of other people's business expresses itself in gossip, snooping, and meddling. . . . In running away from ourselves we either fall on our neighbor's shoulder or fly at his throat. (p. 23)

Meddlers as Peddlers of Anti-Themes

Since meddlers perceive meddlees as engaged in actions the former regard as negative, dangerous, unhealthy, and the like, meddlers are indomitable peddlers of anti-themes. The negative theme is ostensibly more powerful than its positive counterpart. Meddlers meddle out of a self-righteous certainty with which the meddlee can hardly argue. Manichaean dualisms abound in the rhetoric of meddlers. To oppose MADD, for example, is to somehow condone highway carnage "caused" by alcohol. To support the privilege of persons in a free society to use drugs as they see fit is to advocate heroin. To fail to denounce smokers at every opportunity is to endorse cancer. The threat ostensibly posed by passive smoke becomes a grim symbol of our times—innocent people being done in by the seemingly innocuous habits of others. The ubiquitous signs, warnings, and notices prohibiting something or other have become a commonplace feature of the American landscape. One of the authors, while navigating the 100-foot passage between the outside door and the elevator to his office, last counted ten different signs forbidding certain forms of noxious conduct. Such anti-themes have come to permeate our society. From "Just say no" opponents of drugs to animal rights activists who would strip the fur coats off your dinner guests, the world has become a war zone for meddlers armed with a special anti-interest and a totalitarian vision of a world made safe by stamping out those who differ. Everyone seems to have an anti-theme. In fact, assembling, associating, and organizing to *not* do something, though seemingly illogical, has become quite fashionable these days. Yet ironically a language of freedom is increasingly being used by meddlers to cloak their anti-ideology. Adjectives such as *smoke-free, alcohol-free, radon-free, prayer-free*, and *fragrance-free* are proudly touted as identifying settings in which certain behaviors or substances are disallowed. This postmodern freedom for people not to do something that they were never required to do in the first place, replaces the more classical freedom to do what one wishes. Bumper stickers abound with the international "no" symbol (Ø), the perfect icon for an age in which people are coming to be known more by what they aren't than by what they are (see Figure 1.1).

Meddling as Both Avocation and Vocation

Although there are many different species and subspecies of meddlers, most fall into two basic groups: amateur or avocational meddlers and professional or vocational meddlers. Like amateur and professional athletes, they are defined by the role that money plays in their endeavors. And as with athletes, the distinction can be thin, for it is often difficult to say, in any given case, that economic issues are not at stake when people of any stripe meddle.

Nevertheless, avocational meddlers engage in meddling largely for reasons other than the fact that it is their job, and vocational meddlers do so—in spite of lofty protestations to the contrary—because it *is*. Avocational meddlers include snoops and busybodies, whose aforementioned

FIGURE 1.1   Signs of the Times

(continues)

FIGURE 1.1   Signs of the Times *(continued)*

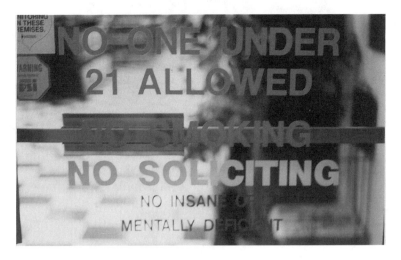

character vices are as universally decried as they are
commonly practiced. This category also includes social-action
groups, "concerned" citizens,
chronic volunteers and board
members, parents and relatives,
"friends" and neighbors, and
those with whom one works. Vocational meddlers, on the other
hand, meddle for money; and
this simple fact considerably alters the relationship between the
meddler and the meddlee, moving it–no matter how much its
honestly motivated and sincere

FIGURE 1.2   A Rare Response to the
All-too-prevalent "No"

incumbents would wish otherwise–from a relational to a cash nexus. Vocational meddlers include a vast and growing array of personnel ranging
from social workers, psychologists, and psychiatrists to lawyers, admin-
istrators, and government bureaucrats. The latter, operating on the belief
that the presence of rules and regulations produces safety, security, and
assurance, attempt to extend their own sphere of influence while claiming the noble justification of protecting the innocent. Despite the loftiness
of motive, however, the primary task of all vocational meddlers is staying in business. Offices must be kept running, positions must be kept
filled, budgets must be increased, promotions and raises must go on
apace. The first concern of the meddling trades is steady work—and, indeed, meddling is perhaps the closest thing there is to a "recession-
proof" business. The only thing that could conceivably depress the economic forecast for professional meddlers would be an outbreak of health,
harmony, and happiness. Unfortunately, however, these virtues have
been so narrowly redefined by those same professionals that they now
function more as utopian abstractions than as achievable realities.

The meddling professions thus constitute a kind of "industry" that interferes with some in the name of protecting others. In the process they
inevitably develop a vested interest in conflicts and difficulties between
the rest of us. The legal profession is, of course, the preeminent example;
but there is also a "divorce industry," that group of professional meddlers who make millions of dollars every year off marital turmoil, much
of which they have a hand in creating themselves. The divorce trade includes not only attorneys but marriage counselors, family therapists, real
estate agents, and those who make their livings off of the inevitable re-
marriages which follow divorce. And of course, there is psychiatry,

which, in concert with the law, has turned the entire human condition into a fertile ground for meddling. These groups are what Thomas Szasz (1994: 35) has called the "montebanks of the hindering professions," and their numbers and presence make it increasingly difficult to live one's life without the interference of those who meddle for a living. Erving Goffman (1961), in turn, has spoken of these occupations as the "tinkering" trades, which have as their goal the "conversion of persons with problems into clients in need of service"–an apt description of the current predicament.

The Cultural Context of Meddling

This has not always been a nation of meddlers. Indeed, America was founded by some of the most virulent anti-meddlers ever assembled. Having been hounded and interfered with especially, but not exclusively, in the practice of their religious faiths by hordes of European tyrants, the founders drafted the Federalist papers and thereby set a definite anti-meddling tone that prevailed at least for a time. "Leave people alone" was the byword. The first coin minted in the United States, the Fugio Cent in 1778, carried the phrase "Mind your own business." Designed by Benjamin Franklin, the coin made it clear that this was to be a limited government for a nation of people involved in their own self-directed activities. Moreover, because these individuals were separated by geography and had only a primitive means of communication, access to and meddling with other people's affairs were difficult; yet meddling would clearly have been unacceptable even if it had been easier.

Such secular founders of the new nation as Thomas Paine and Benjamin Franklin were, however, different from their more devout constituents. Slowly, the actual meaning of such a radical non-interventionist stance began to dawn on believers in the pure and righteous truth. Among its more troubling implications was the realization that a social ethic based on being left alone to pursue one's own interests contravened one's right to interfere with other people's pursuit of interests with which one disagreed. Gore Vidal, writing in *The Nation*, blames much of the historical increase in meddling on religious zealots— sky-godders, he calls them—who were never happy with the paradoxical restraints of secularism:

> From the beginning, sky-godders have always exerted great pressure in our secular republic. . . . [C]hurches were organized in order to make certain that the rights of property were respected and that the numerous religious taboos in the New and Old Testaments would be enforced, if necessary, by civil law. The ideal to which John Adams subscribed–that we would be a na-

tion of laws, not men–was . . . subverted when the churches forced upon everyone, through supposedly neutral and just laws, their innumerable taboos on sex, alcohol, and gambling. We are now indeed a nation of laws, mostly bad and certainly antihuman. (Vidal, 1993)

But religious zealotry, as the present book will show, is regrettably only one of the wellsprings of meddling. The anti-meddling sentiment of the founding fathers has been displaced by a wide variety of interventions foisted on us from a host of sources. Aversion to risk, for example, has become a national obsession and has made meddling in the name of health and safety a virtually unchallengeable argument as well as a growth industry for those who would "protect" us. The regulatory environment of the government bureaucracy, coupled with tort legislation, has turned injury and accident into a national lottery in which every citizen hopes he or she may one day hit the jackpot. Such a deplorable situation has been allowed and even encouraged by a citizenry that wants to be protected from every imaginable risk to which human lives are subject. Accidents no longer exist, it seems, for all such events are seen by the legal profession as "preventable." Tort law in this society has thus become unparalleled in its meddlesome consequences. As Peter Huber (1994) points out in *The Legal Revolution and Its Consequences:* "No other country in the world administers anything like it. Tort law was set in place in the 1960's and 70's by a new generation of lawyers and judges. . . . Some grew famous and more grew rich in selling their services to enforce the rights they themselves invented" (p. 18). In addition, Huber observes that claims that other people's wrong-doings are responsible for life's difficulties generate, in effect, a "tort tax" on goods and services that amounts to a $300 billion levy on the American economy. It accounts, says Huber, for "30 per cent of the price of a step-ladder and 95 percent of the price of childhood vaccines" (p. 36). All in the name of health and safety.

Much of the responsibility for this preoccupation with risk aversion may be traced to the emergence of a new privileged class that works in the burgeoning service sector—including, not insignificantly, government and corporate bureaucracies that do little else but create rules that meddle in everyone else's business. But not only governmental initiatives are at the heart of the dramatic increase in the rise of professional meddling: It dawns on few of us that the more we ask government to meddle into the lives of others, the closer we get to creating an apparatus that will in all likelihood eventually meddle into our own. In a society where civil wars are fought not with guns but with rules, regulatory agencies are under as much pressure to write more rules as to write fewer of them. And although not many of us would argue that rules to circumscribe domestic tranquillity are unnecessary, it doesn't take long to see that these processes can become ends in themselves for the ever-expanding group of people who meddle as a way of making a living. In such a scheme, monitoring and accountability replace personal responsibility and mutual trust as the primary processes of securing conformity in the meddling society.

Intrusions into people's lives in the name of God and on behalf of the magic words *health* and *safety* give us some insight into why people meddle, but the kind of meddling that emerges from the currently fashionable solution to the age-old antagonism between individualism and community tells us even more. This resolution to what Brill (1990: 22) has called "this eternal conflict between the belief in the inherent worth and good of personal and individual freedom versus the belief in regulation and control of others' lives for the presumed public good" has occasioned a rather peculiar vision of what constitutes a "proper" public order. Owing perhaps to the seriously diminished opportunities for either formal political participation or a thriving informal public sociability, people have turned to controlling others as an acceptable and even laudable form of public participation. The lonely void of a self-possessed individualism poignantly noted by so many of Robert Bellah's respondents in *Habits of the Heart* seems to have been resolved for many people in a most unusual way. Meddling has become their attempt at connection with others. But in the process of reaching out to others they neglect the other side of community that involves and even requires a certain civil tolerance, if not an active appreciation, of diverse others–a sentiment that depends so much on what Tennessee Williams called the "kindness of strangers."

Moreover, as we seek community through meddling with others, a proper distinction between privacy and secrecy becomes hopelessly confused or even obliterated. For as Sissela Bok (1983: 10–11) has commented, privacy, or "the condition of being protected from unwanted access by others–either physical access or personal information or attention"—is far different from secrecy or "intentional concealment." But in the consciousness of a nation of meddlers, appeals to privacy are construed as pernicious efforts to conceal matters that undermine the public good. They are seen as symptomatic expressions of the newfound sin of privatization. The commonweal, it is said, depends on everything being out in the open, and if people have something they wish to keep private, they must be up to no good. And if not the commonweal, certainly the media–a group of snoops and busybodies whose major function is making certain that every aspect of life is out in the open, if not for the benefit of us all, then at least for the sake of the stockholders of the entertainment conglomerates who make a sizable fortune airing everyone's dirty linen. We have increasingly come to equate a free press with a meddling one.

So, in the name of a misguided sense of community, the whole of life, particularly those aspects that others wish to keep private, becomes open to the meddler's gaze. The irony, of course, is that those persons who seek community through meddling are themselves engaging in a kind of politics of exclusion. For it is not interaction or mutuality or even "knowledge of" others that they seek but, rather, a self-aggrandizing control or influence over others based on "knowledge about" them; hardly the stuff or fabric of community but, indeed, more akin to the social world of gossips, snoops, and busybodies. Thus, in one very important sense, meddling is individualism masquerading as community. It is difficult to tell whether altruism, caring, and honest concern are the *goals* of meddling as opposed to simply high-minded *justifications* that serve to disguise the meddler's self-interest as philanthropic, public-spirited, and humanitarian. What seems sacred in meddling is not the doing of good works but, rather, the sense of personal accomplishment derived from the meddling act itself. But because we take meddling into each other's affairs as a sure sign of community-mindedness, we may well have reached a point where, as Wendy Kaminer (1992: 56) has observed, "never have so many known so much about people for whom they care so little."

A proper account of the meddling impulse must also recognize that meddling is often accompanied by a certain moral indignation; and although there is much to be legitimately indignant about, we must also remember that moral indignation has much within it that is reminiscent of H. G. Wells's definition of same: "jealousy with a halo." Indeed, Svend Ranulf (1937), among others less careful and profound, has pointed out that, as in other middle-class social movements, much moral indignation betrays a certain disguised envy. This murderous sentiment (one of the seven deadly sins explicated so nicely by Stanford Lyman [1978]) attempts to punish, rather than merely comment upon, those departures from virtue so staunchly supported by the meddler. Reforming the morals of others is clearly one way in which groups act to preserve the dominance and prestige of their own lifestyles. Even the slightest pique of resentment about others doing what meddlers feel they themselves should not, or cannot, do often seems a quick and compelling reason to meddle into these other people's lives. Moreover, for the increasing number of Americans who are dissatisfied or bored with their all-too-proper lives, meddling offers the promise of reaffirming a sense of efficacy and credibility in a world that so often seems totally out of control. Moral indignation is a powerful intoxicant—to say nothing of a vicarious stimulant—for the weary and jaded who object to the raft of unsuitable enjoyments and pleasures of their fellow citizens. And whereas Lionel Tiger's (1992: 62) observation that "powerful people enjoy it when they are able to define and restrict the pleasures of others" is undoubtedly true, it is also true that certain people enjoy power by virtue of their being able to define and restrict others' pleasure.[11]

There seems to be an additional emotional dimension to meddling. To wit: The increasingly popular belief in what Thomas Sowell (1996) labeled the "unconstrained vision" of life has proven to be a cultural backdrop for a great deal of frustration and resentment on the part of certain segments of the populace. For those persons who see a world in which there are no constraints save those that have been put in place by other people, it is only natural that when life goes awry–as it so often does–other people become the cause of the problem. Indeed, if life is not ultimately constrained by forces outside of people's control (e.g., human nature, fate, chance), then taking control of not only one's own life but also of other people's seems the logical path to utopia. For those inflicted with the Rousseauian vision[12] of innocent man enslaved by a society that interferes with their inalienable right to a perfectly actualized existence, and especially for those who have the education, affluence, and opportunity to commandeer such a vision, life often proves to be a disappointing and irritating proposition. When an entire age finds the unconstrained vision alluring, the source of the frustration occasioned by the inevitable constraints of life are laid all too easily at the feet of others. So we meddle.

Finally, there is a pervasive cultural mood that provides both a context and an impetus to meddling in modern society. The reference here is to the seriousness and heaviness that seem to accompany so much of our everyday interaction with other people. As a society, we have become an earnest and pessimistic lot who view most of what people do as balefully consequential. In the process, we seem to have lost our ability to distinguish between major problems and minor vices, for the latter are viewed as simply the inevitable first steps to the former. We have come to believe in, but grossly overgeneralize, the notion that all human maladies are preventable, if only we do the right thing or make the correct adjustments in the way we live. At the same time, we seem to have embraced wholesale the scientific propensity for seeing all human imperfection as interwoven and logically related and, hence, consequently profound and complex. Life has become a weighty proposition indeed, and we seem unable to distance ourselves from the presumed difficulties of our allegedly precarious existence. As a result, we have become a wary clan who go out of our way to fix and change our social arrangements and our fellow man at the earliest opportunity. More important, we seem to have lost our sense of frivolity and our appreciation of the trivial, and have developed such a suspicion of pleasure and play that even minor titillations and major enjoyments have become indistinguishable. And what we fear most, it seems, is ignorance—that wonderful cultural virtue which involves ignoring and disregarding the unseemly but potentially controllable behavior of others. The importance of being earnest has indeed replaced the light-heartedness and playfulness of more tolerant times. As Russell Baker has observed:

> We have survived and come safely to the present age of total earnestness, where we enjoy the governance of an earnest President and his earnest wife on whom earnest Republicans keep a piously earnest eye with the indispensably earnest aid of an earnest clergy, while our oppressed multitudes demand redress with tireless earnestness and our deceased politicians are buried with earnest funerals. (Baker, 1994: A-19)

In the next chapter we discuss the increasing prevalence of meddling and contrast this era's penchant for busybodiness with other times and places that have shown a remarkable aversion to this practiced bit of Americana. As that chapter demonstrates, the roots of meddling lie deep within our social arrangements and the development of our history, but meddling has also arisen in contrast to other traditions and other values that have opposed it and that people might draw on during those times when they conclude that enough is enough. In addition, we show in more detail the historical fact that there were epochs within our own civilization that frowned on this practice to a much greater extent than people do now. In the process, we describe precisely those changes that shaped our movement from a nation that tried to keep the meddling impulse in check to one that in many ways now seems to embrace it wholesale.

Notes

1. Even the Bible weighs in on the question of amateur snoops and busybodies by enjoining us: "Hast thou heard a word against thy neighbor? Let it die within thee, trusting that it will not burst thee" (Ecclesiastes).

2. We will have much to say later in the book about this phenomenon of meddling masquerading as "education." It seems that everyone has a motive for meddling, which, in this information age, more often than not has an educational gloss to it.

3. Max Stirner, a nineteenth-century essayist, thought that a society of altruists was necessarily a society "of slaves."

4. And although in this culture of offense it is well-nigh impossible to say anything without offending someone, ironically we seem less offended by outright meddling than by offhand comments.

5. Anyone unfortunate enough to have been the object of any of these labels can testify to the plea bargains that are struck in the criminal justice system.

6. Perhaps the increase in meddlesome involvement is testimony to the postmodern "decline of the social" that so many social theorists talk about these days.

Since real communities are being rapidly taken over by "virtual" ones, meddling offers people an ostensible way back to connection. But the fact that they may be well motivated in this pursuit does not make their meddling any less problematic.

7. Every meddler is, in this sense, an amateur psychoanalyst bent on cutting through the haze of confusion that they see in the lives of their fellow human beings.

8. As we point out in the concluding chapter, one way to decrease meddling might be to call a moratorium on this babble of rights talk that currently enjoys so much currency.

9. The term *postmodern* is one we will use frequently to describe the contemporary situation. It refers essentially to the interrelationship between several themes: the triumph of the consumer culture of late capitalism (Frederic Jameson); the overwhelming influence of electronic media (Joshua Meyrowitz); the hegemony of transportation and information technologies and their effect on the self (Kenneth Gergen); and the success of democratic movements everywhere bringing about "the end of history" as a struggle between ideologies of elitism and mass culture (Francis Fukuyama), to mention just a few. Although it is an awkward and in many ways unfortunate term, we use it not simply because of its current popularity but also because we believe that when a term has such widespread use in so many different fields of inquiry, it is pointing to something fundamental. For a particularly fine discussion of postmodernism in the social sciences, see Denzin (1991).

10. This point is particularly salient in an era when many people seem dissatisfied with their lives, if for no other reason than the fact that there are so many alternative ways of living being touted by somebody or another.

11. But much meddling these days seems to occur for the sheer joy of extinguishing the pleasures of others. A recent book by David Shaw (1996) aply calls such candlesnuffers who meddle into the personal consumptive practices of others the "Pleasure Police," and provides a useful series of atrocity stories with which many readers will identify. These self-appointed vigilantes of health and fitness, smoking, diet, and exercise are characterized by their insistence that life is a grim business and that fun is of the devil. Hence his subtitle: *How Bluenose Busybodies and Lily-Livered Alarmists Are Taking All the Fun Out of Life.*

12. Charles Sykes (1992) has recently argued that the contemporary fascination with claiming that everyone is a victim of one kind or another stems from the same source.

2

The Roots of Meddling

Attempting to compel other people to believe and live as we do [the sixth mistake in "The Six Mistakes of Man"]
—**Cicero**

What a fertility of projects for the salvation of the world.
—**Ralph Waldo Emerson**

There is nothing more ridiculous than America in one of its periodic fits of Renewal.
—**H. L. Mencken**

How did we come to be this way?

In this chapter we examine in more detail some of the origins and sources of meddling in contemporary society. Following a brief historical treatment of the subject, our discussion centers on the effects of the rising scientific/therapeutic perspective on everyday life that has come to dominate both public and private life since at least the end of the nineteenth century and is the central root of contemporary meddling. As this therapeutic view of life gained momentum, at much the same time that Americans were becoming more socially isolated from one another and the institutions that had kept them together were drowning under the weight of a critical loss of faith,[1] meddling came to be seen as an expedient, socially sanctioned path to individual fulfillment and transformation—a way of making some contact with one's fellow human beings who were increasingly seen as becoming more distant and remote in the culture of postindustrial society. Moreover, the ability to know enough about the lives of others to meddle with them effectively was now, in the second half of the century, just the flick of an electronic switch away. Communication and transportation technologies put us in touch with at least what they thought were other people's lives as never before. The distinction between public and private began to dissolve as the intimate details of our neighbors' lives seemed to leak out from under the doors of their homes and into the discourse of not only their neighbors but also that of the news media, the courts, and virtually anyone else intent on knowing. At the same time, public space—the "commons" in the nostalgic rubric of bygone days—became increasingly privatized as politeness and civility gave way to the rudest displays of boorishness. Even architecture disparaged public space by designing it in such a way as to discourage congregation (Sennett, 1975).

Moreover, as the culture looked to the scientific/therapeutic ethic of expertise for solutions to age-old human problems, it also increasingly came to believe the epistemological baggage that accompanied this ethic. The citizenry adopted its view that there are rational solutions to human problems and that these solutions would come only with the assistance of new forms of healers who had expertise and special knowledge. These neoteric experts were scientifically objective and held the keys to therapeutic efficacy in their offices. Their "new" and "progressive" belief was actually an elaboration on a theme that came straight from the Enlightenment.[2] They had come to believe what the doctrines of the therapeutic state assumed: that human problems are the linear sequential products of the conditions that preceded them. They came to believe, as did the views they increasingly relied upon to sort out their problems, that life is extraordinarily complex, precarious, and dangerous. Insecurity became the cultural climate of the times, as evidenced in such preoccupations as the central overriding importance of the self and of the tender and easily influenced sense of self-esteem. Accompanying the explosion of self talk was the belief that human beings are fragile and delicate creatures, easily altered, traumatized, or even destroyed by the resident hazards of life. This "spun glass" view of the self made it all the more important to seek professional help early and often before one's soul was shattered by those hazards. Meddling and being meddled with thus came to be acceptable—seen, as they were, as a kind of secular/materialistic conversion critically important because the stakes were so high. One offered one's life to be meddled with in the secular world almost as one offered one's life for inspection and transformation in the religious realm—as a declaration of faith in the therapeutic state and those altruistic souls who speak and treat on its behalf. Everyone was a secular sinner of some sort—too fat, too sedentary, riven with mental illness of one kind or another, a victim of this disease or that syndrome. Those who felt that, although life had its ups and downs and problems were inevitable, they were, in the main, doing just fine, were accused of being "in denial," "naive," or "delusional." This social enforcement of the therapeutic was assisted by such luminaries as Ann Landers and Abigail Van Buren, contemporary practitioners of the nineteenth-century advice-to-the-lovelorn columns who bought into the assumptions of the therapeutic state lock, stock, and barrel—probably on advice of their attorneys. They urged readers with problems to "seek professional help," and they became virtual public-relations assistants determined to break down whatever anthropoid stigmata remained about offering one's life for therapeutic inspection.

Tales began to circulate in our national dialogue about remarkable transformations that occurred as a result of allowing the practitioners of the therapeutic state access to one's soul. There was no downside in allowing oneself to be meddled with, and the upside was the promise of personal happiness, wholeness, and the achievement of both inner and outer harmony—notions that rapidly became prime cultural values. Hiding oneself from the meddling intrusions of the agents of the therapeutic state was seen as having something to conceal. People were no sicker than their darkest secrets, so why not let those secrets out? There was always a sympathetic audience within reach who would be, at best, understanding and helpful and, at worst, patient or even amused. The search for individual transcendence came to be deemed an increasingly important personal quest as society in all its complexity, shot through and through with problems of its own, seemed to many to be crumbling all around. Within this unresolvable maelstrom of social problems—crime, racial divisions, economic chaos, and the destruction of community—arose the belief that the individual couldn't even begin to save the world, but *could* save himself if only he did the right things and thought the right thoughts. The search for individual transcendence took many forms, from guru worship to yoga and biofeedback, to the upscale counterculture contradictions of Marin County, where money and sophistication met Mother Earth and eco-feminism. But whatever its form, it was always fueled by the belief that cognitive, emotional, behavioral, physical, and spiritual perfection was both deserved and achievable. "You can have it all," blared the ads, invariably with the proviso "but not by yourself." Transcendence was for sale; it cost whatever you could afford.

Accepting the promises offered by the meddlers of the new healers of body and soul meant, of course, that one had to be open to many new ideas and experiences of which previous generations either were unaware or had kept close to the vest. As a result, the culture saw the emergence of vulnerability, sensitivity, self-awareness, personal insight, and open communication as primary values. Each required a personal trainer if you could afford it, or a self-help group if you could not. Therapy, like freedom and happiness, was a right built into the Constitution. The cultural climate was resplendent with books, magazines, and newspaper accounts, all of which promised a better life through the application of the proper scientifically verified techniques. Access to education widened, and the mark of an educated person naturally came to be his or her understanding and acquiescence to psychotherapeutic knowledge and techniques. Edwin Schur (1976) would presciently call all of this the "Awareness Trap"—a movement that absorbed the individual in matters of the self instead of the social change programs that had occupied many of the same people during the 1960s. One might not be able to change society, contrary to the naive vision of a program that proved to be much larger than the radical imagination, but at the very least one could save oneself.[3]

Accompanying these transformations of consciousness was a certain institutionalization of confusion. Life was simply too complicated to understand on one's own. Experts were everywhere; why not use them? Family and intimate relationships correspondingly came to be disparaged as sources of authoritative knowledge; they were in decline, after all, and in any case were increasingly being seen by the practitioners of the therapeutic state as the main sources of people's difficulties. Murray Straus (1980) and his colleagues, after spending decades studying domestic discord, concluded that the family was "the cradle of violence." Best-selling marriage and family textbooks used in university courses echoed the same bleak theme. Marriage as a lifelong bond held special dangers for women—if not physically, then certainly psychologically. Marriage and family were inherently oppressive institutions, the breakup of the family was a sign of social and gender progress, and even if one survived these bankrupt arrangements there were better alternatives—singlehood, divorce, or open marriage. A *New Yorker* cartoon shows an attractive young woman at a cocktail party introducing her boyfriend: "This," she says cheerily, "is the person my children will someday spend every other weekend with." Such chronic lack of confidence in the age-old sources of authority of family, friends, community, and spiritual advisers came to be replaced by the scientifically accredited experts of the therapeutic state. Few people saw the ideology of therapeutic movements simply as attempts to get rid of the competition. Therapists usually billed themselves as allies to the family, not as adversaries competing for the same business, each having a vested interest in the troubles of the other. One could not achieve happiness on one's own, but the conviction that happiness was expected, achievable, and commonplace in others remained as strong as ever. Others are happy and fulfilled—why not me?

It was not always thus. A necessarily abbreviated and partial history shows that the increasing prevalence of meddling has followed certain historical patterns and themes. It is to this subject that we now turn.

The Increasing Prevalence of Meddling: A Short History

Although there exists no single historical treatise on meddling, and therefore no fully accurate baseline, it is hard not to sense that there is much more meddling now then there used to be. We believe that it is possible to make such a case, despite the fact that, in many respects, America has always been a meddlesome nation, experimenting with first this reform and then with that. Richard Hofstadter wrote as follows about the reformist impulse, which is at the heart of meddling:

> Americans do not abide very quietly the evils of life. We are forever restlessly pitting ourselves against them, demanding changes, improvements, and remedies. . . . [T]here is a wide and pervasive tendency to believe . . . that there is some great but essentially very simple struggle going on, at the heart of which there lies some single conspiratorial force. (Hofstadter, 1955: 16–17)

But whatever the reality of early meddling in this country, it emerged within a set of constitutional conditions that were fundamentally opposed to it; for this society, as we noted earlier, was founded by one of the staunchest bands of belligerent anti-meddlers ever assembled. Since that time, things have changed considerably.

In this necessarily brief chapter we develop some illustrative historical themes (hardly a true history, which would be a project beyond the scope of this book), showing how meddling was viewed in previous eras in American history in order to suggest the development of the meddling impulse we see today. First we deal specifically with the colonial period, when the founding fathers put into place a constitution that was predicated on anti-meddling sentiments; then we move on to the Jacksonian era, when health and religious fundamentalists flourished and the beginnings of formal therapeutic meddling could be seen; next we consider the prohibitionist era, when meddling in the name of the good society, righteousness, and decency resulted in two decades of lawlessness and violence; and finally we conclude with the modern and postmodern eras, which in many respects harken back to previous meddling themes and failed experiments, though with the important difference that much meddling has now become professionalized in ways that earlier reformists might have envied for its effectiveness.

The Puritan Era and Colonial America

This country is what it is partly because some persistent Englishmen known as Puritans landed on these shores in the seventeenth century. Plymouth Colony, founded in 1620 by Pilgrims who arrived on the *Mayflower,* brought with them one of the most adamant forms of fundamentalism ever unleashed. In countless ways we are still living with its legacy. Because of their roots, their uncompromising views about the relationship between God and man, and the persecutions they suffered, the residents of Plymouth Colony were determined to overcome any obstacles that stood in their way as they established in New England "the church unspotted, pure"—a "citty upon a hill."[4] In so doing, they sought to reform everyone else so they could lead an unfettered New Testament life while earning a secular living at the same time. Meddling into the lives of other people in order to achieve these spiritual goals was part and parcel of the Puritan ethic. It still is. God, they believed, had dictated the Bible as the comprehensive guide for dealing with all of life's problems. They took literally passages of scripture that enjoined them to reject pleasure in favor of duty to God. A favorite story once told by Augustine in his *Confessions* is illustrative. He heard a voice calling him to read Romans 13:12–14. "The night is far spent, the day is at hand; let us put on the armour of light. Let us walk honestly, as in the day; not in carousing and drunkenness, not in debauchery and lust, not in strife and jealousy . . . and make no provision for the flesh, to fulfil the lusts thereof" (quoted in Morison, 1965: 62).

The meddling impulses of Puritanism are all the more interesting when one considers that Puritanism was itself framed in the beginning around a kind of anti-meddling sentiment. Not wanting an intermediary between themselves and God, Puritans rejected the ancient liturgy of the Catholic church and insisted on establishing their own version of truth-seeking. Serious dissatisfaction with their situation in England was the main reason the Puritans emigrated to the New World (Morison, 1965). Their anti-Catholicism caused a furor in the monarchy. Called "nonconformists" for their refusal to accept Catholic ritual, the Puritans were purged from the universities and their clergy were told to conform or leave. They left. One thing that can be said for the Puritans is that they were nothing if not courageous. They doubted their own self-righteousness not for a moment, feared no one, and undertook to set everything right while creating heaven on earth. If they were forcibly prevented from doing so in England, they would find some other place to establish their City of God. The contradiction of a group of people who set sail to evade meddlers only to create a meddling empire of their own should not escape us, for this pattern can be seen repeatedly in the history of meddlesome intervention.

The much-vaunted waywardness of the Puritans, identified in recent times by contemporary sociologists of deviance (Erikson, 1968), was undoubtedly so; but the fact that they may have been more hypocritical than previous accounts of their lives have led us to believe—drinking, smoking, and sexual deviance among the Puritans have all been amply documented—should not for a moment distract us from the fact that they were true believers whose daily lives were ruled by a certain brooding conscience and doubts about their sinful nature. Their daily prayers and devotions arose from a profound sense of the worthlessness of their condition. As Stanford Lyman points out:

The conflation of *eros* and *agape* in Puritan thought no doubt proceeded from the difficulties ordinary individuals had in sorting out the nature and objects of their emotions, feelings, and yearning. So devout a divine as Cotton Mather was suspicious and guilty about the love he bore for his children, the indulgence of his sexual impulses in three marriages, and the corruptions of his own body. He sought solace in the intensity of his worship of God, prostrating himself six and later seven times a day in his study, begging, beseeching, and pleading. "The diseases of my soul are not cured until I arrive to the most unspotted chastities and puritie," he wrote at the age of fifty-two, having already buried two wives and married for the third time two years earlier. Yet he hastened to add, "I do not apprehend, that Heaven requires me uterlie to lay aside my fondness for my lovelie Consort." (Lyman, 1978: 75)

Anyone forced by conscience and religious belief to lead such a tormented life, anxiety-stricken by sexual attraction even to his own wife, is unlikely to hesitate in enforcing such restrictions on others through meddlesome acts. The basis of the Puritan ethic, so nicely noted by Alain Robbe-Grillet, was the fear of pleasure itself: "[W]hat virtue does not tolerate, in reality, is not the presumable danger (in which no one really believes) of seeing a few simple souls perverted; what virtue does not tolerate is precisely, pleasure" (1972: 44). As a Johns Hopkins doctor wrote in 1913, Puritans object to tobacco "because it gives its users contentment, peace and a healthful, animal sort of enjoyment, a sublime callousness to the ethical and theological puzzles which fret and frazzle its enemies, a beautiful and irritating indifference to all but pleasant things in life" (quoted in Shaw, 1996: 135). We will continue to see throughout this book that pleasure itself, the heart of the Puritan dis-ease about life, remains the key consideration in attempts to meddle into people's lives; for the complaint that America has become soft and hedonistic is a foundation of and justification for the meddling impulse, especially in matters of the body, and it flows straight from our Puritan roots.

The Jacksonian Era

The era of Andrew Jackson (c. 1800–1845) was a period in which American arrogance, accompanied by an undying belief in the perfectibility of man, conjoined to produce some of the most important ideological and practical roots of meddling. Emerson, commenting on the state of the nation, took for granted the right to fix things: "What is man born for, but to be a Reformer, a Remaker of what man has made?" This popular view, held by many in a new nation that was possessed by an experimental and reformist ethos, could be seen in many forms. Historian Russell Nye captures this reformist spirit of the times in the following passage:

American reform was comprehensive rather than selective; reformers, with supreme confidence, attacked on all fronts. Nothing was too large or too small—one could work for the abolition of slavery or for Sunday mail, or for sensible dress for women and Christianizing Asia at the same time and with equal fervor. Bronson Alcott once even suggested forming a "Club for the Study and Diffusion of Ideas and Tendencies Proper to the Nineteenth Century" that included the study of nearly everything wrong with the world. (Nye, 1974: 32–33)

The source of these ideas came from a mixture of the American tradition of good works and benevolence, philanthropy and mutual aid. If the melting pot of ethnicity had not proven itself workable, the melting pot of meddling reform most certainly had. Everyone from Quakers to Enlightenment Deists had ideas about how to improve things, and little reluctance to foist them on everyone else. As Henry Steel Commanger observed:

The enthusiasm generated by reform may be judged by the fact that in one two-week period in May in New York in the 1840's, there were meetings of the American Antislavery Society, the New York Antislavery Society, the American Temperance Union, the American Women's Educational Association, the American Bible Society, the American Tract Society, the American Female Guardian Society, and the American Seaman's Friend Society, not counting meetings of church missionary societies and other charity-related groups. (quoted in Hofstadter, 1955: 19)

The winds of reform in the nineteenth century, according to Nye (1974), were spurred on by several essential ingredients. First, there was the eighteenth-century Enlightenment legacy of progress. Strongly rooted in these reformers was the idea that all the tools to make the world better were at our disposal if only we would use them: "Americans had science, technology, democracy, and divine guidance to help them; they believed that the process of improvement could be so directed and accelerated that perfection on this earth could be attained and not merely dreamed of. Nineteenth-century reformers were absolutely certain of this" (Nye, 1974: 34). Second, there existed in the nineteenth century a resolute belief in the ability of individuals to see the right and to control and direct themselves in such a way as to achieve it. As a result, there was an "aggressive, almost mystical conviction that each man, by using those powers within him, could achieve in his life and institutions something approaching perfection" (Nye, 1974: 34).

Additionally, the reformers of the Jacksonian era were influenced by the Enlightenment sense of benevolence, which they tied to an evangelical impulse to save their fellow man from the evils that beset him. Unflinchingly accepting the mantle of their brother's keeper, the reformers of the nineteenth century could not imagine having possession of the truth without giving it to others. "It is part of Christian duty," wrote the directors of the American Bible Society, "to rescue one's fellow man from thoughtlessness, ignorance and peril; it becomes Christians to imitate their Master, and to seek the good of those who are careless of their own good" (Griffin, 1960: 46). In 1834, the executive committee of the Home Missionary Society argued that benevolence forced them to work to save their fellow citizens from "infidelity, extravagance, and vice." In the heady atmosphere of reform it never seemed to enter anyone's mind that resistance to such benevolence might be a legitimate concern.

Finally, all of the reforms of the antebellum period of Jacksonian democracy were fueled by one overriding idea—the belief that America was the model of the world. If this country could attain perfection by reforming its people and its institutions, the rest of the world would have held up a shining example of human perfection. Nourishing these ideas were movements on both sides of the Atlantic. Jeremy Bentham's utilitarianism—the greatest good for the greatest number—seemed to Americans as perfect a set of ideas as had ever come along: "[Bentham's] belief that *utility* constituted the final test of ideas and institutions struck Jacksonian America as exactly right" (Nye, 1974: 34). Indeed, "[i]f prisons did not deter crime, change them so they did; if war settled nothing, outlaw it. Nothing could have provided a more practical basis for reform" (Curti, 1940: 73). These deliberate, organized, and conscious attempts to construct a more satisfactory culture were predicated on the principle of simply banishing those things that stood in the way.

On this side of the ocean, the reform impulse drew its most powerful support from the religious evangelism that swept the country in the 1820s and 1830s. Individual salvation was not enough. Putting one's religious ideas into practice, and reforming the world in the process, was the moral imperative. Important to this set of ideas was the belief that legislative meddling and political action were unnecessary: Reform would come automatically if enough individuals were converted. The involvement of churches in politics would come later as the movement for moral reform stalled; but until then, the belief that individual regeneration preceded social reform was solidly rooted in the religious fervor that gripped the nation.[5] Had churches adhered to this simple idea, much meddling in the name of religion might well have been avoided. But they did not. The key reason they chose a meddling course was the emerging discovery of the effectiveness of the principle of "association." As William Ellery Channing wrote:

> Men, it is justly said, can do jointly, what they cannot do singly. . . . Union not only brings to a point forces which before existed, and which were inef-

fectual through separation, but by the feeling and interest which it rouses, it becomes a creative principle, calls forth new forces, and gives the mind a consciousness of powers, which would otherwise have been unknown. (quoted in Nye, 1974: 32–33)

By 1845, reform unions, societies, and collectives were everywhere. Wrote one minister: "Missionary societies, tract societies, education societies, moral societies, and other societies of various names exist for the purpose of feeding the hungry, clothing the naked, instructing the ignorant, saving the lost, and promoting peace on earth and mutual amity among mankind" (Nye, 1974: 34).

Recognition of the principle of "association" meant that the multitude of societies and voluntary organizations that were building rapidly in the fertile soil of reform no longer had to wait for individual regeneration to work its magic, for the journals, tracts, speaker's bureaus, and conventions later formed the basis of powerful lobbies in state legislatures and the Congress. Meddling in the name of advocacy was thus born. Women figured prominently in these reform movements, for the wives of upper-class men often had time on their hands and a socially approved motive for good Christian works. James Buckingham wrote that "while the husbands are in business, their wives could direct their energies into useful channels by joining a charitable or reform society. Visiting the poor, teaching children, gathering old clothes for the sick were, of course, traditionally female activities" (quoted in Nye, 1974: 35).

An overriding theme in this fervor for changing the world through voluntary social action was the unceasing search for human perfection. Virtually no aspect of American society escaped the cold eye of reform: "[M]inor flaws in the conduct of life received the same attention as major social problems. A good digestion, a ten-hour working day, whole wheat bread, better jails, and the abolition of slavery were each considered to be steps that might advance humanity a few paces toward the ideal society" (Nye, 1974: 39).

This inability to distinguish between major problems and minor vices—indeed, the propensity for seeing all human imperfections as interwoven and logically related—was a major source of the meddling impulse, and it still persists. After all, who can say for sure that the problems and stresses of urban living may not ultimately be caused by the ingestion of white bread or the eating of dead animals? Such thinking was common among reformers who were loathe to draw lines in their enthusiasm for making the world right. The reformist tendencies of the Jacksonian era were instrumental in leading to the smorgasbord of meddling reform that occurred at the end of the nineteenth century. By then we saw the establishment of the Social Purity Movement, which urged sexual abstinence before, and sometimes even *during,* marriage. This was joined by the Anti-Cigarette Movement, the Social Hygiene Movement, The Society of Sanitary and Social Prophylaxis, various anti-alcohol movements that in the next few decades would coalesce into the vast experiment called prohibition, and a strident vegetarianism (both moral and dietary) that would radically change, if not the entire world as its proponents had envisioned, at least what Americans ate for breakfast (Carson, 1957). The anti-masturbatory writings of vegetarian pseudo-scientists such as Sylvester Graham would have a profound impact on such visionaries as John Harvey Kellogg, who would eventually create the world's first mass-produced cold cereal in the hopes not only of exercising the colon but also of dampening sexual ardor. Agreeing with the virulent anti-masturbatory climate of the time, Graham believed that the sick and sinful practice of masturbation was brought about by the consumption of what he called "warm and sensuous breakfast foods" such as eggs, bacon, and oatmeal. Cold cereal, thought Kellogg, would be the dietary equivalent of a cold shower—an extinguisher of sexual desire.[6] A pure mind and a pure body went hand in hand, and those who pursued natural foods would surely never go astray in other areas of life as well. Thus was born a movement that came to be known as "moral vegetarianism." Obsessed with the condition of their colons, moral vegetarians such as Kellogg argued that meat was the cause of most of the crises of the age, and the remedy was as simple as eliminating it from the diet. At the time, his new sanitarium at Battle Creek was raking in the dollars from those seeking a quick fix from their purulent ways.[7] Taking his cue from Elie Metchnikoff, director of the prestigious Pasteur Institute and winner of a Nobel Prize for his contributions to immunology, Kellogg came to believe, as did Metchnikoff, that "autointoxication" was the cause of old age, and that it was brought on primarily by dietary deficiency (Whorton, 1984: 219). Kellogg nonetheless scoffed at Metchnikoff's remedy. Noting that his French mentor died at the relatively young age of seventy-one, Kellogg devotes an entire chapter in his book on autointoxication to what he calls "Metchnikoff's Mistake." The "mistake" Metchnikoff made was to add only yogurt and buttermilk to his diet while continuing to eat red meat. Kellogg delighted in quoting one of his mentor's assistants, who said: "Metchnikoff eats a pound of meat and lets it rot in his colon and then drinks a pint of sour milk to disinfect it. I am not such a fool. I don't eat the meat" (quoted in Kellogg, 1918: 311).

For all his silly arrogance and cocksure attitude about the truth of things, the mid-nineteenth-century reformist had not yet laid his hands squarely on the institutional domain. That was to happen later. But the seeds of large-scale meddling were sown, and by the late nineteenth century, economic forces had made this next step a logical and imperative one. The work of Michel Foucault, as interpreted in this excerpt by Andrew Polsky, makes the matter clear:

> The effort to normalize marginal groups took shape in the nineteenth century when it became evident that blunt repression could not prepare them for productive tasks in the emerging capitalist economy. Through fields such as public health, a rising corps of social experts began to accumulate knowledge about marginality and to contemplate new techniques through which it would be possible to refashion the poor and the deviant into positive social assets—initiating, that is, *a discourse on intervention.* Putting their insights to the test in a host of local experiments, the first social practitioners invented a different form of power, one that penetrated to the most minute level of everyday life to evoke higher desires and appropriate economic attitudes. Later, when the value of this constructive power to dominant groups became clear, it was absorbed into the state. This process began, again, through local applications, where the apparent conflict between normalizing discourse and the liberal doctrine of individual rights went unnoticed. The technology of normalization has since attained a secure place within the state, sustained by the ongoing accumulation of bodies of knowledge and an elaborate mechanism of surveillance. (Polsky, 1991: 8–9; emphasis added)

But prior to this incorporation of marginal populations into the institutional framework of the therapeutic state, a move that rationalized meddling into the affairs of first those populations and later virtually everyone else, a grand-scale experiment in meddling would make its elements crystal clear. That experiment was, of course, prohibition.

Prohibition and Its Legacy

By the first quarter of the twentieth century, the enthusiasm for meddling into the lives of fellow Americans was so entrenched that it now seems inevitable that the great meddlesome experiment known as Prohibition would be tried. In the process, much can be learned about how meddlesome interventions arise, for the Prohibition movement offers us a microcosm of meddling at several levels. Moreover, Prohibition hardly went away simply because of its early failure in ridding the nation of killer booze. It has become instead an archetype of meddling. Our inability to prohibit alcohol may simply be seen in this context as an early historical failure, for 1920s-style prohibitionists might well have envied the success of their latter-day cousins in prohibiting tobacco, constructing a multibillion-dollar war on drugs, and fomenting crusades attempting to ban everything from fat to perfume. In fact, so ubiquitous—if not always successful—have these crusades been that their language permeates our culture. We talk freely about "simply prohibiting," "passing a law," "making it illegal," "banning it," "outlawing its use," "turning it into 'a stigma,'" "putting up signs," and "making compliance mandatory." As we pass more and more laws, we then must deal with the contradiction between too many rules and not enough enforcement. Then we "get tough," practice "zero tolerance," "hire more police," and "build more prisons." But as the call to get in on the prohibitionist bandwagon is made for the increasing numbers of bothersome activities in which our neighbors are engaged, it is well to look to the original source for direction in how to think about the problems entailed by such "solutions."

The most important point to be made initially about Prohibition was that it did not arise because of a groundswell of public opinion against drinking. Indeed, the dialectics of drinking and opposition to drinking, then as now, were behaviors deeply rooted in American culture. As Joseph Gusfield, in an oft-quoted work on the meddling context of the American temperance movement, has said:

> Issues of moral reform are . . . one way in which a cultural group acts to preserve, defend, or enhance the dominance and prestige of its own style of living within the total society. In the set of religious, ethnic, and cultural communities that have made up American society, drinking (and abstinence) has been one of the significant consumption habits distinguishing one subculture from another. It has been one of the major characteristics through which Americans have defined their own cultural commitments. The "drunken bum," the "sophisticated gourmet," or the "blue-nosed teetotaler" are all terms by which we express our approval or disapproval of cultures by reference to the moral position they accord drinking. (Gusfield, 1963: 3)

So Prohibition was part of a "symbolic crusade," to use Gusfield's term, designed to celebrate the virtues of a sober society rather than a serious attempt to stop the onslaught of alcohol consumption, which, if it were achieved, would simply have to have been replaced by some other Prohibition anyway.[8] In addition, Prohibition was a boon to the burgeoning medical profession, which used it as an opportunity to further its growing monopoly on drugs via the prescription system. As Thomas Szasz points out, in 1917 the delegates of the fledgling American Medical Association endorsed national Prohibition when it passed a resolution stating: "Resolved, the American Medical Association opposes the use of alcohol as a beverage; and be it further resolved, that the use of alcohol as a therapeutic agent should be discouraged" (Szasz, 1985: 197). By 1928, however, physicians, having taken this moral high ground, had made an estimated $40,000,000 annually by writing prescriptions for whiskey (Szasz, 1985: 197).

But because Prohibition was conspicuously tied to moral and religious movements at the turn of the nineteenth century, its ability to extend its agenda over an increasingly secular America was severely limited. So beginning in the mid-1960s, and supported by the rise of federal and state agencies devoted to issues of alcohol and drugs, a "New Temperance Movement," as Gusfield and others have called it, came into existence (Gusfield, 1991; Wagner, 1997). It's important to note that this movement uses the language of health rather than that of religion or morality to justify its meddling into the lives of people who drink. As Gusfield puts it: "Thus in contemporary American society, the problems connected with the use of alcohol are no longer the ownership of the Protestant churches. They are now being defined as issues of health rather than issues of morals" (Gusfield, 1991: 14). Gusfield goes on to note that since the 1950s an increasing number of professionals in alcohol research, administration, and treatment have emerged, and that this group found an easy convergence with traffic safety professionals in the area of "driving under the influence" (DUI). "The traffic safety community," says Gusfield, "emphasized the automobile as well as road conditions and has included DUI as merely one of several elements in automobile accidents" (Gusfield, 1991: 14). But once alcohol professionals were brought into the mix, isolated from general considerations of traffic safety, they obviously emphasized what they knew best: alcohol and drinking. Thus was the DUI question caught up in the changes in orientation that have occurred in the New Temperance Movement (Gusfield, 1991: 14).

The dialect of meddling ensures that once an evil is identified, meddlers become dependent on it for their cause; and should they succeed in ridding the world of whatever noxious force they are battling, they are then faced with having to identify something to take its place—for what is sacred here is not the abolition of an evil but the sense of accomplishment (to say nothing of a steady job) that comes from the meddling itself. The most recent example of this sentiment is to be found in the current anti-tobacco crusade. The health risks identified in smoking have become the basis for an increasingly strident anti-tobacco movement that has scapegoated this agricultural product to the point where huge numbers of meddlers would be deprived of a convenient source of meddlesome enjoyment, to say nothing of employment, if it were to disappear from the earth. The Clinton Health Plan, for example, proposes to fund its medical utopia via tobacco taxes, which, if the plan is enacted, would ensure that those who are sick are linked inextricably to those who smoke. The smokers may be stigmatized and denounced, but the healthy need them to continue smoking to pay for the health reforms coveted by the healthy.[9] This theme is one that's endemic to most meddling enterprises: Someone or something else is responsible for the carnage of victims in the world, but never the meddler who is innocently trying to make the world a better place and would succeed if only the moral derelicts, addicts, victims of business conspiracies, and those engaged in the dreaded practices being fought could be brought into line through bans, prohibitions, "incentives" and the like.

Before the actual imposition of prohibition, the typical reformer tried to transform his or her audience by argument. The strategy most commonly employed was moral suasion. To change people fundamentally was not merely to change their behavior; it was to transform their character, after which the behavioral changes being sought would occur naturally. As David Burner and his colleagues point out, in the early temperance movements that preceded prohibition, this happened quite often: Emotional appeals conducted by the traveling road shows of temperance persuaded tens of thousands to stop drinking, and their methods were little different from the current moral support supplied by Alcoholics Anonymous, an otherwise nonmeddling organization predicated on the idea that drunks can help each other stop drinking if that's what they really want to do (Burner et al., 1974: 282). But moral suasion has a flaw for the meddler. It leaves too much of the decision up to the person whom the meddler is wishing to change. Moreover, the propagandistic techniques that often surround moral suasion are so transparently exaggerated that many people simply ignore them. Consider the following contrast between an early temperance tract called "The Watchman" and a government pamphlet aimed at rock music in 1988.

Under a cartoon-like illustration showing, on the left, a man having a beer in a tavern ("the first drop") and, on the right, the same man hanging from a gallows ("the last drop") are the words:

> "Come in and take a drop." The first drop led to other drops. He dropped his position, he dropped his respectability, he dropped his fortune, he dropped his friends, he dropped finally all his prospects in this life, and his hopes for eternity; and then came the last drop on the gallows. BEWARE OF THE FIRST DROP. (from Sinclair, 1962: 17; quoted in Wagner, 1996: 67)

Fast-forward fifty years and we discover a more scientific-sounding rendition of the same message, this time about rock music:

> Hard rock arouses the sex drive by changing the cerebrospinal fluid, disrupting the function of the pituitary gland, throwing off the balance of the sex and adrenal hormones that circulate in the blood, in turn causing changes in blood sugar and calcium levels, which in turn affect the brain. This abnormal blood fluid causes moral inhibitions to either drop to a dangerously low level or even be wiped out altogether. This is why rock music has been positively associated with rape, murder, incest, drugs, illicit sex, homosexuality, satanism, suicide, sadomasochism, bestiality, and child abuse. (from a U.S. Government Pamphlet titled "The Downbeat Effect of

Rock Music on an Upbeat Generation," compiled by the National Committee on Music, 1988)

On the other hand, as is often the case whenever people are asked to evaluate alternatives and have the freedom to make their own choices, some drunkards simply failed to get the message. For every citizen persuaded by the moral exhortations extolling the virtues of the abstemious life, there was another who found such a life hardly worth living at all. A historical example may make the point. In the case of temperance, the early reformers met their match in such anti-reformers as the famous entertainer Tom Flynn—a pre-vaudevillian stand-up comedian who enjoyed a substantial following among Washingtonians in the mid-1800s. A group calling itself the "Washingtonian Battery Against Rum" sought to use the Old Chatham Theater (where Flynn performed his act) as a revival tent for its exhortations against liquor.

To the surprise of everyone, instead of denouncing the temperance movement's attempt to commandeer his theater for their cause, Flynn responded graciously: "I have been seriously thinking about this tippling business, and I cannot fail noticing the great good which this temperance revival is causing among thousands in this city. Its good effects have reached even so rum-soaked a sinner as myself, and I am desirous of doing something for the cause. You can only have the theater on certain occasions, but I will address the first gathering that is called together there under the auspices of the Washingtonians" (Burner et al., 1974: 286–287).

When the announcement was made that Flynn was to address a temperance meeting, the response was nothing short of phenomenal. It was as if confirmed atheist Tom Paine were to appear before a group of Baptists to announce his conversion to Christianity. The day finally arrived when the great actor was to renounce liquor and tell the audience why:

> The theater was packed from pit to dome, the very aisles being jammed almost to suffocation with solid humanity. The stage was set with a scene from *The Drunkard's Home* and near the footlights was placed a table, upon which rested a half-filled glass pitcher and a tumbler. At the appointed hour Flynn, wreathed in his most genial smile, came upon the stage, and the thunder of applause which greeted him never awakened such echoes before in the old theater.
>
> Filling his glass from the pitcher, Flynn drank the contents in one draught, and then proceeded with his lecture. He was a brilliant and voluble talker, and his fund of anecdotes never seemed to be exhausted. The pathos and eloquence with which he pictured step-by-step the drunkard's path down the abyss of moral ruin, I will never forget, neither will I forget the laughter I enjoyed while listening to his side-splitting anecdotes. Such an audience was never seen. One moment the sobs of men and women were

distinctly audible throughout the whole building while Flynn drew one of his inimitable pictures of the curse of rum. . . . The audience was worked to the highest pitch of religious enthusiasm, and the lecturer continued for two hours to talk uninterruptedly. At the end of that time, he was seen to totter at the close of one of his sentences, and then fall fainting upon the stage. Such excitement was never manifested in a public gathering before or since; and while some attendants carried Flynn around to the old New England Hotel, the audience dispersed to their homes, loud in their praises of the reformed actor. Some of the temperance people, however, managed to get on the stage, and in nosing around discovered that the pitcher which was supposed to contain water actually contained gin—Old Swan Gin, which was Tom's favorite beverage; and putting two and two together, concluded that Flynn had been drawing inspiration for his lecture from the camp of the enemy, and that his exhaustion and final collapse were not due so much to the mental strain of the lecture as from the seductive and exhausting contents of the pitcher. The story soon got out, and though it caused many to laugh, it made Flynn very unpopular with some at the time. The object of the joke was to prevent the temperance people from again asking for the use of the theater, and they never did. (Burner et al., 1974: 287)

One wonders how many conversions in the face of the pressure of meddlers are of this sort—what might be described as a kind of *noblesse oblige* concession to the powerful status that meddling in the name of consumptive abstinence currently enjoys? In a world of meddlers, moral suasion is too uncertain. If one's cause is right, more direct means are necessary—and certainly justified—in the pursuit of a good society.

Prohibition eventually resulted in the codification of the meddling impulse into constitutional law, but enforcement of its provisions, of course, proved to be unworkable. Attempts to enforce the Eighteenth Amendment ushered in a decade of bootlegging, violence, organized crime, and—interestingly—unparalleled drinking. As Peter McWilliams (among others) has noted, the legacy of Prohibition includes disrespect for the law; erosion of respect for religion; an enormous impetus for organized crime; the corruption of law enforcement, the court system, and politics; an overwhelming burden on the police, the courts, and the penal system; and the destruction of perhaps millions of individual lives. In 1933, the adoption of the Twenty-first Amendment repealed Prohibition and made alcohol consumption legal again.

Since the end of prohibition, scholars have argued about its lessons, and indeed—although singularly contextual history never offers any clear guides to the future—the failed experiment does seem to provide some insights into the nature of American meddling. First, we may say that Prohibition illustrates that meddlers do not require a plurality of public opinion in order to meddle. The public is often no match for a meddler with a cause. Apathy, inertia, and ignorance typically lose to the political machinations of true believers who wish to meddle, whereas those with whom they meddle simply wish to be left alone. Tireless crusaders for public morality, armed with a sure sense of rectitude and fueled by resistance that they enthusiastically overcome, are energized by opposition to their cause. Second, an analysis of Prohibition reveals that no matter how righteous a cause may be, those who meddle in its name frequently create more conflict, trouble, and difficulties than ever are generated merely by the behavior of the miscreants they wish to reform. Meddling always entails risk. The risks of criminalizing consumptive practices (lawlessness, violence, corruption) are clearly indicated by the historical example offered by prohibition. Yet the impulse not only survives, it is thriving. And, finally, there will be unanticipated winners and losers when meddlers meddle. The temperance movements of the late eighteenth and early twentieth centuries wanted to create a society safe from the clear-cut evils that are always present when alcohol is consumed. What they did not anticipate (or perhaps even care about) is that the real winners in this grand-scale experiment in mass meddling were organized crime, enforcement personnel, bootlegging interests, and assorted unsavory characters that the proponents of Prohibition never envisioned.

Prohibition remains a lesson with implications for both the futility as well as the dangers of prohibiting things. Yet in spite of the disasters of prohibition, it remains a model for meddlers everywhere, and various forms of Prohibition still abound. The war on drugs tries to do for harder drugs what it couldn't for alcohol, and with most of the same consequences. Violence, corruption, and contempt for the law are resident once again in the current righteous crusade against recreational drugs. Attempts to change the world in a positive direction through the logic of banning those things which large numbers of people clearly wish to do have become, if anything, even more problematic as the world has grown more complex since the relatively simple visions of the 1920s movement to rid the country of alcohol.[10] In the next section we show how the legacy of this movement continues to be seen in a society that has paradoxically become more, not less, meddlesome since the experiment failed—arguably owing to the institutionalization of meddling that accompanied a new development: the rise of the therapeutic state.

The Scientific/Therapeutic Ethic of Expertise

With this historical background in mind, it is now possible to approach an understanding of why contemporary Americans are so meddlesome and why they are even more likely to meddle now than in the past. The following discussion is organized around the emergence of several essential features that provide a scientific rationale for meddling into the affairs of our neighbors.

The Belief in Rational Solutions to Human Problems

The belief in the idea that human problems will yield to the application of reason is as old as the Enlightenment, but it is only within the last half-century that the intellectual endeavors aimed at sorting out this assumption have gained the public's allegiance. Psychology, psychiatry, social work, political science, and sociology are just a few of the human sciences that traffic in the assertion that human problems are the result of prior conditions that produced them and that a rational understanding of these conditions will lead to solutions. The very idea that there *are* solutions to the human condition is a fascinating proposition that could engage us in endless debate, but the fact is that we have bought into this notion, and those who make their living meddling into the lives of others absolutely depend on it. Governmental agencies, often with deep pockets to fund these endeavors, call on the social sciences to provide a rational basis for public policy based, presumably, on the belief that by understanding the conditions that produced the problems in the first place, one can come up with solutions. The family with a delinquent child, the person who "hears voices," and the couple with "marital problems" are all examples of people seeking helpers who offer the hope that they will be able to resolve their problems through the faculty of reason. Vast bureaucracies emerged after World War I based on the idea that a rational form of social organization was best suited to administer the affairs of those citizens whose problematic lives brought them to their doors.[11]

Moreover, the belief in rational solutions—in the West, at least—has been conceived in a linear sequential fashion. This is why the remedies for the problems that beset us are frequently seen by both professional and amateur meddlers as merely a matter of following certain steps. Alcoholics Anonymous has become the best-known model for self-helpers, by means of its articulation of salvation through twelve steps—so much so that this strategy abounds and is applied to everything from people who beat their children to those who spend too much time on the Internet.[12] As a result of linear-sequential thinking about the human condition, slippery-slope thinking abounds. Meddlers argue that small things lead to bigger ones, that major drug addictions were begun with just one cigarette, that alcohol is a "gateway drug," or even that abstract things like visual images promoting one thing actually promote another. We are told to exercise "zero-tolerance" about a wide variety of matters from drugs and alcohol to sex. Concerning the latter, Leslie Kantor points out that in some sex education programs,

[s]tudents are told that teens develop a sort of "tolerance" to sexual activity
and that it takes increasing amounts of stimulation to achieve the same
arousal over time. Sexual activity, in the exercise entitled "The Woo Scale," is
likened to the analogy of a frog which is boiled to death without knowing it
when the heat is turned up gradually. Another idea promoted by this concept is that sexual activity always gets beyond the control of the people involved (Kantor, 1994: 161–162; quoted in Wagner, 1996: 68)

This kind of linear-sequential thinking is the same logic as that employed by the forces of prohibition. Wagner, in a recent brilliant analysis
of the resurgence of old-style temperance movements, calls it "dry logic."
Proceeding, he says, from the fundamental logical error of decontextual-
izing human behavior from social, personal, and cultural experience, and
presenting it in the form of an anonymous statistical data set, "dry logic"
depends on

a model of human life that assumes no anxiety, boredom, worry, pain, sor-
row, suffering, joy, or excitement. Rather, it regards life as a purely rational-
ist utilitarian venture. Although this view may correspond with stereotypi-
cal Western rationalism, we must question whether it describes anyone's
reality. Most certainly it does not for those people who are neither middle-
aged, nor middle class. (Wagner, 1996: 71)

According to Wagner, "dry logic" entails the following tactics of de-
contextualization.

Blurring Boundaries.   "Dry logic" blurs the boundaries of human behavior and experience by lumping together all activities into categories
that have even the vaguest connection to the worst possible outcome.
Smoking and drinking are talked about in terms of their relationship to
disease and death, never in terms of their relationship to joy, happiness,
and good fellowship. Drug addicts are seen as slaves to their habit, never
as ordinary citizens who incidentally use forbidden substances as part of
their daily lives and get along just fine. And when bad examples about a
person's drug habit hit the front pages or the police blotter, we virtually
always see the problem in terms of the substance or the behavior, never in
terms of its illegality. We also fail to realize that, had the police not been
meddling into the miscreant's life, it would not have been destroyed.

Imposing a False Concreteness.   Tragedies (premature death, illness,
suffering, and sorrows) are presented to us as linear propositions and imply that only the user's misconduct caused the catastrophe. The idea, for
example, that one's lung cancer might have been the result of etiologi-

cally random events, bad luck, or other factors poorly or even dubiously understood are never presented as a part of the equation. Thus, when actor Yul Bryner, dying of lung cancer after a lifetime of smoking, is presented in a posthumous tape saying that if he hadn't smoked all those years he would still be alive, we are not told that he was seventy-six years old, that he had already outlived the vast majority of his statistical cohort, and that his example could as easily be taken as an argument *in favor of* smoking as against it.

Ecological Fallacies. "Dry logic" makes much of associations that may actually be the result of other things. Disease and death are matters that fall out as much along social class and occupational lines as along any others. Everything else being equal, people of higher socioeconomic status have a better chance of living long and healthy lives no matter what else they do.

Creating Judgmental Dupes. The decontextualized logic of the "drys," like that of other meddlers from whom they are descended, treats people as passive, weak, and dumb. Helpless in the face of substances that control their lives, they cannot possibly know the dangers of food, drugs, and sex until it is too late. Incapable of managing life's risks, they are hopelessly mired in the substance in question, well before it dawns on them that they have a problem. Defenseless by then, they can only turn to the professional who offers expert treatment. If, as the cliché goes, an ounce of prevention is worth a pound of cure, then surely abstinence is the road to safety and security; if one never starts, one will never be sorry.

There can be little doubt that the acceptance of such notions, and the fear they have engendered in a populace devoted to consuming the latest in health, safety, and addiction mongering, has been a bonanza for professional meddlers and a boost even to those who practice it on an amateur basis. Standing at a vortex of fate as they practice therapy on those about to embark on a lifetime of evil leading to certain perdition, meddlers have not only the proper eyes with which to see the future but also the proper therapies for heading it off. Popular magazines, too, promote the scientific ideology of therapeutic expertise. Each month's issue is filled with hope about this new therapy or that new pill, the "Ten techniques of . . ." or the 'Five secrets to. . . ," that will certainly improve the readers' lives, raise their consciousness, and lead to salvation and prosperity.

The Decline in the Belief in Fate, Luck, and Chance

If this is a cynical culture, as some critics have maintained (Hughes, 1993; Kantor, 1989), it is also a boundlessly hopeful one. Sharing more in com-

mon with the utopian ideologies and communities of the latter part of
the nineteenth century than some would acknowledge, the therapeutic
state, unwaveringly rooted in science and determined to bring rational
sense to life, also brought with it a corresponding decline in the belief in
fate, luck, and chance.[13] Despite the dramatic increase in various forms of
gambling—casinos, lotteries, slot machines, video games of chance, and
the like—the general trend has all been in the other direction. As Charles
Sykes has noted:

> Before the twentieth century, people had more or less accepted the vagaries
> of fate. Sudden reverses could ruin farmers or businessmen; death, disease,
> and accident were familiar presences. Faith could cushion many of the
> shocks, but it could do nothing to eliminate them. But with the decline of re-
> ligion and the rise of technology and science, society began to lose its belief
> in both the inevitability of suffering and the need for stoicism in the face of
> adversity. (Sykes, 1992: 125)

But by the middle of this century, with the application of scientific and
especially medicalized thinking to the business of therapy, these questions had taken an entirely different turn.

This widespread belief in the efficacy of scientific reason to problems
in living, then, renders irrelevant the bumper sticker slogan "Shit Happens." In the ideology of meddlers, shit never "just happens." There is a
cause for all the shit and a way to banish it forever if only people will do
this or that. Fate, luck, and chance are but legacies of a darker age of su-
perstition; educated, progressive, and right-thinking people simply
"know" that everything that happens is a result of the conditions that
preceded it. "Uh, huh, I knew that would happen" is the self-satisfied response of meddlers drunk on causal chains. No matter what the grim
outcome, they knew that it was coming and that it could have been
headed it off if only someone had intervened sooner. This is why rational
Americans these days spend their time in the arguably irrational pursuit
of the latest "risk factors." The "most recent" finding in medical journals
sets off a wave of chasing. An announced correlation between this substance or that deficiency (vitamins, minerals, food, environmental "poisons") creates a run on the stores that sell the alleged remedy. Governmental prohibitions on cyclamates, a year's supply of cranberries
allegedly tainted by a pesticide that had been used without incident for
twenty years, or alar-sprayed apples give a Hazard-of-the-Week flavor to
contemporary life. At the very least, the seed is planted in the rational (?)
mind. If one believes the paradigm, one can never be sure. One can never
be too safe. One can never be too vigilant in the protection of one's self
and one's children. This uneasy sense of imminent doom and easy

remedy is one of the reasons why Americans seem so mired in perpetual dissatisfaction, the roots of which lie in the curious marriage of the prohibitionist spirit and the new scientocracies that govern our lives.

The Belief in the Expertise of
Specialists and Special Knowledge

Of course, few of these solutions can be accomplished simply on one's own. An increasingly specialized society means that we can no longer rely on ourselves or on the traditional sources of support that for generations have given meaning and direction to life—family, community, religion. A vast array of experts with specialized knowledge must be called upon. Those holding themselves out as authorities on human problems and their solutions have collectively become one of the formidable growth industries in the service economies that have emerged in the postindustrial West. And a booming business it is. Although there are no reliable data on just how large a group professional meddlers constitute, one wing of them—mental health professionals, psychologists (both clinical and counseling), social workers, lawyers, marriage counselors, psychiatrists, child experts, delinquency prevention specialists, drug and alcohol treatment counselors, and those specializing in "emotional problems"—number in the tens of thousands. From "soul doctors" to "relationship specialists," these experts are said to be "objective," a characterization that makes their knowledge more valuable than that of family or friends who, because of their nearness to the problem, are deemed unable to offer wise counsel or intelligent advice. We have to "get away" from our problems in order to see them, it is thought, and the expert specialist provides the desired distance. Scientific objectivity and therapeutic efficacy are claimed as justifications for this vast array of professional meddlers who make their livings tinkering with the lives of others. To be objective is to be set apart from a personal involvement in the problem (though not so distant that one cannot make money off of it), and the vast number of "therapies" that have emerged over the course of the past fifty years are stark testimony to the triumph of the ideology of expertise.

Among the staunchest beliefs in American society is the steadfast conviction that there is always more than meets the eye. Appearances are deceiving, reality is layered, and life is complex. This belief is usually coupled with the equally firm doctrine that certain classes of people (usually experts) have better eyes than everyone else. Despite the fact that much doubt can be cast on this assertion, it continues to hold sway. What do the experts know that we don't? Of course, if the assertion were literally true, we might expect that various classes of experts would be models of whatever it is they hold themselves as experts on. We would expect divorce to be virtually unheard of among marriage counselors, child-rearing experts to have model children, and psychiatrists to be models of mental health. Unfortunately, none of these things true; indeed, if there is a correlation between the possession of expert advice and living the exemplary life implied in the meddler's interventions and exhortations, it is as likely to be negative as positive.

Nevertheless, the idea that there is always more than meets the eye is clearly beguiling. Life is not only complex in the usual sense of a lot of different things going on, it is thought, but also multilayered such that the forces moving it are to be found not on the surface but deep beneath and accessible only to those who have the proper training and understanding. This belief, connected as it is to the language of professionals who not only give us the answers but also tell us that "life is complex," enjoys considerable currency in the contemporary world. It arose out of the professionalization of medicine (Friedson, 1970) and the establishment of the "helping professions" coupled with the academic disciplines that fuel their practice.

The Rise of the Therapeutic Ethic

Beginning in the middle of the eighteenth century, though its boundaries were not expanded until the middle of the twentieth, the ethic of therapy as a justification for meddling into the lives of others has become a way of life. Indeed, the languages of psychiatry and psychotherapy have become part of the national consciousness. Note, for example, how an incident that occurred during a recent summer race meeting at Del Mar Race Track in Southern California was handled by officials:

> NAKATANI SUSPENDED THROUGH DEL MAR MEETING
> Jockey Corey Nakatani was suspended for the remainder of the Del Mar Meeting after knocking apprentice rider Ryan Barber off his mount as the pair were galloping out after Sunday's 7th race.
> During the race, Barber's horse appeared to drift in at mid-stretch, causing Nakatani to take up sharply. After a hearing on the incident, the stewards issued a statement citing the 26-year-old rider for disorderly conduct and conduct detrimental to racing, suspending him through September 10.
> The stewards also directed Nakatani to seek counseling to *"address the issues of impulsive behavior and anger management"* (from Bloodstock Research, Inc., 1997: 2; emphasis added)

If therapeutic accounts of human behavior and counseling as a remedy for misconduct have come to the tradition-bound, nineteenth century world of the race track, they may surely be said to be everywhere. How did this come about?

As Polsky (1991) and others have shown, the therapeutic state arose as a response to marginal populations and then fanned out as the markets became saturated to include almost everyone within its ideology umbrella. Human misery typically speaks of marginality. The problems we see on the evening news have been presented (by both the media and experts alike) as problems outside of, but which threaten, the mainstream. Juvenile delinquency, homelessness, poverty, unemployment, suicide, drug addiction, spouse abuse, the neglect of children—all of these things are presented to us in such a way as to increase the amount of social distance between ourselves and those whose fortunes have led them to become victims of such miseries. Most of these marginal populations came to be so by virtue of their inability to adjust to the postindustrial economies that modernism spawned in the West. The frustrations that stemmed from their economic circumstances spilled over into the kind of behaviors with which the therapeutic state tries to cope.

The governmental/state response to these forms of marginality has been to produce programs that are "therapeutic" in nature. The rapid medicalization of society that has been occurring since at least the turn of the last century (Conrad and Schneider, 1992) has helped this quasi-medical term enjoy a rich vogue. The process begins, says Polsky,

> with the premise that some people are unable to adjust to the demands of everyday life or function according to the rules by which most of us operate. If they are to acquire the value structure that makes for self-sufficiency, healthy relationships, and positive self-esteem [all values and terminologies of the therapeutic state itself], they need expert help. Accordingly, they become the clients of behavioral specialists, clinicians, and social workers. (Polsky, 1991: 3)

The therapeutic approach proceeds, Polsky notes, through a series of steps. First, professionals "diagnose" or "assess" their clients' situation and establish a friendly relationship with them. Then, through a proper series of interventions such as counseling, supervision, reflection, and so on, clients are assisted in overcoming their personal deficiencies and learn to bear the pressures that are placed upon them. No one can change the pressures to which all of us are subjected in the contemporary world, goes the argument, but their impact can be minimized through suitable coping strategies. These strategies, which run the gamut from traditional psychotherapy to such non-Western techniques as yoga and meditation, put people in command of their own fate, at least with the correct personal counselors and trainers. These professionals can then, under the right circumstances, keep tabs on their clients to make certain they do not slip back into their former ways.

We know, of course, that things do not always proceed as smoothly as the ideology of the therapeutic state would suggest. Horror stories abound about treatments that do not work as advertised, clients who curiously fail to respond to the beneficence offered by professional meddlers, and lives made worse by their contact with experts and therapists. But these instances are routinely dismissed as failures of budget, administration of technique, or professional training, or are even blamed on the clients themselves—never on the ideology that underlies them (Polsky, 1991: 4). Although the initiation of this model of "professional intervention" (i.e., meddling) involved marginal groups, its logic now extends well beyond those deviant subpopulations, which were either too ignorant, unfortunate, or victimized by their circumstances to do better on their own, and has ventured into mainstream groups as well. The latter groups—middle class and above—already "know" through education or cultural inclination that the values of the therapeutic state are correct, and it is now a question of using the proper techniques when their lives get off track. Furthermore, they have their own problems with "marginal" populations such as Generation X children who seem to be growing up neither socialized to the values their parents implicitly believed in nor inclined to take the McJobs offered them as entry points into the bourgeois society of their elders. Their rebellious experimentation with drugs, crime, alcohol, and sex make them prime candidates for professional intervention, especially when offered by parents capable of paying the bill. As the money-grubbing demands of a consumer economy escalate, more time is spent working and less time is spent pursuing the venues of those activities and institutions that had successfully avoided many of the problems that therapists now deal with in the first place. As families crumbled and divorce rates skyrocketed, as the Third Places of pure sociability (Oldenburg and Brissett, 1983) characteristic of real communities were taken over by the psuedo-intimacy of the television and the computer, as fictional families and friends became more interesting than real ones, and as the number of human problems said to be amenable to scientific techniques of healing increased, the market for meddlers grew dramatically. In addition, the healing techniques could be attained not simply through face-to-face encounters with expert sources but, under circumstances of less urgency, through bookstores, mail-order catalogs,[14] audiotapes, CDs, and television as well. But no matter what the source, the message was the same: Experts must be relied upon because individuals are incompetent on their own. Fixing their own lives is possible, but not without the counsel of the right people or the right ideologies looking over their shoulder. The marketing of the therapeutic stressed such capitalist truisms as "you get what you pay for," and medicine, the courts, and even the tax system changed in such a way as to render autonomy in critical areas of life virtually impossible, even if the desire was there.

It was also the case, as Norman Fox and T. J. Jackson Lears argue in *The Culture of Consumption*, that near the turn of the century a fundamental cultural transformation occurred within the educated capitalist nations of the West. As they describe this change:

> In the United States, as elsewhere, the bourgeois ethos had enjoined perpetual work, compulsive saving, civic responsibility, and a rigid morality of self-denial. By the early twentieth century, that outlook had begun to give way to a new set of values, sanctioning periodic leisure, compulsive spending, apolitical passivity, and an apparently permissive (but subtly coercive) morality of individual fulfillment. The older culture was suited to a production-oriented society of small entrepreneurs; the newer culture epitomized a consumption-oriented society dominated by bureaucratic operations. (Fox and Lears, 1983: 4)

This change was more than simply cultural; it was also *moral* in the sense that it required much more than a national apparatus of marketing and distribution. In addition, it needed a favorable moral climate that would accept the new urgings to consume:

> [T]he crucial moral change was the beginning of a shift from a Protestant ethos of salvation through self-denial toward a therapeutic ethos stressing self-realization in this world—an ethos characterized by an almost obsessive concern with psychic and physical health defined in sweeping terms. (Fox and Lears, 1983: 4)

The rise of a consumer culture, then, set the stage for therapeutic meddling on a grand scale. But that was not all. Meddlers would also find a fertile field for their wares because of a change that David Riesman (1950) would describe, in an influential book called *The Lonely Crowd*, as the rise of "other-directed man."

The Lonely Crowd

Riesman's analysis of the changing American character focused on a change in the very sources of human direction. There were three possibilities, which he called tradition-direction, inner-direction, and other-direction (Riesman, 1950). We could, as generations of other cultures had, get our sense of where to go and what to do from tradition. But since the land was relatively young and its inhabitants were confronted in their explorations into new worlds with too many situations they had never encountered before, tradition was in short supply. Bereft of that source of direction, we were forced to rely on ourselves. So we became a country of inner-directed types, ruled not by autonomous selves, of course, but by a kind of "psychological gyroscope," set spinning in early childhood and accompanying us wherever we went. Guilt was the major mechanism of the inner-directed type just as shame had been for his tradition-directed predecessor. This character type was well-suited for the development of a wild and new land, but with the taming of the continent, a new character type developed. More suited to the indoor social environments of post–World War II America, the other-directed character type got his sense of things from his interactions with others with whom he was aligned occupationally, geographically, and socially. "Adjustment," "getting along," and "working well with others" became prime cultural values. There was nothing in other-directed man even remotely resembling a psychological gyroscope; his mechanism was more like a radar set, sending out signals and then adjusting his behavior to whatever echoes returned. In short, we had moved from a people who got our inner sense of direction from family, community, or self to one that responded to the other-directed demands of immediate situations, whereby adjusting to social imperatives was the mandate of the age.

A nation of other-directed character types, unlike their inner-directed ancestors, had no choice but to be meddled with because they had no inner core anyway. They could no longer return to the age-old patterns offered by tradition, nor to community sources of help and support—those were either absent or regarded as the source of their problems in the first place. Instead, they looked to others for cues as to how to live. The radar screen was alive with returns, and they could not miss any of the signals. They wished to conform to the expectations of others in terms of the qualities of both outer behavior and inner experience. And they could deal effectively with the demands of the world only by focusing their eyes on how others were handling their problems. But this character type faced a serious problem. The major hurdle to be overcome now was not the outmoded mechanisms for shame or guilt that had served as vehicles of social control for countless generations but, rather, a diffuse and undifferentiated anxiety. Consulting the radar scope for direction was met with a built-in problem. One had to interpret what the signals meant. Fortunately, help was on the way. Anxiety over how one read the responses of others could be resolved by the simple expedient of hiring, or at least listening to, the right meddler.

The Rights Revolution

Beginning with a handful of "inalienable" rights guaranteed by the Constitution, the language of rights has grown to the point where Americans now routinely claim literally hundreds of matters of daily life as "rights."

Every behavior a person wishes to engage in, every hope or dream that anyone possesses, every ideal that has the ring of Utopian good to it, eventually surfaces in the language of "rights." We have operated on the assumption that if "rights are good more rights are even better, and the more emphatically stated the less likely they will be watered down or taken away" (Glendon, 1991: 14). If words lose their meaning not through obsolescence but through overuse (Baudrillard, 1988), rights talk is in eminent danger of losing all meaning whatsoever. Here are but a few of the groups, people, and things that have had rights claimed in their name:

gays	straights
animals	plants
children	fetuses
the handicapped	trees
comatose people	mountains
people who want to die	the earth
men	oceans
women	corpses
smokers	nonsmokers
IBM	art

As each new right is proposed, as each new group is pacified, there is, as Mary Ann Glendon points out, "very little consideration of the ends to which they are oriented, their relationship to one another, to corresponding responsibilities, or to the general welfare" (Glendon, 1991: 26). Never mind these complications; the public wants rights, and politicians seek to deliver them. Rights are, at base, claims that people make on each other, and whether they have them or not depends on whether others validate their claims and on what they are willing to do in the name of such claims. But in contemporary America, "[s]aturated as we are with rights, political language can no longer perform the important function of facilitating public discussion of the right ordering of our lives together" (Glendon, 1991: xi). On the contrary, the escalation of rights cheapens and demeans the entire question of rights by reducing them to the dismal status of yet another pork-barrel smorgasbord inserted into a congressional bill. For politicians to proclaim still other "rights" (often in negative form: freedom from rather than freedom to) costs no one anything since there is rarely any way to enforce these new "rights" anyway.

In addition to the basic constitutional rights mentioned in the Bill of Rights (expression, assembly, search and seizure, etc.) and the new group rights that we noted above a number of freshly minted rights have emerged. John Leo points to a few of the more bizarre ones:

- Post Alpha Bits cereal boxes feature a seven-point "Kids Bill of Rights" that includes "the right to be seen, heard, and respected as a citizen of the world" as well as "the right to a world that's peaceful and an environment that's not spoiled."
- Governor Pete Wilson of California has said that every resident "has a fundamental right not to become a crime victim . . . the right not to live in fear."
- Prisoners on death row have claimed a right to procreate before being executed.
- Gays have claimed a "right to have government and society affirm our lives."
- The environmental group Sierra Club has affirmed the fundamental rights of rocks and trees: "[a] right to go their own way unfettered by man," says Michael McCloskey, chairman.
- In Santa Monica, California, attorney Gloria Allred declared that women "have a right to urinate in any facility at any time." She made this argument on behalf of a woman who had been arrested for using a men's rest room.
- Professor George Gerbner of the Annenberg School of Communication announced "a new civil right" for all people—namely, the right to proportional representation on television. People have a fundamental right," he said, "to be represented fairly and equally in the cultural environment." (Leo, 1997: 8)

To this list can be added the controversy over air bags, which has moved from the language of the "right" to have them (often used by proponents in the original fight over making air bags standard equipment on new cars manufactured in Detroit) to assertions of the "right" to have them disabled (as it became clear that they sometimes kill children and small adults).[15]

The language of rights converges neatly with the language of psychotherapy, for rights now seem to be entitlements—something the government owes each person. It is in this sense that rights encourage "the tendency to place the self at the center of our moral universe" (Glendon, 1991: 8). In spite of these new rights, or perhaps because of them, Americans hardly seem better off. In fact, all of these new rights have merely upped the ante on what it means to be a person, and dissatisfaction has soared. As both social inequality and social distance actually increased, anxious man, now armed with an arsenal full of "rights," looked to a source outside himself for solace. He found it in the marketplace of meddlers selling, paradoxically, "individual transcendence."

The Search for Individual Transcendence

The therapeutic vision seemed to offer the best possible vehicle for what the disciplines that fueled it were discussing as the be-all and end-all of life: individual transcendence. In the secular society of mid-twentieth-century America, the possibilities of transcendence were increasingly less seen as a function of religious views that had fallen into some disfavor than as a question of individual achievement through pursuing the right methodologies, leaders, and purposes. Several central issues defined this search, and each, as we shall see, produced a market for those skilled movement leaders and members of the helping professions who were in touch with their sources and techniques.

Personal Happiness, Wholeness, and Harmony as Prime Cultural Values

The tragic vision of life, held for centuries by human beings who had experienced life on this planet to be an arduous and difficult business[16] and as a result harbored few expectations, has been replaced by an entirely different ethic—one that emphasizes the immediate and painless attainment of everything. As Bernard Zilbergeld points out:

> We want and expect far more than ever before. Parents expect more of their children and of themselves as parents and spouses; children expect more from their parents. . . . [W]hen our desires are not fulfilled, as is frequently the case, we are ready to complain, get assistance, try something else, or file a lawsuit to right the wrongs we think are done to us. Almost everyone seems to feel entitled to all sorts of successes, adventures, and joys right now, without having to make any great sacrifices to get them. (Zilbergeld, 1983: 19)

What we want more than anything else is personal happiness. The United States is the only nation in the world that has the notion of happiness built right into its constitution. We are guaranteed, if not the attainment of happiness, at the very least the *pursuit* of it. In the 1950s Max Lerner observed that "America is a happiness society even more than it is a freedom society or a power society. The underlying strivings may be toward success, acquisitiveness or power, toward prestige or security. But what validates these strivings for the American is the idea that he has a natural right to happiness" (quoted in Sykes, 1992: 29). In earlier times, however, people did not have the luxury of stopping to ask themselves whether they were happy or not. If one attained happiness it was as an unintentional by-product to a life lived according to more socially useful and less trivial standards. But affluence and secularism changed all of that. Theme parks now merchandise "happiness" as though it were a product. McDonalds sells "happy meals." Advertisements for everything from soda pop to caskets and cemetery plots stress how happy we will be if only we make the right consumer choices. We have come to evaluate our own lives in terms of how "happy" we are. Indeed, marriages end with the trump-card argument "I'm not happy." The pursuit of happiness has created, of course, a kind of perpetual infantile tone to things, but it is tolerated because most everyone affirms that this single emotion is the ultimate purpose of secular life. If happiness sounds too childlike for one's taste, one can always adopt the mantra of harmonic wholeness—mind, body, and spirit all united in one concordant package. The search for wholeness takes many forms: Health foods, holistic medicine, and crystals have all claimed their adherents. But no matter how lunatic a particular strategy may seem to nonbelievers, the basic idea has endured: The American dream is failing and people have a right to more than they are getting. Such ideas have emerged as prime cultural values in American society in the past thirty years. Beginning as fringe movements of hippies and underemployed intellectuals, the language and the technologies have become mainstream. Gestalt therapy, biofeedback, assertiveness training, transactional analysis, transcendental meditation, rational-emotive therapy, EST, primal therapy, feeling therapy, encounter groups, aromatherapy, and bioenergetics are just a few of the more popular therapies that sprouted up in the 1960s and 1970s. Today the genre has exploded and has been joined by such new glosses as acceptance therapy, drama therapy, art therapy, survivor therapy, be-good-to-yourself therapy, and even angel therapy. And if these are too time-consuming for a culture of conveniences, there is now a host of "brief" therapies that get the job done much sooner.[17] Each of these approaches offers the prospect of individual transcendence in a world gone awry. Therapy books have become to the twentieth century what etiquette books were to the nineteenth. But unlike etiquette books, those touting a therapy were not designed to grease the machinery of social interaction by smoothing over potential conflicts with commonly agreed-upon rules. The search for individual transcendence was primarily an individualistic movement designed to save the person, to make him or her fit for coping with life in a world viewed as having gone mad. It was an acting out of the desire to rise above it all; and more than any thing else, it was an *individual* remedy. It was a thorough-going rejection of society rather than a celebration of it.

In this climate of a therapy for everyone, turning oneself over to either professional meddlers or to amateur helpers became a way of establishing innocence in an era of pollution. One had to come clean in order to gain the nirvana that was said to await those who would only follow the right procedures. Opening one's life for inspection became a way of showing others that one had "nothing to hide"—a legacy from the 1960s, when "letting it all hang out" became confused with therapeutic good intentions. Therapy was akin to the spiritual practice of confessing one's sins and rededicating oneself to God, and the secular post-1960s generation took to it with an enthusiasm that must have surprised even its creators.

The Emergence of Vulnerability, Sensitivity, Openness, and Self-Awareness

The legacy of the 1960s that fueled the meddling impulse as much as any was the rapid emergence of vulnerability, sensitivity, openness, and self-awareness as both languages people used and values they dearly held. These were not significant issues in earlier times, when the demands of life led to little inner reflection;[18] but in the 1960s, other-directed man— economically prosperous but trapped in an indoor world and surrounded by a diverse array of others intent upon face-to-face encounters—found that very different standards were being used to assess character. These standards were talked about as being more internal than external, and the talk included a generous helping of the idea that the new character type most in demand was one engaged in a process of self-awareness. Much of this new awareness was engendered by the movement for women's rights. Its particular efforts included not simply legal questions of discrimination but also the more important question of consciousness-raising and altering the interpersonal environment. "Sensitivity" emerged as a major social good. "Insensitivity" became a despised epithet. To be sensitive was, by definition, to be self-aware, and self-awareness was the ultimate goal of Americans disenchanted with a culture of affluence in which their economic success was regarded as having shut them off from their "true selves." Personal insight and open communication were regarded as the keys to restoring a sense of balance and harmony with others. Moreover, Americans became interested in "relating to one another," a phrase that came to mean more than simple interaction. Rather, it implied a process of "sharing," "caring," and being attuned to the concerns and needs of others. Relational skills such as "expressing" and "communicating" were workshop fodder in the new climate, where, as it turned out, there was a market for the rising tide of people who wanted to "get in touch." Encounter groups appeared, each led by a trained counselor who tried to put people in touch with their inner feelings as well as with each other: "Encounterists offer both verbal and nonverbal exercises expressly designed to enhance relating. When group members . . . publicly state the good feelings they have for each other, or when they hug, stroke, and cradle each other, this is supposed to free them up to giving and receiving affection more openly" (Schur, 1976: 99). As a result of such "encounter therapy," people were said to understand each other better and to avoid making unrealistic demands, because, in the words of primalist Arthur Janov (1970: 47), "each person becomes a viable human being, content to live and let live."

The new ethic of honesty, openness, and 'relating', as it turned out, was a complete reversal of what previous generations thought of the matter. As Philip Rieff notes: "Reticence, secrecy, concealment of self have been transformed into social problems; once they were aspects of civility, when the great Western formulary summed up in the creedal phrase "Know thyself" encouraged obedience to communal purposes rather than suspicion of them" (Rieff, 1987: 22). Now it was the community that was the target of suspicion, having played, it was thought, a decisive role in the repressive structures that psychological man was rebelling against. Civility was a veneer anyway, it was thought; better to tear away the facade and express oneself openly and honestly.[19] But in order to do so effectively, one had to have the proper techniques. These could, in the new environment of psychological man, be gotten for the small price of opening up one's life to therapeutic inspection.

The Belief That Human Beings
Are Fragile and Delicate Creatures

Accompanying the new self-awareness movements of the latter part of this century was the belief, largely kindled by therapeutic and psychological views of the world but contradicted by thousands of years of history, that human beings are fragile and delicate creatures, their selves composed of "spun glass," easily shattered, but which could be remade by contact with the right therapies. Stressing, as Freud did, the importance of early childhood experiences, but also extending this view to a host of later experiences, human life was regarded as a vale of traumas, each resulting from negative experiences suffered years before. The idea of "psychological pain and suffering" began to be seen in court litigation, often resulting in large payouts to those whose psyches had been damaged through the careless or reckless behavior of others. What in previous eras had been regarded as the ordinary and inevitable troubles of life were now being transformed into avoidable issues. Our myths began to move from "something beyond" to "someone else," and those "someones" were increasingly seen as the source of our difficulties and grief.[20]

Whatever the movement one sought, individual transcendence could not be achieved on one's own. Gurus, counselors, and those in command of the specialized languages of the new truths were needed. The idea that these "helpers" might actually be meddling into people's lives ceased to be a form of speech with which we were either acquainted or comfortable. The term *meddling* was translated into the array of euphemisms we discussed in the previous chapter: Social workers engaged in "professional intervention strategies" and performed "crisis intervention"; therapists and movement leaders "empowered" people and engaged in "treatment"; psychologists and psychiatrists had a "professional involvement" with "clients," "patients," or "cases"; meddling was transformed into "assessment" and "negotiation." There remained little recognition in this therapeutic milieu of overstepping one's bounds, for invading another person's life was seen as an important "professional confrontation" that, in turn, was simply a part of what adroit "therapy" was all about. If the "clients" disagreed, they were, of course, "in denial," a phrase that further reinforced the idea that meddlers knew what was best and the objects of their meddling did not. Misery meant opportunity.

The Triumph of the Therapeutic

When Rieff's classic work on what remained of the uses of faith after Freud was revised in 1987, he observed in a new introduction that what he had called *The Triumph of the Therapeutic* was now better termed "the unconditional surrender" to it. No longer simply a theoretical exercise in the implications of what the Americanization of the Freudian worldview had done to sacred versions of morality, the therapeutic had in every practical sense totally won the battle.[21] The therapeutic had become a vicarious faith, serving as a surrogate for religious traditions that were in full retreat:

"[T]he spiritualizers, who set the pace of Western cultural life from just before the beginning to a short time after the end of the nineteenth century, have given way now to their logical and historical successors, the psychologizers, inheritors of that dualist tradition which pits human nature against social order" (Rieff, 1987: 3). Few of the inheritors of this tradition were willing to concede, as Kenneth Burke (1965) claimed, that psychiatry was a "secular religion," a substitute for people who had lost their capacity to believe in God but needed one more than ever.[22] Instead, they attached themselves tenaciously to the medical/scientific ethic, a view whose currency was ascendant, and whose firm grasp on the public consciousness ensured that everyone along for the ride would be elevated to the status of prophet or guru. Psychologists, like the scientists they both envied and emulated, were realists, and they believed, along with Freud, that religious questions induce the very symptoms they seek to cure. "The moment a man questions the meaning and value of life," Freud wrote, "he is sick, since objectively neither has any existence." But as Rieff has shown, the earliest professional adherents to Freud's doctrines were dissatisfied with the limits that such a form of realism imposed. Freud thought that the proper use of psychotherapy was to assist people in adjusting to the pathological demands imposed by a culture of repression by helping them to understand their plight. Said Rieff: "To be analytical is to be a realist. It is not required of a realist to be hopeful or hopeless, but only truthful" (1987: 34). Freud's followers, unhappy with this neutral position, insisted on a better alternative. Faith reappeared, but this time it was understood as therapy.

Whatever else it may have meant, the rise of the therapeutic ethic indicated that people who intervened in the lives of others weren't simply meddlers anymore. They were scientific therapists armed with a method that would ensure salvation. Fortunately for their cause, the basic ideas had so many secular uses in this rapidly changing society that there was an instant appeal—a bond to be forged between meddler and meddlee. There was something in it for anyone who would respond to the solicitations of the meddler. It is to this issue that we turn next.

Notes

1. It is worth pointing out that *The Triumph of the Therapeutic*, Philip Rieff's (1987) brilliant early effort to document this change, was subtitled *The Uses of Faith After Freud*.

2. This belief also has clear-cut social control and institutional power implications. For a particularly enlightening discussion of this aspect of the rise of the therapeutic state, see the trilogy by Michel Foucault: *Madness and Civilization* (1961), *The Birth of the Clinic* (1963), and *Discipline and Punish* (1975).

3. The chronological career line looked something like this: In the 1960s we thought we could save society; in the 1970s and 1080s we thought we could save ourselves; and now, as the millennium runs out, we think the only way we can save ourselves is by stopping others from doing what they're doing.

4. More than three centuries later, President Ronald Reagan would, revealingly, call his vision of America by the same name.

5. For a full discussion of these ideas, see Smith (1965).

6. For a revealing historical summary of the connection between dietary practices and sexual purity, see Money (1984).

7. A recent film version of the novel *The Road to Wellville*, by T. Coraghessan Boyle, documents some of the sillier beliefs of Kellogg and his time, though the viewer cannot help but note that many such beliefs are in the process of making a major comeback.

8. The American humorist Will Rogers seemed to sense this slippery slope in his lectures on prohibition, for he observed with considerable prescience: "[T]he

minute they get prohibition they will hop on to something else—cigarettes . . . or baths or something" (Rogers, 1975: 15).

9. In the 1980s the Nebraska state legislature built a new multimillion-dollar basketball complex on the campus of the University of Nebraska. The building was funded by a special 5-cents-per-pack tax on cigarettes. Seemingly ungrateful for the source of their largesse, the legislators promptly prohibited smoking in the building.

10. The uselessness of the war on drugs in terms of meeting its stated goal of creating a "drug-free" America is evident in several respects, as documented amply by scholars. See especially Szasz (1985).

11. As discussed by Polsky, two such bureaucracies were critical. First, "[a]dvocates of institutional reform had settled upon the necessity for centralization . . . [S]ome form of state oversight, they had contended, would provide the needed antidote to local interference in the management of remedial asylums, and so assure that these would fulfill their moralizing mission" (Polsky, 1991: 102). Second, during the progressive era, it was presumed that through state administration, institutions would be further sanitized of politics, and the cardinal virtue of efficiency would be realized.

12. We're not kidding, although the following news item may well be. According to this report, a new disease called Internet Addiction Disorder (IAD) is characterized by such diagnostic criteria as "[a] need for markedly increased amounts of time on the Internet to achieve satisfaction," "withdrawal symptoms," "fantasies or dreams about the Internet," and so on. Whether the report is real or fanciful, no great leap is required to see that some serious authority will come up with such a syndrome soon enough. Psychologists are already earnestly talking about it, in any case.

13. Howard S. Becker (1994) has recently examined some of the ways to get at this question in his "'Foi por Acaso': Conceptualizing Coincidence."

14. A trip through the aisles of any mega-mall bookstore chain will give ample testimony to the popularity of the therapeutic vision of life. Shelf after shelf offer help and sustenance for every conceivable problem. One gets the distinct impression that life is a disease, God is a doctor, and help is only a few pages away.

15. Once it became clear that air bags had the potential to take as well as save lives, a campaign to give car owners the "right" to disable them was commenced. After much debate (a circumstance that has significant implications for our notions about meddling), the issue was settled with a compromise. Consumers could have a switch installed on their dashboard that would disable the bag, but only after establishing that they met certain criteria such as height restrictions and so on. In effect, their bodies still belonged to a meddlesome nanny government bent on protecting them at all costs.

16. "Nasty, brutish, and short as Hobbes called it.

17. George Ritzer (1993) might call them "McTherapies."

18. Or if such reflection *did* occur, it was more likely to be communicated only to intimates or confined to personal diaries.

19. We have only to look at the crude and boorish behavior being played out in public places to see the results of this ethic.

20. Following this view there even came to be court cases in which "repressed memories" of past abuse—usually sexual—were successfully argued.

21. Despite periodic outbursts of religious revival, the long-term trend toward secularization is no longer disputed. Even churches have surrendered to the therapeutic, offering counseling services, divorce mediation, and the like. Many therapeutic self-help groups with completely secular agendas now meet in underused church facilities.

22. Michael Lerner's (1997) movement to establish what he calls a "politics of meaning" is the latest incarnation of this trend. For a less-than-enthusiastic endorsement of such efforts, see Marin (1996).

3

Running Scared: The Appeal and Acceptance of Meddling

The biggest business in America is not steel, automobiles, or television. It is the man-ufacture, refinement, and distribution of anxiety.
        —Bernie Zilbergeld

Meddling continues to flourish in America in part because people allow themselves to be meddled with. Why this mutual conspiracy between the meddler and the meddlee? What is the allure of the meddler? If everyone simply told others to mind their own business, as they were much more likely to have done in previous eras, meddlers would find little to occupy their time. But like many other issues having to do with meddling, the matter is complicated by the fact that people receive numerous benefits from submitting to the intrusions of others. And even though the promises are typically greater than what is delivered, the entreaties of the meddler are clearly beguiling. And for what reason? In this chapter we will provide the beginnings of an answer as to why so many Americans allow others to meddle in their lives. The fact that people tolerate, accept, and endorse the meddling of others is analyzed through a discussion of the promise of meddling to resolve the institutional and interpersonal confusions in American life. We begin with a theme that is dear to the heart of the meddling enterprise: the uses of confusion.

The Institutionalization of Confusion

Part of the reason people allow others to meddle so shamelessly into their lives lies in what we might call the "institutionalization of confu-sion." Most people say they abhor confusion and seek to resolve it with understanding. Indeed, surveys regularly report that a majority of Amer-icans long for a "simpler life." Yet in this culture bewilderment has come to be institutionalized with literally thousands of business and service ac-tivities relying on a baffled public to purchase their wares. A prime example is the kind of confusion brought about by the gender wars. The swelling puzzlement over relationships with the opposite sex has created a mushrooming cottage industry composed of dating services, personal ads, 900 numbers, divorce lawyers, relational counselors, politicians ever-ready to legislate—the list goes on. These new services gain financially from the contemporary mystification of male/female relationships and use it as a rationale for butting into the lives of those who can't cope.

Even more widespread is the anxiety that has become the national air we breathe. The less people know and the more anxiety-ridden they are, the greater is their dependence on people who claim to know. Confusion breeds questions, and questions, after all, are what supports meddlers, many of whom do little more than peddle advice. Who are we to believe? Is fat bad for you? A spate of books bolstered by some science (pseudo- or real—who's to say?) claims that it is. Does caffeine cause cancer? Are air bags truly life-savers, or are they themselves agents of death? Is date-rape epidemic on college campuses? Which child-rearing technique is best? By what standard do we judge our marriage to be a good one? Meddlers not only have answers—they have the right ones. The message of the meddler is that life is simply too confusing, so one needs advisers—preferably paid ones—to sort things out.[1]

Exaggerated Claims and the Promotion of Anxiety

There are many sources of such confusion and anxiety. One is the hyperbole of postmodern society shouting from every media source. Those who would meddle into our lives tend to portray the particular problem with which *they* deal as the most serious threat to human life since the great plague. As Howard Leichter notes, this "crying wolf" is particularly prevalent among those who would meddle in the name of health and safety: "Road accidents have been characterized as 'the most intractable challenge of the second half of the 20th century,' cigarette smoking as second only to 'nuclear annihilation'; AIDS as a 'peril to our entire species'; and alcohol abuse as 'the major public health problem of our time'" (Leichter, 1991: 255). We could easily add to this litany of the hazards of modern life such things as obesity, poor diet, lack of exercise (the latter two being the putative cause of the first), cancer, heart disease, economic insecurity, crime—the list seems endless. And all this wolf-crying persists despite the fact that America is arguably the safest and healthiest society on the face of the earth.[2] Lacking a sense of perspective, we thus become mired in millennial thinking. A spate of books trumpet the "end" of something—the end of work, the end of history, the end of sex—their combined apocalyptic weight adding to the consensus that life is not nearly as safe as we could make it if only we did the right things, and the "right things" frequently involve the meddlesome banning of this substance or that behavior. Many of these books, of course, contain wise insights about changes in the context of our lives. Collectively, however, they are an invitation to disaster thinking and the anxiety it breeds. People can't be sure anymore of where they are going or what their life means. Think you have a good marriage? Just take this test or talk to us. Believe that your children are doing well? Consider this fact or that interpretation. Have a behavioral problem? It could be a chemical imbalance in your brain. Our clinic, with its access to the latest science, can help. The confusion industry includes a wide variety of practitioners in the human service fields, including psychiatrists, social workers, counselors, lawyers, and marriage and family therapists, as well as the mighty media empires whose quenchless appetite for material that purports to solve problems gives voice to these groups.

Edward Tenner (1996: 147) notes that we are suffering from "an epidemic of apprehension," arguably brought on by this confusion. "We seem to worry more than our ancestors," writes Tenner, "surrounded though they were by exploding steamboat boilers, raging epidemics, crashing trains, panicked crowds, and flaming theaters" (1996: 147). A recent newspaper article reported on eleven new things to worry about. These include the helpful notice that syphilis cases are up dramatically in the United States; that your toothbrush could give you the flu; that one in every ten people is allergic to penicillin; that naturally occurring carcinogens are found in oranges, celery, mushrooms, and spinach; that your carpeting, upholstery, insulation, and plywood may be emitting formaldehyde gas; that someone dies at work every forty-nine minutes; that according to U.S. environmental protection agency research, bleached-paper coffee filters may leech dioxin (a poison) into your coffee when you pour hot water through them; that dental fillings contain silver amalgams (another powerful poison); and that in a recent survey, college students responded that given a choice between two jobs—one manufacturing weapons-grade plutonium for $48,000 a year, and another paying $24,000 per annum for making socially benign products—they would take the plutonium job. But the more we try to insulate ourselves from the resident dangers of life, the more problems we create. Various laws designed to protect people actually increase the very hazards they seek to alleviate. Examples abound. Improvements in fighting forest fires produce more fires by building up flammable materials that feed new fires. Residents of California, emboldened by improvements in construction technology, build on increasingly hazardous hillsides, leaving themselves vulnerable to mud slides. Charles Murray reports that when laws were passed mandating that tractors be equipped with roll cages, the number of fatalities remained about the same because farmers, armed with their new "safer" equipment, simply began to grade steeper hills (Murray, 1994). Armed car-jacking has increased in part, says Tenner, because thieves, frustrated by alarm systems that make the theft of parked cars more difficult, resort to more direct approaches (Tenner, 1996). Home security systems produce so many false alarms that police resources are wasted on checking them out, thus making crime easier. And automobile air bags, as we noted, may cause more injuries than they prevent, especially in children.

Adding to the managed confusion created in part by professional meddlers who have a stake in ensuring that no one is confident in his or her approach to life is the allied problem of the meddlers' inflated claims. A prime example is health. So much has been avowed about the benefits of health and fitness that it is practically impossible for any organized movement to live up to such billing. Ideologists with truths to sell, of course, may be *expected* to inflate their claims, but among the more grandiose ones relating to health and fitness are such astonishing (as well as humorous) assertions as those avowed in a 1983 article on the objectives of "wellness" programs:

- To precisely document in numerical terms a person's overall level of health and fitness.
- To prevent rather than cure: The way to reduce hospital costs is to keep people out of the hospital.
- To convince people that they are responsible for their own health. More than 53 percent of disease is self-controlled. More than 80 percent of cardiovascular disease and cancer are preventable phenomena.
- To foster positive lifestyle changes in smoking, nutrition, weight control, blood pressure, stress and tension, aerobic exercise, lung function, strength fitness, and lower-back problems. (Plyman and Perkins, 1983: 7)

When Oscar Wilde called *health* "the silliest word in the English language," he may well have been thinking about such exaggerated claims, which only add to the confusion these meddlers seek to resolve. Since even a definition of *health* is elusive, if not impossible (*health* tautologically being defined as the absence of disease, and *disease* being defined as departures from health), the claim that we can develop a quantitative measure of it seems to represent unalloyed hubris. The idea that "the way to reduce hospital costs is to keep people out of the hospital" almost begs for satire rather than serious analysis, for the matter is considerably more complicated than such an easy diagnosis of the problems of the health-care system would suggest. Although it may be true that prevention cuts costs (thereby saving insurance companies money in the short run), all it does in the long run is to delay the inevitable illnesses and ultimate death that await everyone—this along with the costs that the system as a whole will eventually incur from people living longer lives and dying from chronic diseases, the control of which already seems to have reached a point of diminishing returns (Callahan, 1990). It might as easily be argued that if the country did become successful through its citizens' individual diligence in staying out of hospitals, the cost of hospitals might well increase, since every endeavor (especially expensive hitech ones like hospitals) needs a steady stream of customers to keep its infrastructure going. In view of the fact that healthy people get sick, too (and have on occasion been known to die)—even if we concede that upstream interventions like wellness do, indeed, decrease the cost of acute health care in America, as its proponents claim—the financial burden of inevitable illness and death will simply be shifted to society at large in the form of increased social security and Medicare benefits, since the majority of medical costs tend to pile up in the last few weeks of life.[3]

Moreover, there is mounting evidence suggesting that the "cost-to-society" argument, often claimed as a justification for intervening in people's lives in the name of health, actually sorts itself out on the side of the health miscreant. Although the exact ratio of smokers to nonsmokers varies slightly from study to study, it is clear that the net cost to society of each smoker is a negative one; in other words, smokers pay more to society in the form of taxes than they get back in the form of additional health-care benefits necessitated by their smoking. In short, because cigarette smokers die on average six to eight years sooner than nonsmokers, the amount they cost in additional medical care is more than offset by their shorter life span (see Figure 3.1). Data compiled by Duke University economist W. Kip Viscusi (1994: 33) and others suggest that the economic advantage to society of each smoker is between 20 and 30 cents per pack.

Peter Huber, writing in *Forbes,* agrees that smoking kills people—but, for the most part, not when they are in their prime, during the most economically productive years of their lives. It kills them, he says, "before they live long enough to burden the social welfare system" (Huber, 1995: 42). Dennis Zimmerman, an economist for the nonpartisan Congressional Research Service, uses slightly different numbers to reach the same conclusion. Smokers cost society 72 cents a pack, he estimates, but because they die earlier, they save society the equivalent of 39 cents a pack in nursing home and Medicare expenses. That leaves an average gain of 56 cents a pack (Zimmerman, 1994). Once again, it is the smokers who are subsidizing the nonsmokers rather than the other way around. All we have to do to understand this rather obvious relationship between health sins and the cost to society is to take the rhetoric of the healthists at face value. Let

FIGURE 3.1   Offset Costs

SOURCE: Bok, Chip. *Akron Beacon Journal* (August 10, 1995). Reprinted with permission from Creator's Syndicate.

us say, for instance, that a person smokes, drinks to excess, eats unapproved foods, follows a sedentary lifestyle, and practices unsafe sex. And let us say, theoretically, that as a result of these health and fitness sins she dies in her early sixties. It is obvious that, on the eve of her retirement, she has saved society a pile of money in social security and Medicare benefits alone. And let us say, on the other hand, that the pure and virtuous healthist does not smoke, abstains from drinking, eats only approved foods, exercises regularly, and practices safe sex. And let us also say—theoretically, of course—that as a result of this pure and wholesome life that would make the most priggish Puritan proud, she lives to be ninety. Put this way, it is not difficult to see which type is the heavier drain on the public treasury. Now, there are many reasons why one might wish to pursue what is understood to be a healthy and virtuous lifestyle. But the alleged savings to society is not one of them, for the facts indicate just the opposite.

In spite of such obscure data, untouched by the media and largely hidden from view, an anxiety-ridden society where confusion has been institutionalized is ripe for the siren call of the meddler. Increases in moral fervor that often accompany conversions to new lifestyles make tolerance of contrasting lifestyles not only more difficult to accept but positively dangerous to one's newfound truth. A society on the move not only geographically, but also in terms of its own understanding of itself, makes such conflicts more frequent and more contentious. The stakes, it seems, keep rising as the meddlers increase the decibel level while sounding the alarm about various maladies that plague us. New expectations—perfect bodies, minds, and spirits—all create a climate in which those who do not "live up" are seen as having something inherently wrong with them. They must, for their own good, as well as the good of those around them, be meddled with.

The Decline in the Prestige and Durability of Family and Intimate Relationships

One of the less salubrious effects of the massive breakup of the family we have witnessed over the last three decades is a precipitous decline in the belief in the wisdom and durability of family and intimate relationships. There was a time when we were likely to believe that the word of the family was, if not the last, at least the most definitive and authoritative word on any subject. Even such esoteric subjects as medicine and law were likely to be dealt with primarily in terms of the wisdom of the family, and only secondarily in terms of doctors and lawyers, members of those fledgling professions that were neither well regarded nor particularly competent at what they did.[4] But much of that ethos has disappeared. Indeed, the decline of the family means that families are increasingly viewed as the problem, that everyone is sick, and, above all, perhaps, that people can always point to someone as the source of the litany of problems that almost everyone's life seems to have become. As Charles Sykes remarks: "Almost any of the anxieties and failings of adult life can now be attributed to a toxic or unenlightened upbringing. One leading psychologist argued on 'The Phil Donahue Show' that 'much of what we consider normal parenting is actually abusive,' while a best-selling book warns of the dangers of 'Toxic Parents'" (Sykes, 1992: 141). Scattered to the winds by geographic and social mobility, the postmodern family is a *bouillabaisse* of loose connections without any particular basis of respect or commitment. Conjugal gatherings frequently turn out to be reminders of how little we have in common with our relatives except for the increasingly loose connection called "family." Furthermore, the term itself has been coarsely cheapened by its appropriation to institutions that in many ways are the antithesis of family—work settings, television newsrooms, restaurants, and other commercial enterprises that urge us to view them as "family."[5] These pseudo-places fill the void that was once held by real families. As Ray Oldenburg has argued, the rise of the companionate marriage in which husbands and wives were supposed to be wed in blissful intimacy was conjoined by the rise of suburbs, a development encouraged by cheap government loans and the total abandonment of society to the requirements of the automobile (Oldenburg, 1989: 246). Safely distanced in these new suburban locations from the inquiring eyes of in-laws and acquaintances who knew them as youngsters, people subscribed to a new ideal of togetherness that took root around marriages conceptualized as sweetheart dreams of romance whereby each partner would spend the rest of his or her life sprinkling happy dust into the eyes of the other.

The results of the pursuit of this idyllic dream proved to be a bonanza for meddlers. Divorce rates soared, making marriage and family "therapy" a growth industry.[6] Moreover, those who did not succumb to divorce *per se* increasingly sought alternatives to companionate marriage. Oldenburg quotes data suggesting that by the twilight of the pre-AIDS era, between 2 and 5 percent of the nation's married couples were regularly involved in mate-swapping, that rates of extramarital involvement likewise were on the rise, and, perhaps most astonishingly, that the number of single-person households is projected to grow twice as fast as that of all households in the United States (Glick, 1984: 21–25; quoted in Oldenburg, 1989: 247). Clearly, this "new family" vision of intimate relationships was not working out very well.

Likewise, intimate relationships, whether they involve marriage or not, are said by various meddling groups to be seething cauldrons of pathology and depression. Trumpeted, of course, as the be-all and end-all of life, these relationships are much more interesting when addressed in terms of problems and difficulties than in terms of possibilities and constraints. A mere sampling of the wide selection of titles on the shelf of any urban bookstore will show what we mean. Such books as *Women Are from Venus, Men Are from Mars, Codependent No More, The Dance of Anger, Broken Blossoms,* and *Raging Heart* all characterize intimate relationships as cesspools of alienation, violence, and despair. (One could say that Nicole Brown Simpson is the poster child for married women everywhere.) No one really gets along because power and exchange issues are to be found in all human relationships, your intimate other is merely using you, and people who think they do get along are living in a fool's paradise of ignorance—which, of course, this book or that workshop will apprise you of, raise your consciousness about, and teach you to handle. Even the IRS joins the fray by offering a helpful government pamphlet titled "Divorce: An IRS Perspective."

The Promissory Appeal of Meddling

The appeal of meddlers stems in part from the promises they implicitly offer. They are grandiose indeed. Among the more prevalent ones are the purchase of friendship and community, the allure of becoming a victim, and the myth of denial. We will discuss each of these in turn.

The Purchase of Friendship and Community

Friendship and community, those traditional gifts that the presence of others offer us, have become, in the promises of the postmodern culture of late capitalism (Jameson, 1991), simply another commodity that can be purchased.[7] The price? Meddling intrusions. Meddling confers instant friendship. Mention that you have a problem and strangers as well as mere acquaintances come forward to offer advice. One's intimate circle of real friends may have dwindled, but the television offers an immediate array of pseudo-friends ever-ready via electronic signals and videotape to amuse, entertain, instruct, meddle, and provide scripts for life. The only tangible cost? Watching hours of advertisements. ("Don't touch that dial, we'll be right back," says the commanding voice of one whom we have identified as a friend already.) And watch we do. According to a report in the *Chicago Tribune*, the A. C. Nielsen company reports that, despite the fact that television viewing is down slightly, Americans still watch an average of twenty-one and a half hours per week (Jones, 1996). Children watch somewhat more and adults somewhat less. In spite of criticism and even the occasional bumper sticker that proclaims "Kill Your TV," the number of cable channels is escalating rapidly and 24-hour services are coming on-line on a regular basis.[8] "I'm continually surprised by the appetite of the American viewing public," says Fred Wray, president of TN Media in Chicago (quoted in Jones, 1996: 44). Such "virtual" communities clearly compete with real ones, and it is probable that the slight decline in viewing is testimony only to the fact that some Americans are spending more time in front of the computer, surfing through the vast array of "programming" offered there, rather than in front of their conventional TV sets. If we then add the amount of television viewing to the amount of isolated time in front of the computer, we can easily conclude that the attraction to non-face-to-face forms of relationships is overwhelming the amount of real time that people spend with one another. Given this enthusiasm for watching, pointing, and clicking, as opposed to traditional conversation and the enjoyment of one another's company, the gifts bestowed by real community are under considerable pressure. These essentially one-way relationships, no matter how "interactive" they claim to be, are essentially the union of strangers, and they constitute a growing segment of the lives of contemporary Americans.

Being meddled with is often the price we pay for the time we spend in these pursuits. Among the vast array of programming on television and information on the electronic billboards of cyberspace, increasing portions are given over to telling people how to live their lives. The meddlesomeness of television may be seen in the constant offering of shows that are nothing but thinly disguised advertisements for various products (extended "infomercials"), predicated on the idea that something is wrong with the viewer's life and offering a remedy. Touting this therapy and that cure, meddlers find a ready audience in the anxious American. Whether it be weight-loss advice (hundreds of hours of programming per week are given over to assisting the corpulent American with such advice), spiritual counsel, exercise regimens, or health and beauty tips (the two becoming increasingly synonymous), we are saturated with meddling in the name of any number of ideologies (many of which we will discuss in the next chapter). The net affect of all this problem-mongering is the view that something must be wrong with us. The standards are so voluminous—albeit contradictory—that we adopt the view of the meddling electronic gurus: Something must surely be wrong with us.

The instant celebrity offered by the culture at large is mirrored by the interpersonal celebrity offered by meddlers. "Let us into your life and we will be your friend" seems to be the message. Although human interaction has always been characterized by a preoccupation with problems, we seem to be paying the price in the form of more and more meddling interventions. But as we have come to discover, meddling is fundamentally unlike friendship in that it consists of the elimination, not the provision, of alternatives. The meddler, unlike the true friend, is full of ways of telling us what not to do as opposed to offering precious and well-motivated advice regarding the various consequences that emerge from our making this decision or that. Historically we allowed these intrusions into our lives because we felt that our friends were not after our money but were interested in our welfare. But as this "welfare" became a commodity for sale in a marketplace of therapies, nostrums, and cures (many of which are necessitated by the manufactured diseases, maladies, and syndromes of the therapeutic state), the absence of real friends is substituted by the lure of the meddler. They *seem* to care. They *seem* to know.

Moreover, since the basis of our myths has moved from "something beyond" to "someone else," the meddler offers someone to blame our problems on. We can now purchase, at nominal cost (or so it seems, inasmuch as the true costs are never known), an understanding of the adversary that is at the source of all our problems. Take the matter of obesity. Judging from the words of those who meddle in the name of sveltness, the number of people held accountable for the plight of the fat American is legion. Listen to those who offer advice to the corpulent and you will discover a rogue's gallery of villains including doting parents who made you unconsciously associate food with love, friends who use food as an excuse to "get together," the fast-food culture of a "McDonaldized" society (Ritzer, 1993), and the plague of food advertisers who link food to identities, emotions, and the good life. Happily exempt from this enemies list are, of course, the meddler themselves, who are making a nice living promoting anxiety and who, as the preeminent historian of bodies and fat Hillel Schwartz has said, turn our bodies into "test-sites" for a series of thoroughly different ways of being, restless or peaceful, public or reclusive, ascetic or indulgent" (Schwartz, 1996: A-2). The meddler cashes in on our angst. The more restless we can be made to feel, and the more public we regard our body as being—as not our own at all but, rather, as the wholly owned subsidiary of viewers repulsed by its imperfections—the more the solicitations of meddlers will be purchased and the greater their claim will be on our lives. In the consumer culture we can purchase anything: happiness, peace of mind, perfection in every human sphere. Our minds, bodies, and souls are not only perfectible (as thousands of testimonials claim), but since others have achieved this perfection we can too. The only price is to pay heed to the counsel of the meddlers, to buy their wares, and to live our lives according to the formulas offered. The willingness to accept meddling may be the perfect mesh of economics and the search for a mode of transcendence—a truly secular and materialistic conversion.[9]

Moreover, the availability of health and fitness for a price redefines community in a way that has the capacity to let loose its most virulent fascist strains. However inviting, bodily perfection can be a particularly tyrannical concept. As Schwartz has observed:

> [I]f there are few true "health nazis" among us, certainly there are exercise executives and fitness infantas who encourage us to "go for the burn," who shame us into stair stepping, who berate us toward ever-lower pulse rates, and whose motto is "no pain, no gain." Boldface headlines on boxes of adult breakfast cereal hector the overweight and the undervitamined; some scales now scold us for not following our diets; a fat person's belly seems to be common property for others to pinch, josh, and bully.

And then, the critical question: "Why do we unswervingly accept an ideology whose judgments of moral integrity are based upon evidences of abstinence, leanness, efficiency, and stamina rather than upon proofs of charitableness, compassion, mercy, and foresight?" (Schwartz, 1996: C-F). At least part of the answer to Schwartz's question is that such an ideology sells, and that those who argue it are making a fortune out of the products sold to perpetually dissatisfied Americans. But economic arguments always founder on the more provocative and useful social psychological question, "Why is anyone buying in the first place?" An answer to this question lies in the observation that as community has dissolved into a postmodern pastiche of possibilities, clarity of perspective has become obscured by the richness of the view. So many competing voices compelling us in different ways is not the sort of thing out of which confidence emerges. Contemporary Americans are riven with confusion and anxiety. To use Kenneth Gergen's term, we are "saturated":

> [W]e become pastiches, imitative assemblages of each other. . . . [I]f the conditions are favorable, we can place these patterns into action. Each of us becomes the other, a representative, or a replacement. To put it more broadly, as the century has progressed, selves have become increasingly populated with the character of others. . . . [E]ach of us comes to harbor a vast population of hidden potentials. (Gergen, 1991: 71)

We listen because the babble of voices seems to know what we do not; and, perhaps even more significantly, it claims to know about the most important things of all—self, bodies, relationships, spirituality, and the welfare of those about whom we are supposed to care the most: our family, friends, children, and communities. Never mind that, in the final analysis, the dissatisfactions stem not from such mundane issues as fat, food, and pulse rates but, rather, from more central existential issues, a point made nicely in the last stanza of a poem by Margaret Atwood (quoted in Schwartz, 1996: C-3):

> *you aren't sick and unhappy*
> *only alive and stuck with it.*

This is not a message that would be sellable in the marketplace of the meddler, but it states the prime essence of the problem nonetheless.

Even friendship becomes an exercise in meddling interventions. Although friendships are still established through the age-old exchange of secrets and trust (Bok, 1983), they now seem even more likely to originate as a function of the willingness to meddle and be meddled with. Meddling confers "instant friendship" in a society where the allure of having a friend is very much a modern motif, but it also gives in to the therapeutic ethic whereby one should tell the whole story and hold nothing back. Friends can be depended on to listen and help solve problems or, failing that, to at least offer a sympathetic ear. But to accomplish these supplications the friend must be given the whole story. Holding back is sure evidence of having something to hide, and friends don't lie to friends. We are told it is good to "get things off your chest," to "clear the air," or to "come clean." After all, a specialized society means that we can no longer rely on ourselves, and why should we? There is a whole series of cultural resources out there to be tapped, if one concedes to being meddled with—especially when the meddling is not offered as meddling at all but, rather, is euphemistically transformed into "helping," "caring for," and so on. It is no wonder that being meddled with is so beguiling. It is seen as the passport to friendship in a society where true friendship is becoming increasingly problematic.

In addition, the more people utilize meddlers, the more accepted (and acceptable) the latter become. If only a few brave hearts are going to see psychiatrists, opening their lives up for inspection on the *Oprah Winfrey Show* or intervening boldly into the lives of their friends and acquaintances about intimate things, that would be one thing. But everyone seems to be doing it, and the fifteen minutes of fame that Andy Warhol predicted for each of us is surely coming true as the meddlers and the meddlees engage in their revelatory dance. So the more people meddle and allow themselves to be meddled with by utilizing various professional meddlers, the more acceptable meddling becomes for everyone.

The Allure of Becoming a Victim

Likewise, victimage is increasingly becoming our national currency—the ticket to ride. We accept the advice and counsel of the meddler because he or she offers us the chance to become pitied as a victim of this disease or that syndrome, and previous inexplicable behavior is now rationalized by the alleged "condition" that one has. Communities once held their hands out to the poor and downtrodden, not because they were victims of diseases but because they needed help, just as we might one day, and it was the right thing to do. Charity was a community obligation rather than a business. The emergence of professional social work, psychiatric thinking, mental-disease-mongering, the widespread acceptance of the myth of mental illness (Szasz, 1961)—in short, the medicalization of human behavior—has changed all that. With the advent of mass media and the postmodern institution called the television talk show, there now exists a forum for almost everyone to splay out the intimate details of their lives. This is what all too often passes for community—people sitting in their living rooms watching what amounts to game-show contestants trying to out-victim one another.[10]

- **The Rise of Self-Help.**   To add to this confusion, we have seen an eruption of support groups, support relationships, and supportive others, all of which operate on the ragged edge of meddling. Not necessarily coercive, they are nevertheless meddlesome. Getting into each other's lives is the ostensible reason for bringing people together. Sometimes they act out their meddling under the patina of voluntarism, but at other times the distinction between voluntary and coerced is thin indeed. These groups are sometimes seen as a laudatory sign of improvement in our collective lives, and personal testimonies abound concerning their effectiveness in leading people to new heights of self-actualization and problem solving. Indeed, these support relationships have become big business. From Weight Watchers to Jenny Craig, there is a commercial group for every overweight American. The corpulent who feel beset by the culture of thinness, tired of being meddled with by what they consider the weight obsessed, have organized a "fat liberation" movement that is becoming increasingly militant. Composed of such groups as the National Association to Aid Fat Americans and a more overtly political group called the Fat Underground, these groups have claimed victim status themselves and have even gone to court to secure the "right" to be fat (Martin, 1995). The commodification of alcohol and drug rehabilitation serves a clientele that runs into the millions. And you don't even need money. A quick look at the weekly meeting schedule in any newspaper will show that churches, in order to get a quorum for underutilized worship facilities, have offered, rented, or leased their space during the week to a host of self-help groups. For example, the Sunday paper in a town of only 40,000 people contained an announcement listing groups such as the following:

Nicotine Anonymous
Singles Alternative
Co-Dependent Anonymous
Parkinson's Support Group
Smokers Anonymous
SAVES (Sexual Abuse Victims Emerge Survivors)
TOPS (Take Off Pounds Sensibly)
Narcotics Anonymous
Secular Sobriety
Overeaters Anonymous
MENders (for wife beaters)
Sex Addicts Anonymous
Sandwich Generation Support Group
Overcomers (for overweight people)
Alcoholics Anonymous
Al-Anon
AMAC (Adults Molested as Children)
Al-Ateen
"Came to Recover"
Concerned Parents
Motherwell (for women seeking maternity fitness)
Emotions Anonymous
ADD (Attention Deficit Disorder) Parents
Community AIDS Network
Challengers (for the disabled)

Each of these organizations is staffed by a solemn collection of chronic volunteers and board members who presumably receive a sense of satisfaction and accomplishment or who engage in such activities as part of the "community service component" of the expectations of their jobs. Anyone who lives in a larger town will find a correspondingly longer list that would include such groups as Pill Addicts Anonymous and Dual Disorders Anonymous. It would seem that America is a nation populated by massive numbers of sick people, each with his or her own circle of helpers dedicated to the formal offering of self-help.

What could possibly be wrong with such a salutary phenomenon? The problem, of course, is that alongside the rise of these groups we have witnessed a transformation of "support" from a secondary to a primary mode of human affiliation. In its secondary form, we have traditionally supported others because we had primary affiliations with them. They were friends or members of families, or they belonged to a network of others in our community to which we felt a kinship and an obligation. Our support was required and was merely "the right thing to do." In more recent times, however, "support" has metamorphosed into a primary form of interaction—it is what people do both avocationally and vocationally. It is, as we pointed out earlier, the hallmark of good friends and a "caring" community. Moreover, it is a respected way of making a living. That these endeavors are largely bureaucratic and even entrepreneurial in nature is beside the point. Community and friendship are increasingly purchased commodities, packaged, marketed, and sold in much the same way that travel agencies sell vacation "experiences" (Brissett and Lewis, 1981).

Self-help groups may also enforce the very confusion they seek to erase. Dependent as they are on a view of the world as complex and dangerous (the very ideas that engender so much meddling in the first place), these groups cash in on the idea that since the family and other sources of intimate help are no longer available, one has to look elsewhere for support. Opening up one's life to others has become the price of admission. Lines are blurred; participants are given the sense of outsiders looking in. The "voyeur's gaze," as Norman Denzin (1991) once called the cinema, is legitimated as a group activity.[11] The forthright admission of imperfections in one's life gives others a license to meddle.

Victims All.   In a compelling article in *Harper's*, David Rieff asks us to

[i]magine a country in which millions of apparently successful people nonetheless have come to believe fervently that they are really lost souls—a country where countless adults allude matter-of-factly to their "inner children," who, they say, lie wounded and in desperate need of relief within the

wreckage of their grown-up selves. Imagine the celebrities and opinion-makers among these people talking nightly on TV and weekly in the magazines not about their triumphs but about their victimization, not about their power and fame but about their addictions and childhood persecutions. (Rieff, 1991: 49)

Of course, the country of which Rieff speaks is not some underdeveloped Third World enclave but the richest country on earth—America. Whereas the citizens of other countries go to great lengths to get in, increasing numbers of those who have lived here all their lives see themselves as victims of this disease or that syndrome—done in by their parents, abused by their spouses, and generally down-trodden, even in the face of all that material wealth. It seems that everyone you know is recovering from something—a veritable army of sick people trying to sort out their desperate lives with the assistance of authors and therapists, many of whom were instrumental in defining their problems in the first place. The "Me" generation characterized by Tom Wolfe in the late 1970s has devolved into what Charles Sykes (1992) calls "a nation of victims."[12] One need only look to the cozy relationship between victims and meddlers to see what is happening. Every new class of victims has a new class of meddlers, usually professional, standing in the wings to attend to their wretched plight. Even the most cursory look at what Jane Shattuc calls the "teletherapy" emanating from television talk shows, will demonstrate that victimage is in full bloom (Shattuc, 1997: 80). And the numerous books with such titles as *Co-Dependent No More* and *Healing the Child Within* that constitute this genre compete with the lucrative talk-show market where contestants vie for victim status and the recognition that comes with it. This profusion of victims all complaining about the hand others have dealt them must be what Pete Hamill is talking about when he says that "[l]ife in these semi–United States often seems to be an illustration of Jean-Paul Sartre's dictum that hell is other people" (Hamill, 1991: 26—30).

Being a victim is powerful because it forces attention on you. Those caught up in this way of life sometimes move from meddler to meddler. Thus, for example, persons who were sexually abused may find that in presenting themselves for therapy to one professional, they will eventually make contact with dozens of others as well. The resulting attention is itself part of the allure of being meddled with. Like the child who acts out because at least someone is watching, victimhood has a kind of narcotic, self-enhancing quality. And in a nation that increasingly celebrates those who claim to be the casualties of the unfortunate wreckage of our civilization, people can actually extract useful benefits from playing a role that our ancestors would certainly have regarded as humiliating and demeaning.

There are also monetary rewards to be had from claiming victim status and allowing oneself to be meddled with by the array of professionals ready to help advance their clients' cases. Indeed, the social construction of "helplessness" has emerged in the late twentieth century as a powerful political catalyst for funding various programs designed to help "victims." Many of these programs were originally targeted for groups that most everyone could see genuinely needed help. But as with just about every other boundary in the postmodern world, the coverage of victims has expanded to include virtually anyone who wishes to claim the status. The traditional distinctions between people who were hurt by either malevolent or natural forces outside their control and those who were harmed as a result of their own bad judgment, poor choices, or actual misconduct have now largely disappeared. As the human sciences have grown in their power to define human behavior as symptoms of various constructed pathologies, and as expert witnesses are increasingly used in courts of law to persuade juries of the validity of their claims, more and more victims emerge to ask for money. Thus we find the surprising case of stupidity elevated to the status of victimage when a woman sued McDonalds after she spilled hot coffee on herself on the grounds that the coffee was "too hot." Or the case of a tort lawyer who sued a bicycle manufacturer on behalf of his client who was seriously injured when struck by a car while riding the bike on an interstate highway at night without a light. "My client was lulled into the false belief that the reflector system was sufficient to protect him," the lawyer disingenuously asserted. Or the case of a couple hit by a train while making love on the track of the New York subway and later suing on the grounds that the train was moving too fast to see them. The fact that they were trespassing on transit authority property became simply another "variable" in the case to be decided in litigation.[13] Or the case of a man who ran up a $25,000 bill on his American Express card at a Las Vegas casino and refused to pay on the grounds that he was an alcoholic and American Express and the casino had "let him do it." Many of these cases, of course, are thrown out of court or reduced on appeal, but there are enough victors to make the game both attractive and lucrative—always for the lawyers who file the cases, and sometimes for the clients who win them. Victimage has indeed become something like America's version of a national lottery.

In addition to monetary rewards, being a victim and allowing oneself to be meddled with by others have actually become sources of prestige. Following protracted campaigns to convince Americans that various kinds of behaviors are actually the result of known diseases and syndromes for which there is "help," it seems that being in recovery can now be worn as a badge of honor. The fault lies not in bad habits or poor choices but in "denial" or refusals to accept the help that is so generously pro-offered. In the new consumer culture, being a victim has a certain chic to it, a cachet. And in an era when people are constantly being urged to change their lives, and are so bored that they want to, victimage is enchanting. Consider the case of former model and current talk-show host Christina Ferrari, who received national acclaim—and a considerable boost in ratings—when she revealed on her show that she had lost all of her sexual desire. Praised as a "courageous woman," she was instantly mobbed by a phalanx of meddlers, both amateur and professional, who saw her as a new poster child for self-awareness and dauntless problem solving. She subsequently announced that she had found relief in a "testosterone cream" that restored her to her former libidinous self.

In a society of spectators and consumers, watching, being watched, and drawing attention confer status. Instead of participating in a rich and vibrant community life, we go to the mall, surf the net, or watch pseudo-people engage in pseudo-events on television.[14] We are fascinated with "virtual" experiences to the exclusion of real ones—the distinction increasingly being seen as void of difference. The culture of victimage conjoins with the culture of newness in such a way that being first on one's block with the latest therapy, the latest disorder, or the latest disease actually confirms status and attention. And why not? There might be something that someone knows that we don't. There might be a better way if only we knew it. We can help people best, the meddler thinks, by offering the latest model of anything—cars, therapies, books, pills—they are all commodities to be purchased and distributed to the raft of victims in a world come apart. The more meddlers are listened to and utilized, the more accepted they become. So the rise of victims can thus be seen as a consequence of this symbiotic relationship between meddlers and victims.

The Melodramas of the Electronic Media.   In this context we are reminded of Max Frisch's definition: "Technology—the knack of arranging the world in such as way that we don't have to experience it." Formulaic and predictable, television talk shows like *Donahue, Maury Povich, Sally Jesse Raphael, Rickie Lake,* and *Geraldo* present us with the dramaturgy of victimage. Longing for heroes, villains, and rescuers, victims of the terrors of postmodern life receive wide exposure on such shows. Their stories, both bizarre and mundane, can, because of the nature of television as a medium, be physically disassociated, making them safe for viewer consumption. As Joshua Meyerwitz suggests, television is "evanescent, it is consumed and leaves no trace" (1986: 83). The conditions of attendance have changed. Watching a program on television is therefore like stopping to watch an event in a public park. One can view it and not be associated with it in any way. "Many people would be uncomfortable going into a bookstore and buying a book on transvestites but have no qualms about watching a program about transvestites on television. Talk show hosts like Phil Donahue have built their careers on this dual response to the same content in different media" (Meyerwitz, 1989: 84) Just a few of the recent victimization topics that have been discussed on these shows include idiot savants, teenage alcoholics, porno movie stars, male strippers, herpes sufferers, and women whose silicon-gel breast implants have sprung leaks. One program on *Donahue* explored the psychopathology (with appropriate experts) of one Sabrina Aset, who claimed to have had sex with 2,686 men. The *Donahue* imitators (*Sally Jesse Raphael, Oprah Winfrey, Jerry Springer, and Maury Povich*) are equally fascinated with victimhood, having done shows on subservient women, satanic abuse, shopaholics, necrophiliacs, and "women who catch their husbands in topless bars," to mention just a few. Moreover, the ante is being upped daily to find more outrageous instances of victimhood. "You can no longer just put prostitutes on," says Ed Glavin, a *Donahue* producer. "It has to be prostitutes who are sex addicts" (quoted in Kurtz, 1996: 52). The electronic voyeurs who watch these shows can therefore observe at a safe distance, meddling vicariously as they identify with both the victims and the professional meddlers who are showing their wares on national television.

Like nineteenth-century romance novels (a genre that continues to be popular itself), the individual stories of these poor souls are usually held together by a hero who rescues the victim from their intractable plight. But unlike the rescuer in romance novels, who is typically a tall, dark, strong male (the victim tends to be a beautiful woman who finds herself in perilous straits), the contemporary rescuer is most likely a therapist or an expert. As Shattuc suggests, "She or he narrates the overall story of victimization in the culture, the master narrative of the program's drama, but moves beyond just narration (a function shared by the host) to become an active participant in the drama, performing therapy or offering solutions" (Shattuc, 1997: 80). These electronic *Dear Abby's* follow the well-worn formula of translating most human problems into illnesses that require "professional counsel."

Victims of the class structure in American society are also prevalent on talk shows. Women, minorities, the poor, and the homeless compete with the abused, the harassed, the handicapped, and the co-dependent for star victim status. No attempt is made to sort out what constitutes a victim:[15] Anyone making the claim who has an interesting story is fair game— these being, above all, ratings-seeking television entertainment shows. Because the audience members are more likely to be female themselves, a common theme is feminine unhappiness. The inarticulate longings of the

American female wallowing in her wretched plight conjoins with the feminist movement to offer interpretation and reflection—consciousness raising as therapy. These shows also compete with each other in providing women a forum in which to whine, complain, and sometimes confront their tormentors. A case cited by Shattuc (1997) in her analysis of tele-talk, *The Talking Cure*, is instructive. After learning about an unemployed nurse who cut the silicone breast implants out of herself, the producers of the *Maury Povich* show rushed to beat the producers of the *Sally Jesse Raphael* show who had previously contacted her while she was still infected and on painkillers. The *Povich* producers reached her at a hotel, asking only if they could "talk" at their office. Within an hour the woman was being taped, Maury Povich leading off with the question on everyone's mind: "Just two weeks ago at one A.M. in the morning, in the privacy of her bathroom, she took a razor blade and attempted to perform surgery on herself. I mean, we can't even imagine—the audience is breathless, and so am I. What would make you do such a thing?" (Shattuc, 1997: 141).

Talk television is one more demonstration that the allure of victims is powerful because it forces attention on them. Being meddled with pushes people to the front stage, their lives now the object of analysis, curiosity, sympathy, and fascination: Meddlees get automatic friends who pay attention to their plight. Meddling is in this sense another example of what William Schofield (1973) saw as the primary appeal of psychotherapy: "the purchase of friendship." But in contrast to psychotherapy, the cost of being meddled with by the media is not a professional fee but merely the loss of one's dignity—a small price to pay, it seems, for a moment in the sun.

The phenomenon of talk television is worldwide and suggests that electronic media are rapidly becoming a new form of community for those who find ordinary life too dull. According to a recent report, Swedish television plans to show a woman undergoing a gynecological exam in front of a studio audience. "The examination was taped for next Thursday's episode of *Lotta*, an Oprah Winfrey–style talk show. "When the little camera the doctor held in his hand was switched on and people saw the girl's genitals on two big TV screens, it was absolutely silent." Some viewers, however, were repulsed. "It was distasteful. How far are TV channels prepared to go in the hunt for viewers?" asked an unidentified spectator (Associated Press, September 20, 1996).

Scripts for Life. The issue to be faced is that television is not a neutral, self-contained ground. We are being more than entertained by such shows; they also offer us, as the media have always done, scripts for life.[16] As Kenneth Gergen (1991: 55) has argued, the media in general, and talk shows in particular, expand the range and variety of relationships available to the public. But despite any pretensions of being "interactive," such shows are for the most part one-sided and virtual, offering no opportunity for reciprocal exchanges and negotiated meanings. The scripts taken from them as solutions to the riddles of life are thus stripped of the contextual complexities in which everyone's life is housed. So we wind up with such postmodern absurdities as the following:

> A timid appearing junior college student meets a tall, blond, drug-using housepainter and invites him to dinner. He gets amorous and rapes her in the bedroom of her apartment. She files charges but less than a month later she posts his bail and moves in with him and plans to be Mrs. Rapist. . . . When asked how she could marry him after what he did to her, she referred to a soap opera in which one character rapes another and later marries her. "It's like Luke and Laura on "General Hospital," she said. . . . In keeping with the TV flavor of the whole affair, he asked her to marry him while they were watching the *Oprah Winfrey* show, and they are considering an invitation to appear on *Donahue.* (quoted in Gergen, 1991: 54)

The traditional excitement of creating relationships from scratch are replaced by packaged versions that seem, to many, far more interesting than their own. "The powers of artifice may indeed be in the superior position," concludes Gergen. "So powerful are the media in their well-wrought portrayals that their realities become more compelling than those furnished by common experience" (1991: 57). So we meddle into each other's lives not only over our own sense of values and purpose but, now, with scripts gotten from the media itself. This "mediafication" of life can be seen all around us. A student reports on a long-awaited vacation to the Grand Canyon. After driving for two days, she and her family arrive at the rim. Tired, but happy to be there, they soak up its majesty and grandeur for a few minutes, and then someone pulls out a camera to dutifully record the moment for posterity. As soon as the pictures are taken, someone asks: "What do we do now?" It was as though the event hadn't occurred until it was photographed, and after that there was nothing left. In this sense, much of contemporary experience has been reduced to a search-and-destroy mission, bereft of any lasting effects. "Been there—done that" is the bored refrain of the sated American.

Even more bizarre are the serious national conversations now being waged through the vehicle of situation comedies. The *Murphy Brown* show has become the contemporary *Face the Nation*, a nationwide political forum on matters of lifestyles and morals. Not only did former Vice-President Dan Quayle involve himself in the question of whether the fictional (virtual) Murphy Brown should have a baby out of wedlock, but when the character contracted breast cancer, the Women's Healthcare Educational Network took the show to task for a line regarding a prosthetic breast in which Murphy joked, "Should I go with Demi Moore or Elsie the Cow?" Following suit, two other groups, the Northwest Center for Health and Safety and the Coalition for Healthy Communities, contacted CBS to complain about a later episode in which Murphy uses marijuana to deal with the side effects of chemotherapy.

In the realm of what is still sometimes euphemistically called the "mainstream" press (a postmodern contradiction, indeed, as the fine line separating the old mainstream from the new tabloids continues to fade), the confusion over the press's proper meddling role and what is out of bounds has never been more pronounced. William Safire, a columnist and conservative critic for the *New York Times* news service, believes that revelations about the private lives of Presidents John F. Kennedy and Richard Nixon have created a situation in which reporters are not even remotely queasy about invading the private lives of presidents: "[A]ccounts of immorality in Camelot, coming on top of Watergate, had an unfortunate fallout: In most media, what used to be nobody's business has become anybody's business" (Safire, 1997). The wholesale commodification of news has become a boon to the meddlesome impulse everywhere. If we cannot or will not draw a line between the public duties and private lives of public officials, we are not likely to draw them in our own lives either as we respond to the same forces that have privatized the public and publicized the private.[17]

These examples show that television programming, both fictional and otherwise, are rapidly becoming scripts for life. The postmodern citizen, absent of any clear-cut visions of how to live, and cut off from traditional communities that provided them by example, is increasingly likely to derive them from television itself. Meddlers looking for an efficient technology with which to market their wares need look no further.

The Myth of Denial

Encouraging and promoting the allure of victimage is a device created by the meddlers of the therapeutic state to secure conformity to the demands of its view of the world. It has been so effective that it now may be seen in other venues as well. We are talking here about the prevailing myth of "denial." Routinely used in discussions of alcoholism, denial can be said to be the centerpiece, if not the driving force, behind an increasing array of rehabilitation therapies.[18] It is prominent not just in the treatment of alcoholics but also in therapies that treat any kind of substance abuse or drug addiction, in diet, fitness, and exercise programs, and even in the popular and shifting therapeutic approach to crime and deviance.[19]

The concept of denial is a pivotal component upon which the identification, treatment, and recovery of a person is said to turn. Like mental and psychological disorders themselves, denial is a "taken-for-granted" and self-evident fact in rehabilitation circles (Landeen, 1978). Speaking in the context of treating alcoholics, J. Wallace remarks that "[t]herapists working with alcoholics are so familiar with their clients' unwillingness (or inability) to see the facts of the[ir] drinking and its consequences that nothing further needs to be added here" (Wallace, 1985: 37). Therapists working with these "addicted" populations assert that denial is the most common "defense mechanism" that patients use to continue their destructive patterns of behavior; indeed, in the clinical treatment of alcoholics, "protestation on the part of an alcoholic in question that he or she is *not* an alcoholic . . . is one allowable criteria for the diagnosis of alcoholism," according to the national Council on Alcoholism (Owen, 1984: 4). Moreover, the professional therapists working in clinical settings can draw on a backdrop of scholarly literature that assures them that denial is not even a deliberate and conscious act of the patient, so victim blaming is unnecessary. This literature (e.g., Leaffer, 1982; Anderson, 1981) supports the contention that denial is virtually automatic in sick people: "[I]t is not usually a matter of deliberate lying or willful deception," says D. J. Anderson (1981: 42). Rather, it operates unconsciously and involves a distortion of perception and an impairment of judgment such that the person with the problem becomes self-deluded and incapable of accurate self-awareness. Breaking the patient's denial system is an essential first step in recovery, it is believed, for as long as an individual asserts that his or her "addiction" to liquor, food, sex, fat, tobacco, or other modern consumptive taboos is *not* a problem, little of a therapeutic nature can be accomplished.

As is the case with many phenomena said to be "self-evident," one must look long and hard to find a discordant voice over the concept of denial. Against a heavily fortified garrison of psychological research and favorable social opinion, the reality of denial itself is undeniable. Why this unanimity on the subject? Because the concept of denial is the cornerstone of effective meddling. It places the meddler in a superior, unassailable position. No wonder the practitioners of the meddling trades hold so tenaciously to its conceptual heart. Meddlers know the truth; the pitiful sick person with whom they are working does not. The meddler's perceptions of reality are the correct ones—the meddlee is deluded. The meddler's view of the world is accurate—the meddlee's is self-serving and fatuous non-sense designed to rationalize his or her own purulent condition. It has not been surprising, then, to discover that meddlers almost always believe in denial, and that they practice their craft in organizational and clinical settings that promote it heavily.

There are some, however, who have dared to question the very concept of denial. Craig MacAndrew's was one of the first voices raised against the arrogant and totalitarian implications of this popular idea (MacAndrew, 1969). To him, the heart of the interpersonal situation where one person alleges another to be in denial was simply a difference of opinion, disguised by one side as something else. Some persons who recognize the negative consequences of their behavior simply do not change it. Since the behavior in question so clearly (at least to the meddler) has negative consequences, the question of why such people don't change boils down to one of two propositions. Either they *won't* change (they suffer from a weakness of will) or they *can't* change (they are innocent victims of a disease). If the first proposition is true, then drunkenness, for example, is avoidable and therefore morally reprehensible; if the second is true, drunkenness is an unavoidable outcome of having a disease, and moral judgments are therefore irrelevant. Since society's historic attempts to deal on moral grounds with drunkenness, drugs, sexual deviance, and, to a lesser extent, gluttony and fitness have been spectacularly unsuccessful, subsuming these behaviors under a medical model of the human experience has had the happy consequence of providing a rational, culturally approved explanation for the miscreants who are no longer responsible. The point is not that these people don't want to alter their behavior; it is that they can't. What some less enlightened souls historically saw as moral choices are actually the symptoms of diseases. In his discussion of the concept of denial in the literature of alcoholism, Dennis Brissett expressed this view of the matter: "As the concept of alcoholism rationalizes the unavoidability of drunkenness, the concept of denial rationalizes the apparent discrepancy between the drinker's and other people's versions of the nature and consequences of the drunkenness" (1988: 388). In this sense, Brissett went on to say, "denial is . . . an acceptable definition of the situation that emerges from the interaction that drinkers have with certain other people. The identification of denial does not necessarily reflect something about the drinker's psychological process as much as it establishes the nature of the drinker's relationship with others" (1988: 388).

So, when meddlers assert that a miscreant is "in denial," that very assertion rests on a difference of opinion concerning the "reality" of a person's comportment and its consequences. All the social consensus to the contrary does not alter this basic fact. When meddlers invoke the idea of denial, they are obscuring this fundamental disagreement under a preferred rhetoric of scientific authority. They are rendering not scientific facts but moral judgments about the persons and the problems with which they deal. But instead of saying outright that their patient's view of reality is simply wrong, they instead use a language that discredits anything a person might say as further evidence of being "in denial"—yet another symptom of the disease entity being treated. It is in this sense that therapeutic relationships have the unmistakable ring of Star Chamber proceedings.[20] "Because of their denial system," says Anderson, "information received from alcoholic persons themselves is usually not very reliable. To get a more valid assessment of the extent and seriousness of the illness, corroborating information should be obtained from others who have been closely involved with that individual" (Anderson, 1981: 29). Clearly, then, the idea of denial is as much a political as a therapeutic act (Vatz and Weinberg, 1983), for it rests eventually on the relative power, both epistemological and ontological, held by the two sides. Given the ever-increasing power of the therapeutic state (Szasz, 1984), it is often no contest.

A close examination of the assumptions that underlie the myth of denial is instructive. Brissett's discussion of them in the context of alcohol provides a model for understanding denial applied to other issues as well (1988: 389–390). Consider the four major assumptions that follow, which are often made by people asserting denial in those alleged to be alcoholics:

Assumption 1.

- **There exists a recognizably optimal level of drinking or at least a maximal standard that should not be exceeded.**

This assumption may be based on survey data about how much most people usually drink or gleaned from one's social circle. Either way, the question is whether the person drinks more or gets drunker than most other people one knows. In the case of alcohol counselors who typically make an ostensibly "clinical" judgment about "denial," part of this question may be translated as "other alcoholics I have known." Furthermore, the idea that certain persons can be certified by experts as drinking "too much" is a function of the contemporary Protestant cultural view that regards drinking as unnecessary and as a waste of time that could be more productively used in other pursuits.

Assumption 2.

- **Problems in the lives of alcoholics are due to their drinking.**

This is perhaps the most critical assumption of all. In establishing the "reality" of denial, the basic disagreement is the line taken by the alcoholics (they drink because they have problems) and the meddler (they have problems because they drink). Aside from the gross difficulty involved in determining retrospective causal linkages between any piece of behavior and the conditions that are alleged to preceded it, the cultural biases in Puritan America are all on the side of those who claim that problems in living can be attributed to drinking and not the other way around. The often serious difficulties that people who drink sometimes get themselves into underscores the therapeutic assumption that if a person drinks *and* gets into trouble, it is the drinking that must be either causing or aggravating the difficulties. It is important to point out, however, that these arguments are often assumptive rather than factual. Indeed, "[k]ey terms have been defined vaguely and used ambiguously; statements which sound authoritative and factual are often guesses, opinions, and ideology" (Levine, 1984: 45). Such statements, if they are to be made with any certainty, require an enormous leap of faith in the worldview of the meddler. It is in this sense that alcoholism, like mental illness and other kinds of "non-disease diseases," operates as a scapegoat for personal and social problems for which we have no other ready explanation or solution (Szasz, 1984).

Moreover, there exists in the game of alcohol treatment a presumption that is astonishing, given the scientific and objective pretensions of those meddlers who play it. Unable to recognize the possibility of differences of opinion about matters of personal pleasure, such meddlers often make professional pronouncements about alcohol consumption that look suspiciously like the writings of Carry Nation clothed in pseudo-scientific language. A colleague in Florida recently reported on an extensive review of the alcohol education books in his university library. "Nowhere," he says, "could I find books which cited *any* benefits from consuming alcohol."[21] Similarly, a review of the psychological and sociological literature on alcohol makes it abundantly clear that the meddling "scientists" who generated this literature regard drinking as pathological (Brissett, 1984). Rarely if ever does one read that people drink because they feel good, because they are happy, or because they enjoy high self-esteem or some other positive attribute.

Assumption 3.

• **An individual's control over his or her drinking behavior is something that can be identified, measured, and documented.**

Perhaps more than any other, this assumption is the key to understanding the therapeutic rationale for imputing denial to a client. Because the meddler assumes that the alcoholic is "sick," all of the client's protestations serve to confirm the original diagnosis. The critical point here is that such therapeutic meddling assumes that a piece of defined symbolic behavior has only *one* meaning and that meaning itself is something that can be measured scientifically. Like the previous assumptions, this one is based on the widespread belief in our culture that people *should* always be in control, exercising careful diligence over everything they do. The popular view that alcohol "looses inhibitions" (MacAndrew, 1969) serves as a vocabulary of motives for both drinkers and those who are trying to stop them from drinking. But when are we to know when a person's drinking is out of control, particularly in light of the protestations of many alcoholics that it is not? It is here that professional meddlers act as traffic cops or behavioral referees, determining with their alleged therapeutic expertise that a "clinical" judgment is something more than simply one person's opinion against another. One wonders if these judgments are not in fact less a matter of whether people can control their own drinking than a matter of whether those around them can control the drinkers. Differences of opinion are often resolved with the hammer of power. But the problem with the power of the therapeutic state is that it disguises itself in the garb of medical diagnosis and treatment. As Howard Stein suggests, often "the family's and 'society's' inability to constrain the alcoholic is projectively translated into [a] perception of the alcoholic as [the] one who cannot be constrained" (1985: 221).

Assumption 4.

• **Other people have a clearer vision of reality than the drinker does.**
Critical to the meddling stance is the view that the meddler has a clearer vision of reality than everyone else does. In the case of alcoholics, it is assumed that people who behave the way they are supposed to—particularly if they previously had not done so, as in the case of many alcohol and drug counselors—have a monopoly on truth and knowledge. Because alcohol blurs one's vision, it is said, users cannot see what is obvious to everyone around them, especially those who are certified as experts by virtue of the fact that they have had experiences in higher education. Their Ph.D. or M.D. degrees are thought to give them special insights into the plight of the wretched souls they treat. The ironic twist to this definition of a situation is that in discounting the beliefs of alcoholics as unreliable rationalizations for their drinking, these experts also put themselves in the position of believing the alcoholics' version of truth only if and when it comes around to theirs. Only by accepting other people's versions of their life history and personal identity can the alcoholics be said to no longer be in denial. But then the "reality' of the situation consists of treating persons who are now acting like people they previously said they weren't.

If this sounds convoluted, it's because it is. By asserting the existence of a psychological construct called "alcoholism" and then offering no evidence for it except the behavior that defined the construct in the first place, meddlers trap alcoholics in a vicious circle where everything they do confirms the initial diagnosis. Only by accepting versions of reality by those in a position of power over their lives can they convince them that they are not "in denial."

The denial that is routinely alleged about alcoholics who wish to keep drinking has become a model for the meddling impulse everywhere. Drug users, the obese, the maritally incompetent, smokers, and almost anyone else engaged in behavior that offends the New Puritanism of the age are said to be in denial if they deny the entreaties of the meddling industries. The consequences of employing a psychological conception of denial in the identification and treatment of these issues constitute an affirmation of social over personal control of a person's life. The use of the concept of denial allows for and justifies other people's attempts to change individuals' lives against their wishes. If these individuals occasionally express some doubt about their lives—as practically everyone does at some time or another—the issue is sealed. The miscreants don't want to live the way they do and thus need the help of the meddler. Resistance is part of the disease pattern, and it confirms the accuracy of the diagnosis in the first place.

The essential point, however, remains the same. The behavior of these individuals flies in the face of the social judgments that have been made about them. The fact that meddlers offer these judgments with such rectitude and certainty only makes them more difficult to resist. Because of their degrees and certificates, meddlers are presumed to know what they are talking about. To argue that one is not denying anything, but only wants to live the way one has been living, is to confirm the fact that one has a problem. Differences of opinion do not ordinarily lead to the conclusion that one person is absolutely right and the other is wrong—but in the case of the meddler armed with the rhetoric of psychological science, it does. This is the same predicament in which those who are adjudged to be "mentally ill" find themselves.[22] Insisting that one *isn't* only confirms that one *is*. The argument here, however, is that those persons who deny the judgment that they have a problem are, as Brissett says,

> not necessarily wrong, do not necessarily suffer from some illness, nor are they necessarily being governed by some psychological defense mechanism that is outside their awareness. They simply may be announcing an identity which has a long history of validation by others despite current heavy disagreement. (1988: 394)

In one sense they are reluctant to surrender the "irreplaceable and incomparable quality of their individuality . . . to the socially constituted abstraction" (Berger, 1963). Whereas meddling others may see their lives clearly from their own point of view, the individual stubbornly and persistently sees it another way. The question is, Who should be the primary definer of a person's situation? Increasingly, it seems, if that behavior has a negative impact on the lives of others—and, indeed, the definition of what constitutes a "negative impact" seems to be increasingly inclusive—the answer is everyone *but* the person. Rather than viewing alcoholics as powerless in the face of liquor, we might as easily view them as powerless in their negotiations with meddlers who have equally strong convictions about the power of alcohol.

Interpreting a person within a single frame of reference, in keeping with the myth of denial, seems a particularly devastating and outrageous thing for meddlers to do. The meddlers, of course, see it differently—as do their newly acquired converts. This new insight of alcoholics, who have been mired in a bog of denial, offers serious benefits. It allows them to reconstruct their biography in light of the frame of reference provided by treatment personnel and fellow patients (Berger, 1963). If one buys into this frame of reference, it becomes a way to obtain the validations of a circle of newly acquired significant others (i.e., to obtain a "secular conversion," to use the language of Kenneth Burke [1965]); or if one does not, it offers a way out of treatment. By telling alcoholics what they want to hear, meddlers open the door to their departure: "Persons passing through different alcoholism programs come to highlight different strategies, beliefs, and explanations regarding their alcoholism. Some learn that their behavior is a consequence of a disease and others that it is a habit. Some learn that they have an allergy to alcohol, while others learn that they are orally fixated" (Rudy, 1986: 54). Like the religious convert who discovers a new language with which to understand his old life, the secular convert to the myth of denial provides "the person with a convenient explanation . . . for much of his behavior" (Wallace, 1985: 33). And like the religious convert, the latter also gets a new before-and-after time line whereby he can date himself in terms of the old life of drinking and the new one of sobriety.

None of these are minor details if one has a drinking problem. But neither should they obscure the fact that what they involve in essence is the acceptance on the part of the alcoholic of the views held by those who meddled with his life. This is the basic move of all professional meddlers and many amateur ones, no matter what the subject of the intervention. Persons who find themselves caught up in the web of their service net (whether "voluntarily" or not)[23] are told that they are "insightful" when they describe themselves and their problems in the language of their rehabilitator's view of them, and are said to be "blocking" and "resisting" when they do not (Scott, 1979). Converts, then, of whatever stripe— smokers, fat eaters, sexual deviants, couch potatoes—by denouncing their previous denial, offer to the meddlers who interfere with their lives an apology for the wretched behaviors in which they were previously engaged (Goffman, 1971). Like other apologies, it splits the self into two parts—a good self and a bad one—and furthers the argument that the bad self was not the real person but the good one is. The good one, of course, is now doing exactly what the meddlers want him to do.

An intriguing question implicit in all of this is how these addiction meddlers have been able to get away with such a manifest failure of logic in their basic view of substances and their effects on human behavior. Substances so strong and addictions so powerful would hardly seem to be controllable by simply dropping one's denial system. Yet that, apparently, is exactly what is taking place. It isn't the substance at all—whether drugs, booze, or fat—that controls one's life but, rather, a simple act of faith and affirmation of consciousness; recognizing that we have been engaged in denial gives us the power to manage our problems. But if overcoming denial is the secret to controlling our "addictions," it holds the much bigger secret of how professional meddlers have managed to exert so much influence on American life. Again, in talking about alcohol, but with much broader implications, Brissett points out that

> [a] belief in the psychological reality of denial has enabled treatment personnel to consolidate and legitimize their efforts with regard to the alcoholism problem in society. Aside from legitimizing the power of alcohol counselors over their individual patients, denial serves as an apologia for the existence of the alcoholism treatment profession itself. On the one hand, it legitimizes the counselors' position of being in possession of knowledge that others, by definition, are unaware. The idea of denial imparts an almost mystical character to the treatment process in that counselors have insight into matters of which the general public and practicing alcoholics do not. (Brissett, 1988: 396)

Perhaps even more important, the myth of denial serves as a convenient way of explaining away treatment failures. Thanks to the language of denial, those who persist in doing what the professional meddler is "treating them for" do not call the treatment system into question but, instead, tend to be individuals who refuse to develop insight into their own condition. In a world awash in "educational" strategies of one kind or another, failure to change in the face of compelling and universally validated evidence to the contrary is regarded as the ultimate sin—an assault on reason itself. The miscreant can then be dismissed with a moral label—alcoholic, drug addict, and so on.

A final contribution made by the myth of denial to the work of professional meddlers—and that of the phalanx of amateurs who support them—is what denial gives to arguments regarding the significance of problems in society. "Claims-makers," to use Joel Best's (1987) terminology, are frequently confronted with the problem of how to deal with people who refute their claims. And, indeed, the myth of denial presents an easy way to explain away what Room (1984) has labeled "problem deflation." Just as claims-makers often inflate their claims, they assert that those who do not agree with them "deflate" theirs. Those who disagree with the claims of the meddlers are passed off as products of a cultural denial system that makes it more difficult for the meddler to do his noble work. And those who question the money poured into the enterprise, or criticize it from the outside, are similarly ignored as part of the problem.

Why People Meddle

In this chapter we have traced out some of the major sources of the appeal and acceptance of meddling, as well as provided criticism of the underlying claims of meddlers. In the course of that discussion an answer to the question of why people meddle has begun to emerge, along with the dialectic that explains why others allow them to do so. The following points summarize this analysis, starting with the first question—why people meddle.

1. *Meddling generates money.* Meddling has become an industry in which large numbers of people make huge profits by nosing into other people's business. These meddling businesses now have an enormous financial stake in constructing a culture where meddling and being meddled with are accepted as hallmarks of good citizenship. They sell the rhetoric that they are not meddlers but "problem solvers," and through their research they legitimate the existence of the very problems they offer to solve. Lawyers, social workers, psychiatrists, doctors, all those who do "clinical" work, have a vested interest in seeing to it that as many diseases, maladies, conditions, syndromes, and disputes as possible are elevated to the level of professional practice.

2. *Meddling establishes power.* Meddling is also a way of showing that one has power over others. The superior position of the meddler is in sharp contrast to the subordinate position of the meddlee. This meddling is situationally an exercise in the high and the mighty versus the low and the downtrodden. No matter how much meddlers wish to humanize their humble task, sub- and superordinacy are built into the meddling situation. The dramaturgy of meddling typically involves a scene that communicates power, knowledge, and prestige. This is certainly true of professional meddlers who work in clinical settings. The meddlee is the one who makes the appointment, waits in a room to be called, and then is shown into an office festooned with plaques, diplomas, and the trap-

pings of power, all of which demonstrate decisively who's on top. Who is having the problem? The meddlee of course, not the meddler. Those who meddle unavoidably set themselves up as superior to the persons with whom they are meddling.

3. *Meddling is entertaining.* For the meddler and the meddlee, being a busybody and being meddled with by those who engage in the practice are hugely entertaining in an era when being amused has been elevated to the status of a national right. Talk shows, radio call-in formats, gossip columns, and magazines such as *People* and its many clones entertain us with stories of gossip, scandal, and sexual adventure in high places and among celebrities. The rise of electronic media has provided even wider forums for the entertainment payoffs that come with meddling, as well as for the anonymity that fuels bolder and more salacious versions of it. When the late Princess Diana called a press conference to announce that she was going to pursue a more private life of raising her children, and asked the press to respect her decision by leaving her alone, she effectively, and as it turned out consequentially, sealed her own doom by vastly raising the price of paparazzi photographs of her. Perhaps no public figure in our century has been meddled with more than Diana (although Jackie Kennedy might have disagreed), and many believe it eventually resulted in her death. Yet it must also be pointed out that she was a master of manipulation—the "Queen of Surfaces," as Maureen Dowd (1997) called her—who understood that the press, her most hated liability, was paradoxically also her biggest asset.[24]

4. *Meddling develops self-knowledge.* Allowing oneself to be meddled with is one way of developing understanding about and insights into oneself. Taking our cue from the rise of the industries of the therapeutic culture, we believe that only by splaying out our lives for others to discuss can we gain true insight into ourselves. The traps of self-awareness are obscured; the benefits of meddling are highlighted. Because one's self is inextricably tied up with others, with interpersonal relationships, and with the society at large, meddlers have a distinct advantage in their claim that only by allowing others access to his or her life can a person attain the gifts of self-awareness. This is one of the primary strategies of the therapeutic culture.

5. *Meddling establishes status differentials.* From the powerful podium of doctors, attorneys, therapists, and media mavens we receive the impression that those who meddle are better informed, more compassionate, and more objective, and understand more about the world in which we live, than the meddlee. As the family declines as a source of wisdom it has been recast by the meddling trades into the source of the problems of its members. This new image of the family as a cauldron of pathology creates the largest possible role for those saviors who rush in with meddling advice about how to repair the damage done to individuals by this

leviathan institution. The members of the meddling trades are then seen implicitly as higher than, smarter than, and more compassionate than those who traditionally worked with human problems that, in turn, were perceived as a natural part of life.

6. *Meddling confers intellectual superiority.* To meddle is to regard oneself and to be regarded by others as being intellectually superior to everyone else. In a nation where such intellectual supremacy is the road to wealth and riches (as opposed to common sense, wisdom, and other remnants of our traditional past), it is not surprising that the information explosion has also produced a spate of meddling mandarins. It is difficult to remember that the mere fact that people are good at their craft doesn't mean that they hold privileged insights into everything else as well.

7. *Meddling offers a way to be remembered.* Meddlers frequently succeed in being remembered by those with whom they meddle. Successful meddling produces a warm glow in the meddler. Professionals and amateurs alike thus bask in the sunshine of phrases such as "I will always remember what ____ told me about that." Given that the memory of the average American is now selectively short, this is no small achievement. Meddlers almost never recall, or even know about, the instances in which they meddled badly and things didn't work out. There surely must exist, in most instances of meddling, a far greater list of meddlees who responded silently to the solicitations of meddlers with resentment, anger, rage, and a sense that they were violated by the presumptuousness of those who believed they knew better how to run someone else's life.

8. *Meddling confers cultural superiority.* As the so-called culture wars rage around us, meddling into the affairs of others has the further benefit of establishing a certain cultural superiority for the meddler. Both "conservative" and "progressive" movements seek to demonstrate their superincumbency through their success in meddling into the lives of those who disagree with them. Thus drug warriors meddle to show the superiority of their own abstinent lifestyles. Similarly, the sober and the reformed meddle in the lives of drunks and smokers, proving that their way is better. This is why those who claim to be "recovered" from the endless list of substances and activities now forbidden—alcohol, cigarettes, food, co-dependency, sex addiction—often find that the next stage in their career is "helping" others still unenlightened and caught in the grip of the diseases, disorders, or bad habits they see as "wrecking lives." The superior position of the meddlers' new life is affirmed; the debauched life of those they seek to help offers verification.

9. *Meddling masquerades as altruism.* As it gets to be more and more difficult in the postmodern world to escape the charge of self-interest, meddlers can sometimes claim an altruistic interest in others by meddling into their lives. It is in this sense that meddling constitutes a toll-free road

to community. One gets credit for "caring" without shouldering the responsibilities that traditionally went along with such a role. Volunteer organizations, even when their motives are pure and their purposes noble, are nonetheless often peopled by those who meddle in the name of altruism. Significant misery can be exacted from our fellow human beings in the name of altruism. This is what H. L. Mencken was getting at when he claimed that "[m]en are the only animals who devote themselves, day in and day out, to making one another unhappy. It is an art like any other. Its virtuosi are called altruists" (quoted in Green, 1984: 138)

10. *Meddling advances the belief that "what goes around comes around."* Meddling represents one response to the many recurrent cycles of pain and suffering that seem to come with being human. Life is difficult, this line of reasoning goes, and both the meddler and the meddlee are joined in their mutual interest in each other's life. Thus, there is the belief that what happens in your life may well happen in mine, so meddling becomes another instance of a misguided attempt to "do good." Neighbors and friends often meddle out of such a belief.

11. *Meddlers have nothing better to do.* Some types of meddlers clearly engage in these practices because they have nothing better to do. Meddling out of boredom, or to create the impression of "busyness," is part of the practiced behavior of many different kinds of meddlers. As American public life has moved from genuine involvements in a connected commonweal to exercises in the subjective use of common space, meddling has become an entertaining and socially accepted way of observing other people's behavior. Meddling allays boredom and at the same time gives the impression of "caring" for the one with whom one meddles. In addition, some categories of meddlers—namely, those who meddle in the name of organization—do so because they see their job as involving meddling into the lives of others. Petty bureaucrats such as assistant and associate heads of organizational units meddle as a way of giving the impression that they are good "managers." Having few production standards and therefore no clear way of showing that they are doing a good job, they meddle in order to give the impression that they are at least doing something. Indeed, as the managerial classes have escalated, and as the society and its work have increasingly retreated indoors, these kinds of meddlers have sprouted in a wide variety of work settings. This is one reason why so many bureaucratic organizations are such frustrating and draining places in which to work.[25]

Why People Allow Themselves to Be Meddled With

By the same token, here are some of the reasons why people allow themselves to be meddled with:

1. *Meddlees believe in expertise and qualifications.* As the educated middle classes have burgeoned, so has the belief in credentials and expertise. In short, we allow others to meddle with our lives because we have bought into the belief system that has convinced us that only experts with the proper qualifications know about life and problems in living. In a society drowning in certificates, diplomas, qualifications, and claims of expert status, the handling of one's own problems through traditional sources—family, friends, and local institutions—seems an exercise in futility: They can't possibly know. Even parenting has been transformed into yet another specialty, with classes now being taught on "parenting skills."[26]

2. *Meddlees possess vulnerabilities born of confusion.* The various confusion industries we've discussed often succeed in creating an enormous sense of vulnerability. Communicating their message through a credulous media system that finds its own interests well served by doom-saying, the contemporary American may seem outnumbered and vulnerable when it comes to the central question of how to live. Overwhelmed by so many conflicting voices, each claiming expertise, the individual is beset by a sense of vulnerability and, not surprisingly, often gravitates to the siren-song of the meddler offering advice and council.

3. *Meddlees are overcome by doubt and fear.* Some people allow themselves to be meddled with out of little more than a profound sense of doubt and fear. And, indeed, the postmodern culture has been called the "culture of ontological doubt." Frustrated baby boomers who grew up in the 1950s and 1960s have come to believe that self-actualization is a right—and that if they aren't self-actualized, then something is wrong. The meddler offers a solution. Such doubt frequently leads to fear and anxiety, and, as we have shown, the latter emotions create many opportunities for meddling interventions.

4. *There's something in it for us.* Finally, we must not forget that meddling offers a host of both tangible and intangible benefits to those willing to play the role of meddlee. Sympathy, identity, compassion, attention, and celebrity are frequent outcomes of allowing oneself to be the target of meddlesome interventions. These intangible benefits may even be accompanied by monetary rewards, if only people will give up their lives to others to analyze and manipulate.[27] If meddling is an industry, then the meddlee offers the raw material that the business of meddling is willing to pay for.

And so we accept the solicitations of the meddler. We wallow and bask in the attention offered us. But appealing as it is, meddling still needs a rationale to give it dignity and sensible-sounding explanations for the clearly presumptuous act of intruding into the lives of others. This is the role that ideology plays in our lives, and the major ideologies that provide the necessary rationale are the subject of the next chapter.

Notes

1. Many members of the growing class of divorcing Americans can testify to what happens when the news of their divorce hits the community. They will be besieged with calls and literature from matchmaking services, some of which "guarantee" remarriage within a certain period of time. Their pitch centers on the idea that whereas family and friends are poor judges of mates, their sophisticated computer tracking systems will ensure that the person they introduce you to is the one for you. They ask how the last mating system you used worked, knowing the answer in advance since you just came out of a divorce.

2. By virtually any measure—average life expectancy, rates of poverty and disease, declining risk of accidental death—America is the safest and healthiest society on the face of the earth. A documentation and analysis of this can be found in Wildavsky (1988).

3. "Twice cured, once dead" is the way Daniel Callahan (1990) puts it in his exploration of the moral dimensions of this dilemma.

4. In this connection, see Friedson (1970).

5. For example, there has been an outbreak of new restaurants in the last ten years with "family" in their names. But one would think that if people wanted to have "family experiences" they would simply stay at home and eat with their families.

6. A rough estimate of the number of marriage and family therapists working in the country today runs into the tens of thousands. There are, for example, 46,000 registered family therapists who belong to the American Association of Marriage and Family Therapists (AAMFT) and countless more clinical psychologists, licensed psychologists, psychiatrists, and social workers who practice their noble craft on the growing army of casualties in the marital wars.

7. Frederic Jameson is regarded by many as *the* American Marxist theorist of the postmodern condition. He asserts that "anyone who believes that the profit motive and the logic of capital accumulation are not the fundamental laws of this world is living in an alternative universe" (Jameson, 1991: 354).

8. In just the past year alone, 24-hour news channels have been launched by ABC, NBC, Microsoft, Rupert Murdoch, and the Fox television network. Turner Broadcasting is considering a 24-hour sports network to challenge the hegemony of ESPN, and new business and financial networks have been started.

9. One has only to listen to the snake-oil salesmen of the meddling trades to see that nothing less than holistic salvation is being offered at an affordable price.

10. Critic John Leo put it this way in a 1992 interview: "Almost everybody is clamoring to *become* handicapped. A woman in Virginia was arrested for trying to poison her two-year-old son by mixing mouse poison with breakfast cereal and ice cream, and the defense was that she is suffering from 'Munchausen's syndrome by proxy.' Now, Munchausen's syndrome is a mental disorder in which people mutilate themselves to elicit attention. So to get this women into Munchausen's syndrome, it had to be by 'proxy' since she had attempted to harm not herself but her child. The devil made her put the mouse poison in the ice cream. That's the manufacture of disability" (quoted in Winokur, 1992: 227).

11. What with the extension of the twelve-step model of Alcoholics Anonymous to every other conceivable kind of human problem, we have often wondered about the voyeuristic strain in these helping activities. For example, among those who gather to assist and support persons who claim that they are victims of "sexual addictions" (Sex Addicts Anonymous) there must surely be those who obtain erotic satisfaction from listening to the stories of the victims of this new "disease."

12. The number of academic and popular references to this crisis of responsibility is now on the rise. For example, ABC News airs "The Blame Game," a report on how Americans are increasingly blaming everyone but themselves for life's problems, and the study of "victimology" is a popular subspecialty in various academic disciplines, complete with workshops, conferences, and a journal.

13. These examples were discussed on ABC's "The Blame Game."

14. This notion of a "pseudo-event" is drawn from Daniel Boorstin's (1964) *The Image*. He defines it as a happening that has the following characteristics: (1) It is not spontaneous, but comes about because someone planned, planted, or incited it. Typically it is not an earthquake, but an interview. (2) It is planted for the purpose of being reproduced. (3) Its relation to the underlying reality of the situation is ambiguous. It wouldn't exist if no one talked about it. And (4) it is designed to be a self-fulfilling prophecy. We take it that much meddling qualifies as "pseudo-events" under this definition.

15. "Today's talk shows celebrate the victim and the victimizer equally; they draw no lines and have no values except the almighty dollar" (Nelson, 1995: 22).

16. The naiveté of otherwise perceptive critics of talk television is evident in Howard Kurtz's conclusion that talk television, rather than playing any substantive role in "the decline of civilization and other assorted sociological ills, simply mirrors the best and worst of society" (1996: 156).

17. This theme is explored more fully in Brissett (1988).

18. The recent Clinton-Starr-Lewinsky imbroglio promises to make this particular source of the meddlesome impulse even worse.

19. Increasingly being voiced is the argument that even criminal activities, especially if they involve juveniles, should be treated in clinics rather than courts because the people involved are victims of various disorders that "cause" them to be criminal.

20. A Star Chamber is a secret proceeding with no provision for cross-examination of the accused.

21. Ray Oldenburg made this comment during a personal communication.

22. See the entire corpus of the work of Thomas Szasz for documentation of this point, beginning with *The Myth of Mental Illness* (1961).

23. Whether the meddlee is in a "voluntary" relationship with the meddler is a matter open to considerable interpretation. For example, in the case of involuntary hospitalization for mental illness, some patients who are technically there involuntarily actually want to be and some who are there "voluntarily" have agreed to be so only under the heaviest duress. For more on this point, see Goffman (1961).

24. These points, among others, were made in a *Frontline* documentary entitled "The Princess and the Press," aired by the Public Broadcasting Company (PBS) in November 1997.

25. When the work is a part of the new category described by Arlie Hochschild as "emotional labor," in which people do not make a product but instead provide a service that includes the acting out of certain emotional states such as happiness, the toll it exacts on workers can be particularly high. In this connection, see Hochschild's (1983) study of flight attendants who find that a major component of the job is to assist the company in trafficking in the image that the skies are "friendly" and the mood and ambiance are "professional."

26. An older member of this author's family commented sarcastically: "It is little wonder that previous generations had so many problems with their children—they had no 'parenting skill training classes.'"

27. President Clinton's accuser, Paula Corbin Jones, is but the latest to gain instant fame and monetary rewards by allowing her life to be analyzed and manipulated by others.

4

The Ideologies
of Meddling

The spirit of the age favors the moralist and the busybody, and the instinct to censor and suppress shows itself not only in the protests for and against abortion or multiculturalism but also in the prohibitions against tobacco and pet birds. It seems that everybody is forever looking out for everybody else's spiritual or physical salvation. Doomsday is at hand, and the community of the blessed . . . can be all too easily corrupted by the wrong diet, the wrong combination of chemicals, the wrong word.
—Lewis Lapham

In this age of busybodies, meddling is most often done in the name of something else. Few meddlers have the temerity to rely on their own prejudices to justify openly tampering with the lives of their fellows. So rather than engaging in Talmudic disputes about their reasons for meddling, today's meddlers, when challenged to explain why they are poking their noses into somebody else's business, explain it away with a preordained appeal to one of the many ideologies in common currency—health, safety, God, the children, and so on. Their rationale gives legitimacy to what is a foregone conclusion—that meddling is both justified and called for. The range and variety of reasons for meddling into each other's lives have increased to the point where it is difficult not only to avoid the meddlesome interventions of our neighbors but also to dispute the implied rationales for such intrusions. After all, the meddler appeals to some of the most powerful rhetorics of our time, and a person's fitness to belong to a community seemingly hangs in the balance as he listens to the reasoned intolerance that justifies an intervention, which is, of course, for "his own good" or "the good of the children," "the good of society at large," and so on. The following list suggests but a few of the ideological rationales available to the contemporary meddler:

Health
The Children

Safety
Society
God
The Unborn
Public Morality
Community
Virtue
Family
Prevention
Protection
The Common Good
The War on Drugs, Fat, Tobacco, Alcohol, etc.
The Law (i.e., rules)

These common ideologies of meddling represent the belief systems that propel meddling social movements. Ideologies are essentially discourses composed of what people think and say (Garner, 1996: 15). Many of them function as secular religions for their adherents, offering quasi-theological comfort in a secular age when everything seems to be falling apart. Like other belief systems they are usually taken for granted by their advocates. They are socially constructed realities that have no life other than what people give them, yet they are employed to create the very realities they project. The sociological mystery has always been how people can construct these realities in their relationships with others and yet claim that their constructions exist independent of them, emanating instead from God, nature, higher laws, and so on (Berger and Luckmann, 1966). Moreover, they serve to justify the vested interests of those who hold them, thereby leading to the suspicion that they are simply levers that individuals and groups use to get their definitions of what is important enacted into reality. The true believer is less likely to examine his or her beliefs than to act on them without question. Beliefs save us time and energy because they blithely bypass thought or debate—luxuries that people can ill-afford in a fast-paced world.[1] Moreover, as Ralph Turner and Lewis Killian have noted, the ideology of a movement facilitates collective action by providing not just internal guidance for its members but also a sense of who, what, and why they are. Ideologies are peddled with an identity thrown in for the believers, free of charge; they also include the offer of a group with which the believers can identify through the simple act of believing as they do (Turner and Killian, 1987). To meddle from the standpoint of an ideology is to *be* someone, to elevate one's self to the level of a noble warrior in the "service" of the community—an abstraction that, all too often these days, exists primarily as a rationale for meddling in the first place. But once the question of identity is placed in the equation, the stakes rise, for now the meddlers are not simply busybodies or candlesnuffers but individuals with a personal investment as well. Their very selfhood is on the line as they grimly interfere with the choices of others. Meddling "for the sake of the children" puts the meddler on the side of the angels regardless of whether such interventions are ultimately helpful to the interests of children. Political meddling in the name of God identifies one as a true believer with a sure route to heaven even if the goals of the meddling are at variance with the Constitution. None of the belief systems that we will explore in this chapter can be said to rest on an unequivocal scientific foundation; and even if they did, it is important to notice that they would still be ideologies, sets of beliefs held by some (scientists and those who choose to believe them) and imposed on others. Science, whatever else it may claim to be, is still an ideology, a belief system that serves the interests of some and is aligned against the interests of others. Peter Berger has noted that since most people cannot claim expertise in the physiology or epidemiology of the matters that they have passionate convictions about, it must be that the convictions are based on a faith in one authority or another:

> But since authorities conflict, the individual chooses which authority to give credence to. Thus it is at least noteworthy that people who believe very little of what government agencies tell them on other important matters (foreign policy, for instance) will regard an issue as closed because the surgeon general has spoken on it. [We] will want to know why faith in the surgeon general is plausible to people who will not believe one word uttered by the secretary of state, and this question may be asked quite apart from the . . . question of who is right in the final analysis. (Berger, 1994: 82)

So, we pick our authorities and believe what we want—the beliefs usually being organized around some vested interest we share in common with someone else since the analysis is never "final" anyway. Because there are so many possible ideological rationales available to postmodern meddlers, this chapter considers only the most prevalent of these belief systems and their relationship to interpersonal conduct. It includes an analysis of the veritable explosion of meddling into people's lives in the names of health and safety, along with such venerable favorites as the aforementioned meddling in the name of God and meddling "for the sake of the children." The features of these belief systems, as we will see, tell us much about the rise of meddling in general.

Meddling in the Name of Health

Today's major pathogen is, I suspect, the pursuit of the healthy body.

—Ivan Illich

It would be difficult to find an arena of meddling more common or accepted these days than that of health and fitness. The individual effort to control the tormenting vicissitudes of that ever-expanding aspect of modern life called "health" has become a socially sanctioned excuse for meddling into and controlling the behavior of our fellow human beings as never before.[2] And whereas the pursuit of health is not new, the meddlesome chutzpah of its advocates is. In the Age of Theology, life was regarded soberly as a brief and testing vale of tears before an eternity with God; now, however, in the Age of Eternal Bliss, it seems to have become an inalienable right to live eighty-plus years of untrammeled well-being, with medicine working steadily on that last heretofore intractable disease—death (Edgley and Brissett, 1990). Health is presumed to underlie all achievement and is said, therefore, to be the fundamental precondition of everything else. ("At least we have our health" is the default position of the dispossessed who have lost everything else.) As our previous discussion has indicated, the increased medicalization of society, especially in the 1960s and 1970s, went a long way toward establishing the preeminence of the metaphor of disease as a way of making sense of people's personal and social problems (Conrad and Schneider, 1992). As a result of this revolution, the avoidance of disease, sickness, and illness has become an important cultural motif—if not the dominant one. Robert Crawford, in an influential piece, summarizes the change in this way:

> In short, health has become not only a preoccupation, it has also become a pan-value or standard by which an expanding number of behaviors and social phenomena are judged. Less a means toward the achievement of other fundamental values, health takes on the quality of an end in itself. Good living is reduced to a health problem, just as health is expanded to include all that is good in life. (Crawford, 1980: 380–381)

At the same time, many Americans began to question the effectiveness of institutional medicine, both in dealing with health problems and in promoting healthy lives. Again, as Crawford puts it:

> The well-known inability of medicine to find a cure for many of the chronic and degenerative diseases, especially heart disease, stroke, and cancer, combined with the cost crisis in medicine and the accumulation of data which even question the contribution of medicine to the declining mortality from

infectious disease, have all pushed policy discussion toward the consideration of more effective strategies of disease prevention. (Crawford, 1980: 372)

Accompanying the growing awareness that health was not guaranteed by simple acquiescence to medical treatment regimes was the realization that being healthy might have more to do with personal volition and diligent effort, a theme that played into American individualism and its preoccupation with personal salvation. In 1986, for example, 93 percent of Americans agreed with the statement of a Gallop pollster: "If I take the right actions, I can stay healthy" (Glassner, 1988). As a result, we have seen an explosion of health, exercise, running, dieting, and fitness programs. Holistic health movements, popular magazines, newspaper articles, health food stores, home health-care kits, vitamin regimens, dieting protocols, exercise mavens ranging from the formerly radical but still politically correct Jane Fonda to the sexually ambiguous Richard Simmons, television cable channels, and Internet Websites are merely the more obvious examples of the mushrooming market for health through individual achievement.[3] Even the conversational environment, at least among the middle classes, has shifted dramatically from the ubiquitous subjects of sex and money to the more ethereal topics of health and fitness.[4]

Much of this change, of course, is just talk. As Dave Matheny has said, "Reducing our likelihood of heart disease is great, but look more closely and you'll see that we're not really exercising and watching our fat intake more than we were before, we're mostly just talking about that stuff more" (Matheny, 1989: 48). Further evidence that health represents primarily a change in rhetoric and little else is the fact that the number of steakhouses in the country has increased by 60 percent since 1994. We may be discussing the alleged poisons on our plate, but we are eating them more than ever. Changes in the conversational environment do matter, however. As symbolic interactionists keep telling us (Perinbanayagam, 1984), transformations in the way we talk are among the most profound social changes we know, for talk essentially constitutes much of our collective experience. We are, in this sense, what we talk about. And talk we do, often in a meddlesome and militant manner. As noted previously, meals now seem less a celebration of food and fellowship than an excuse to offer cautionary advice on the quality and quantity of the provisions on our neighbor's plate. Inviting someone to dinner increasingly involves an inventory of what our guests will and will not eat in order to avoid an embarrassment, which is more likely to be the host's than the guest's since health-conscious people these days are inclined to assert their food aversions in stridently moral tones, even as the entree emerges from the oven. "I don't eat fat." "I'm avoiding cholesterol." "I won't allow sugar in my house much less in my body." These are just a few of the common declarations of the nutrition meddler using the occasion to declare his or her belief that food is a moral issue and that the host is insensitive to the health needs of the guests. It is no wonder that the fine art of having guests for dinner is dying, not just in the sea of fast-food outlets that line our streets but also in the Holy Grail of health.

None of this has gone unnoticed, but the growing critical literature on the health and fitness movement often concentrates on an analysis of what it regards as an overemphasis on individual salvation and self-absorption at the expense of social change (Crawford, 1979; Schur, 1978; Stein, 1982a, 1982b). Crawford, for example, claims that healthism situates the problem of health and disease at the level of the individual and formulates solutions on that level as well. "By elevating health to a supreme value," he argues, "healthism reinforces the privatization of the struggle for generalized well-being." In the same vein, Howard Stein notes that the "wellness" ideology not only treats complex human problems simplistically (e.g., by promoting running as a cure for depression or smoking cessation) but also diverts attention from pressing social issues by preoccupying each person with his or her own individual well-being. These analysts denounce the health movement for its subjectivism and apolitical nature, its focus on what Russell Jacoby (1975: 101–118) calls "the permanent emergency of the individual," and its consequent ignorance of the social matrix in which all such movements are imbedded.

But in our view it is a mistake to believe that the health movement has opted to avoid society and politics altogether in favor of an individual and narcissistic emphasis on personal salvation. Far from it. For although it is apparent that the individual is deemed in this form of consciousness to be the ultimate executor of his or her own wellness, the new individualizing health ethic contains within it the notion that each person is also responsible for the health achievements of others. In fact, the idea that most anyone can be healthy given the proper combination of diet, exercise, and lifestyle has been translated into an ethic that everyone *should* be. The belief that health is both an individual responsibility and a moral obligation has become a justification for meddling into the lives of those persons who seem either ignorant of that "fact" or unable or unwilling to act on it. Indeed, self-righteous intolerance appears to be the driving force behind this new health movement. As Crawford observes, "There seems to be an inevitable progression from seeing health as a goal requiring choice and active commitment, through seeing the 'problem' of health as a matter of control, discipline, denial and will-power, to expressing a moral verdict for the inability of self or others to meet the rather extensive expectations for optimal health behavior[5] being elaborated in the media and throughout largely middle-class social networks" (Crawford, 1984: 70). Given this view of health through individual achievement, failure to comport oneself in healthful ways has become a sign of social, not just individual, irresponsibility. The influential health-policy expert John Knowles set the moral tone of the health meddler early in the development of the contemporary health movement:

> The idea of individual responsibility has been submerged to individual rights, rights or demands to be guaranteed by government and delivered by public and private institutions. The costs of sloth, gluttony, alcohol intemperance, reckless driving, sexual frenzy and smoking are now a national, and not individual, responsibility. This is justified as individual freedom, but one man's freedom in health is another man's shackle in taxes and insurance premiums. I believe that the idea of a "right" to health should be replaced by the idea of an individual obligation to preserve one's own health—a public duty if you will. (Knowles, quoted in Crawford, 1980: 379)

Joseph Califano, former secretary of health, education, and welfare and a reformed smoker, has echoed this theme by calling for nothing less than a political and cultural transformation:

> We must acknowledge both the limits of medicalization and the breadth of factors that affect health. We must recognize that our quixotic desire to drink from the fountain of immortality and the well of cosmetic perfection can demean the dignity of human existence and trample on . . . basic health needs. And we must temper our insistence on absolute individual autonomy while we accept more responsibility for our own health. (Califano, 1994: 53)

Since health in this scheme of things is both an individual responsibility and a public duty, what we have seen escalate over the past few years is a powerful mixture of devices designed to regulate health miscreants. The political apparatus of the commonweal (legislation, regulation, and organizational policy) as well as the smaller (though perhaps more effective) interpersonal strategies of intimidation, harassment, and stigmatization have been commandeered as power vehicles with which to establish a certain totalitarianism around the banner of health. In an AIDS-, tobacco-, and cholesterol-infested age, "health fascism" seems to be the emerging political order of the day, with various meddling groups and agencies exercising increasing vigilance and control over what people put into their bodies and what they put their bodies into.

The Quest for the Perfect Body

Neither science nor medicine has ever found the perfect body. That has not kept people from looking for it. If science has failed to locate it, current popular culture most assuredly has, too. It is slender, fit, and glowing. It, of course, does not smoke. And if it drinks, it does so in moderation, and only for the purpose of ingesting flavonoids, which protect the body against heart disease. It carefully regulates its diet in terms of calories, carbohydrates, fats, salt, and sugar. It exercises regularly and intensely so that its heart rate climbs to prescribed levels and stays there for prescribed periods of time. It showers (not bathes). It engages only in safe sex, preferably in the name of health, not pleasure—or, at the very least, healthy pleasure (pleasure, for the moment, having been relegated to a subcategory of health). It sleeps regular hours. It has the correct amount of body fat. It is flexible, supple, and has appropriate aerobic capacity. In short, the perfect body is one that is biochemically, physiologically, and autonomically balanced. Moreover, it does not allow toxic substances and activities to disturb its inner harmony. It has wrapped itself in a protective membrane. It is, in a word, "healthy."

That the perfect body is, for the most part, an ideal and not a reality is obvious from even cursory observations of those who pursue it through exercise, nutrition, and other virtuous habits of life. But like other consummations devoutly to be wished, its promise drives a large segment of society to temperance, moderation, and control in all things that have been deemed healthy. And the promise is more than just biological perfection, for good things are said to come to people with perfect bodies. Better relationships, better work performance, better self-images, and less stress: All are laid at the feet of biological fitness. The advertisement of a recent aerobics class summarizes the fit with its title "Healthy, Wealthy, and Wise." Social and psychological salvation await those with perfect bodies.

There is perhaps no more vivid testimony to the cult of the perfect body than the amazing popularity of running. The serious runner has become the prototype of fit, healthy individuals. Running is the microcosm of the fitness movement as a whole, given its emphasis on the body as a finely tuned and perfectly functioning machine. The marathon—and there are countless numbers of them staged throughout the land each and every week—has become a Cynthian celebration of the integrity, steadfastness, discipline, and achievement of the fitness mentality. It is a spectacle of "health," lived by its participants and vicariously experienced by its spectators. Running has indeed become a kind of religion among its participants, replete with gurus, testimonials, places of worship, conversion stories, rituals, self-denying practices, and sacrifice. It is estimated to have attracted as many as 40 million devotees. Moreover, much of the rest of the health ideology has apparently been inspired by, associated with, and followed the same pattern laid down by the running movement, for healthism at large is filled with spiritual rhetoric. Before-

and-after stories abound as runners talk about the changes that have occurred in their lives as a result of their newfound faith. These transformations range from trivial ones such as getting up and going to bed at different times of the day, making new friends, and becoming involved in new activities, to more profound ones such as shedding sedentary friends, divorcing spouses, rejecting smokers, and finding a whole new set of others who can be counted on to validate their new healthy selves. "I have abandoned the non-running world" is the way one runner summarized his conversion (Higdon, 1978: 76).

"Pure as Well as Perfect": The Puritan Underpinnings of Health and Fitness

Of particular interest to us in this book, however, is the observation that exercise and fitness are no longer movements content to celebrate the achievements of the individual who either accepts or rejects the hedonistic temptations and health-hazardous inducements of those who have not yet accepted their newly found faith. Instead, the lives, habits, and behaviors of the unfit are increasingly being viewed as the enemy that must be changed in order to make the world safe for the pursuit of health. Indeed, the religious underpinnings of the health movement spring from a Puritanism that has always seen the problem of controlling others as central to its mission. As Robert Briffault pointed out in 1931: "Puritanism does not regard ascetic self-torture as virtue, but regards enjoyment as sin. It is therefore not concerned with practicing the former, but with suppressing the latter" (Briffault, 1931: 996). If health, then, may be characterized as a secular religion, then it seems to be advocating an increasingly right-wing and Puritanical version of its faith. Those who live will ultimately see their pleasures constrained, if not banned outright. In the meantime, those who die from what will surely be regarded as their own dissipated health habits may well be accorded the same amount of sympathy we have recently seen directed to people with AIDS.

In the face of this new health militancy, it is not surprising that, as Richard Goldstein has noted, "nearly everyone . . . has given up some formerly cherished 'sin'" (Goldstein, 1986: 23). Saying "no" to the temptations of drugs, tobacco, fatty foods, lethargy, and unsafe sex has become almost fashionable. For

[u]nder the reconsecrated tweed, the body must be pure as well as perfect. Yesterday's stud is today's carrier, yesterday's head is today's substance abuser, yesterday's smoker is today's public health menace. As the war on drugs conflates with the war on porn, as AIDS becomes the buzzword for

depravity, as drinking and smoking are rated R, giving it up has become a fashion statement. Antonovich the furrier advertises an "I-Stopped-Smoking-Coat"—the perfect tradeoff of pleasure for prestige. (Goldstein, 1986: 23)

This heavily proscriptive tone of the modern health movement seems remarkably akin to the obsessive abstinence ethic of old-time Puritanism. For in that scheme of things, suffering, denial, and self-sacrifice were positive virtues in and of themselves because they paved the way for productive work, freed from the temptations of hedonism. This is an idea that Max Weber has shown was, and apparently still is, seen by the children of Puritanism as the surest route both to heaven and to the prosperity created by the fruits of capitalism (Weber, 1930). If this is indeed what the health movement is all about, then pleasure itself is the enemy, and the fundamentalist, ascetic tone of its advocates, who regard themselves as among the elect, suddenly becomes clear—as does H. L. Mencken's pithy definition of Puritanism: "the haunting fear that someone, somewhere, may be happy" (Mencken, 1921). The key to understanding Puritanism is to note that, despite its otherworldliness and emphasis on salvation, older-style Puritans thought they would see a payoff in this world as well. The grace of the deity would shine on the elect in real and tangible ways. Their children (the "New Puritans," as Dinitia Smith has called them), bereft of their sense of the sacred, but still armed with righteousness, also want to see early results in exchange for their strenuous purity:

> New Puritans are part of the American tradition that equates exercise and good eating habits with material progress and spiritual well-being. In the 19th century, the Muscular Christianity movement advocated regular exercise to improve one's moral state and reduce lascivious thinking. Sylvester Graham, inventor of the eponymous cracker, preached "moral vegetarianism" and collected a band of followers, the Grahamites, who liked nothing more than a hearty meal of honey, apples, and cold water . . . [T]he New Puritan is the secular equivalent of the muscular Christian. "People believe that if you run a marathon you will somehow, mystically, become president of your corporation. You martyr yourself in order to achieve." (Smith, 1984: 27)

This is a very old American theme: Deprivation is spiritually ennobling and will pay off in this life. But whereas these examples show that health and purification movements are nothing new in American society,[6] what substantively distinguishes the new health movement from older ones is the strident attempt by its devotees to enforce this ethic on everyone else. If the decade of the 1960s saw the reign of the "Me" generation, the 1980s and beyond have displayed the power of the "No" generation (Seeley, 1987) whereby restraint, purification, and environmental control line up on one side and drinking, smoking, corpulence, and sexual excess line up on the other. In such a setting, "[h]ealth maintenance is a matter of abstentions and renunciations. In other words, self control, discipline, denial, and will-power are precisely the qualities of character needed to combat 'bad habits' and to negotiate the mine fields of health hazards" (Crawford, 1984: 72). This enthusiasm for a perfect body and the Puritanism that it implies occurred during a period when morality in other arenas of life seemed by many to be on the wane. As Barbara Ehrenreich has observed:

> Morality is no longer a prominent feature of civil society. In the 1980's politicians abandoned it, Wall Street discarded it, televangelists defiled it. Figuratively speaking, we went for the sucrose rush and forgot the challenge of fiber. But only figuratively. For as virtue drained out of our public lives, it reappeared in our cereal bowls, our exercise regimens, and our militant responses to cigarette smoke, strong drink, and greasy food.[7] (Ehrenreich, 1995: 59)

In short, virtue, which previously had been a lofty ideal applied to such things as honesty, decency, fidelity, integrity, and trustworthiness, was now being applied to health: "To say that we want to be healthy is to gravely understate the case. We want to be good" (Ehrenreich, 1995: 60). One of the great advantages of translating health into virtue is that commodifying it in this way transforms it into something that is relatively cheap and easy to obtain. Although the complexities and costs of such eternal verities as trust, honesty, and loyalty are all too well known, health is a bargain. Faithfully adhere to a regimen such as diet and exercise, eat the right foods, take the right vitamins, and abstain from the correct pleasures, and you too can achieve biological perfection and the imputation of virtue that comes with it. If all else fails, medical science increasingly offers a panoply of options—liposuction, implants, and body sculpturing[8]—to assist with the quest. Even convicts and moral derelicts, unable to pursue anything else, can pursue health.[9] The road to Wellville is open to everyone; just get on it and start running.

The pursuit of the perfect body has also gained impetus from certain changes in the way Americans view themselves. In the shift from modernism to the postmodern culture of high mass capitalism (Jameson, 1991), viable distinctions could no longer be drawn between what could be marketed and sold and any other features of social life. In this world, bodies were not only commodified but also became a way of establishing who and what one is in terms of selfhood. It is not so much a matter of selves having bodies attached to them (a modernist notion observed by such scholars as Erving Goffman) as of bodies having selves hooked to them for display to others. Not just sex, but also fitness, has become tangled up with marketing—and for many of the same reasons. The avalanche of images of idealized bodies that spew forth to Americans from every media source have become dominant symbols in the race to be regarded as morally good in the eyes of others. And these eyes are everywhere: "In front of the television set, washed in torrents of disconnected images of exemplary talking bodies, bodies prescribing health clubs, fiber-enriched cereals, and mini-skirts, the individual has little time or space to experience 'his' body as apart from generalized insistent others" (Glassner, 1989: 224). The ideologies of wellness are totalitarian by their very nature.

Health Fascism

But in the midst of all this virtue in the name of health, this desire to save one's own life and live forever, what does one do with those who do not pursue the dream of biological perfection held so devoutly by others? What of those careless eaters, drinkers, smokers, and sedentary souls— or, in other words, those individuals who choose to engage in activities that in former times were considered to be privileges of the aristocratic leisure classes? Two fates have awaited them. On the one hand, they may be considered sick, if indeed words like *compulsive* or *addictive* are attached to their behaviors. On the other hand, and at the very least, they are considered potentially sick and, as such, are then pressured into minimizing that potential by altering their bad habits. In fact, persons who predispose themselves to sickness by lighting up cigarettes, eating fried eggs, drinking martinis, and watching television—particularly if they do so repeatedly and after proper warning—are now considered by some to be actually ill:

> Positive wellness, not just the absence of disease, is the goal. The conventional physician considers a person well if he has no symptoms and falls within the normal range in a series of diagnostic tests. Yet this "well" person might smoke heavily, take no exercise, eat a bland, sweet, starchy diet, and impress all who meet him as glum, antisocial, and emotionally repressed. To a New Medicine practitioner, such a person is quite sick, the carrier of what biologist René Dubos calls "submerged potential illness." (quoted in Crawford, 1980: 6)

So here we see the nub of the meddling impulse when it comes to matters of health and fitness. Through various linguistic legerdemains, one can be "well" but still be "sick." And the sick must be attended to; for whether sick or only potentially so, the unhealthy person's condition is viewed as a consequence of "individual and moral failure" (Crawford, 1980: 380). Since the illness is essentially his or her own fault, the unhealthy individual becomes a legitimate target of moral revulsion. It is not enough for the persons directly affected to waste away in their own polluted condition; they must be rehabilitated and their wretched behavior controlled by the healthy. Prime examples include obese people and alcoholics who have long been the object of both structural and interpersonal ostracism in American society. But although the disease metaphors of obesity and alcoholism have conveniently disguised the more direct accusations of weak willpower and defective character, they have not refuted the nagging suspicion in this culture that fat people and drunks are still their own worst enemies. And, of course, the expectation that individuals be neither fat nor drunk, no matter how much scientific evidence piles up on the side of the many virtues of sveltness and sobriety, remains clearly a moral rather than a medical judgment, a point made nicely by David Mechanic: "Those persons who wish to reform the unhealthful habits of others give as their stated motive for changing certain habits the damage caused by the habits upon the individual's health. But their real reason—conscious or otherwise—might simply be moral revulsion to the habits themselves" (1978: 14).

Blaming the Victim

Medical settings increasingly mirror American society in their enthusiasm for blaming the victim. Paul Marantz, writing in the *American Journal of Public Health,* notes the case of a friend who died suddenly and unexpectedly of a myocardial infarction. Because he was in seemingly excellent health, this epidemiological curiosity prompted discussions among the medical staff at the hospital where he worked. A resident offered the helpful theory: "Well, he was a real couch potato" (Marantz, 1990: 1186). Marantz goes on to say that medicine and popular culture have coalesced on the deterministic view that nothing "just happens" and that the reasons given for tragedies such as the death of his friend increasingly "blame the victim" for his own disease, illness, and infirmity. All one has to do is listen to the talk among the staff at any hospital—"She blew her IV," "He flipped an embolism"—to discover innumerable instances of blaming patients for their own plight. Marantz says that many members of the medical profession now believe that anyone who has a heart attack "must have lived a life of gluttony and sloth" (Marantz, 1990: 1186). In this new scheme of things, we seem to view raising a cheeseburger to one's lips as the moral equivalent of holding a gun to one's head.

Such intolerance of real diseases is particularly striking when one considers that it exists alongside the increasingly prevalent view that alcoholism, drug problems, and sexual abuse should be classified as "diseases" and their "victims" placed under the auspices of medicine. In other words, at the very time when we are coming to see people as not responsible for what Thomas Szasz (1984) calls "non-disease diseases," we are also coming to see people as utterly responsible for their real ones. This well-nigh total reversal of the traditional view of medical compassion gives rise to a spate of questions: In the future will we ration health care based on moral categories? Will those who are determined to be responsible for their own diseases be stigmatized? (This is increasingly the case now with alcoholics and tobacco users.) Will we add diet and exercise to this mix? If everyone is responsible for his or her own diseases, what happens to medical compassion? As it turns out, there is a kind of predictive case study under way that might point to an answer to these questions.

Demonizing Smokers

In the last twenty years, the battle over tobacco has become perhaps the greatest single morality play of our time. Always a controversial habit—the first anti-smoking ordinance in the country was established in 1630 among the Puritans in the colony of Massachusetts—tobacco moved from the status of a disgusting nuisance to a major health hazard with the publication of the Surgeon General's report in 1962. The United States is the only country in the world that has a "Surgeon General" to lobby on behalf of right thinking about matters of health, and much of the moral revulsion of the incumbents of this office over the past forty years has been reserved for tobacco companies that, as a result of their relentless crusades, are now widely dismissed as moral outlaws. Never content simply to state the scientific facts, however, the war on smoking has devolved into a major assault on smokers themselves. Meddling into the lives of people who smoke clearly represents a much larger agenda than is sometimes claimed by the elevated health pretensions of those who lead such movements. Evidence of this lies in the fact that the health consequences of the age-old behavior of smoking tobacco products is less the target of healthists than the degradation, denunciation, and humiliation of those who smoke. As Jay Epstein observes: "Just now the five most menacing words in the English language may well be: 'thank you for not smoking.' One feels about these five words that a sixth word is missing but strongly implied, and it could be any of the following: chump, creep, pig, scum, leper" (Epstein, 1989: 7). Such degradation efforts may also be seen in a *Wall Street Journal* article in which it was reported that smoking is now hazardous not simply to people's health but to their career advancement as well, and that smokers are being harassed and shunned, criticized by their superiors, herded into ever smaller sections of the office or out of work settings completely, or even discretely terminated as a drain on worker health insurance programs and HMOs. "I've become almost like a junkie, sneaking around as if I take illegal drugs," says a manager at Johnson & Johnson. "In a corporate culture like ours, where everyone is looking good and smelling good, the last thing you do is stick a cigarette in your mouth" ("Harmful Habit," 1987: 1). Furthermore, this organizational meddling into the lives of workers is justified by the imputation of various characteristics presumed not only to reside in the personality of the smoker but also to "cause" his smoking. For example, an industrial manager was quoted as saying that he wouldn't hire a smoker, even though his company has no official policy against it, because "I look upon smokers as being weak and not at the same level of intelligence as I am. At some point their progression up the career ladder will be stopped because, to me, they're slobs" ("Harmful Habit," 1987: 1).

So, although often disguised as benevolent concern, the meddling response of the "healthy" to the "unhealthy" in the case of smoking is clearly one of ostracism or, at least, distancing. For, as Irving Zola predicted two decades ago, "in addition to the basic depoliticizing effect of the labels 'health and illness,' there is also an exclusionary one. [W]here once one was excluded from jobs because of race, ethnicity, gender and age, now one will become ineligible for promotion, inappropriate for work, pushed to early retirement—all on the basis of one's physical status or health" (Zola, 1977: 65–66). Smokers, as well as drunks, gluttons, and sedentaries (now derisively called "couch potatoes" in the new pejorative of healthism), are viewed as an inferior class of people, certainly unfit, undependable, inefficient, and probably unclear in mind and spirit as well as body. Indeed, the feeling of discomfort that the healthy feel while in the presence of the unhealthy seems frightfully akin to the disquiet experienced in former times by "good white folk" when in the company of blacks.

It is important to remember, as Joseph Gusfield has observed, that the process of stigmatization may take one of two forms: It can be either "assimilative" or "coercive" (Gusfield, 1963). The meddlesome response to smokers has involved both. Assimilative interventions attempt to persuade the individual smoker to kick the habit. They involve educational programs, warning labels, television ads, co-optation of the medical community, and school programs. Because such meddling is done in the name of two of the sacred icons of American culture, education and medicine, it is often seen as wholly positive. And yet, if assimilative stigmatization does not work, coercive forms are always waiting in the wings. They include such heavy-handed tactics as prohibition, segregation, and, in the case of tobacco, banning any mention of it from the airwaves. All of these actions represent meddling at its worst, for they adopt police-state tactics to enforce personal life choices, all in the name of the public good—even though such actions represent little that is truly public but are more often an attempt on the part of individuals to wrap themselves in a largely illusory membrane of safety and security.[10]

Elevating a Nuisance to a National Crisis: The Meddling Career of Secondhand Smoke

The excesses of the movement to banish tobacco from the American land-scape have engendered one of the most astonishing chapters in the history of meddling. We are referring here to the social construction of "passive smoke" as a health problem for those who do not smoke. As if stigmatization of those deemed unhealthy were not enough, they are now also being blamed for the unhealthful habits of those with whom they live, work, and socialize. Secondary smoke, admittedly a nuisance for some who do not smoke, is now alleged to be physically harmful to the nonsmoker, just as alcoholic behavior is said to spawn the disease of "co-dependency."[11] Late in this century, smoking has become akin to the solitary vice of the previous century—masturbation. Do it if you must, but only in absolute secrecy. The leviathan data dredge[12] set out by epidemiologists has caught in its net dozens of diseases among nonsmokers that are now claimed to be "associated" with contact with secondhand smoke. Indeed, passive smoking has been linked to heart disease, cancer, crib death, vitamin deficiencies, and endothelium arterial dilation in otherwise healthy people, to mention just a few of the horrifying effects on human beings who involuntarily associate with the outcast of our age, the dreaded smoker. Peter Berger traces the career line of the movement against tobacco on the basis of passive-smoking claims:

> Seen in the perspective of the antismoking campaign, a perspective frequently reflected sympathetically in the media, the issue is quite simple: not only is ETS [environmental tobacco smoke] an annoyance to nonsmokers ("an invasion of their private space") but it is more important, a matter of public health. ETS, albeit in a less intensive way, promulgates the same diseases that smoking supposedly does. Smokers thus constitute not only an annoyance but a health hazard to nonsmokers. The scientific basis for this belief is allegedly conclusive, having been legitimated by an authority no less than that of the U.S. Surgeon General. Anyone who questions the belief, therefore, is either motivated by wishful thinking (smokers in the main) or by vested interest (the tobacco industry). (Berger, 1988: 81–82)

Caveats are, however, in order. For in the face of this "overwhelming" medical evidence of the dangers of passive smoking to the nonsmoker, many people, including those within the regulatory community, have begun questioning the "science" that the Environmental Protection Agency (EPA) has used to arrive at a set of conclusions that have led to enormous costs, draconian programs, and even discussion of an outright prohibition against smoking. The Consumer's Research Council reports that at least some facts are finally catching up with the "political" science of the question, suggesting that the entire matter may simply be one of yet another group meddling in the name of science. As Peter Samuel and Peter Spencer claim in commenting on the Congressional Research Service's recent study of passive smoking:

> [T]he government is admitting the erroneous nature of much regulatory policy. In particular there is a rising consensus that a good deal of what has been cited as a science-research basis for that policy has been constructed the other way around: The policy has dictated or influenced the "science," and the evidence has been sorted out to fit an existing mind-set, if not a preconceived conclusion. (Samuel and Spencer, 1993: 10)

These authors, who write for the Consumer's Research Institute, condemn government reports that claim in excess of 3,000 lung cancer deaths a year from exposure by nonsmokers to tobacco smoke. They say that the Congressional Research Service (CRS) of the Library of Congress, along with leading epidemiologists, have now concluded that the EPA's claims are completely unsubstantiated. The CRS points out that of thirty studies, "six found a statistically significant (but small) effect, 24 found no significant effect, and six found a passive-smoking effect opposite to the expected relationship" (quoted in Samuel and Spencer, 1993: 14). In addition, a study by the National Cancer Institute found "no statistically significant relationship increase in risk associated with exposure to environmental tobacco smoke at work or during social activities" (Stockwell, 1992: 1422). Worse yet, when the EPA's studies did not fit the policy conclusion they were attempting to support, the agency cooked its own data:

> The EPA based its report on 11 earlier studies. But even after manipulating the stats, ten of the 11 studies referred to by the EPA still failed to reveal a statistically significant effect of secondhand smoke on health. The EPA responded with a technique it had never before employed. It simply combined data from the 11 studies into one report. Even then it couldn't demonstrate a connection between passive smoke and cancer within the 95 percent accuracy required of all previous EPA studies. So the agency changed the

rules. This time, a statistical conclusion with only 90 percent predicted accuracy would be acceptable. (Scheer, 1994: 49)

In Greece, the European country with the highest number of cigarettes consumed but the lowest number of deaths from lung cancer, the notion of "passive smoking" is unknown. A villager, laughing, told journalist Telemaque Maratos, who had just explained the concept of "passive smoking," that passive smokers should be taxed because "they smoke for free." Maratos also relates an experience in which he appeared on a Greek talk show. The subject of the program was smoking:

> The host immediately asked for an ashtray, lit up—"on the air"—and said that he had recently been in America where he was so disgusted by the restrictions on smoking that if he was not a smoker already he would have started then and there. The chairman of [a Greek anti-smoking group] was not allowed to go on with the death statistics. "We do not want death here. This is about liberty. Freedom and the rights of the individual. We shall discuss cancer another time," said the host, summing up the Greek attitude on the matter (Maratos, 1995: 46).

But back in America, where the tobacco police are in full cry, things are quite different. In 1990 Congress banned smoking on virtually all U.S. domestic flights. City after city has passed stringent anti-smoking rules for restaurants, and some have implemented a ban on vending machine sales as well. Jan Ferris reports that anti-smoking groups are putting pressure on publishers who print tobacco advertising. Among the magazines they are targeting are *Glamour, Essence,* and *People* (Ferris, 1994: 16–18). Federal excise taxes on cigarettes can be raised virtually with impunity. In California, the state is using $28 million from a 25-cent-a-pack increase to fund an advertising campaign that Jacob Sullum says "depicts smokers as inconsiderate slobs and cigarette manufacturers as gleeful murders." The government is, in effect, forcing tobacco companies to pay for a campaign to vilify themselves (Sullum, 1991: 29). None of this, of course, is meant to suggest that tobacco companies are saints or that tobacco isn't a carcinogen. Rather, the point is that the slippery slope of justifications that fuels the meddlesome impulse can be seen clearly in such cases, which call to mind the censor who, when hacking away at obscene materials, always seems to know where to start but seldom can figure out where to stop. Once tobacco is deemed a "health hazard" to nonsmokers, any number of paternalistic interventions are ostensibly justified. Moreover, the rationales for the interventions are selective and arbitrary. For if the reason for raising taxes and banning smoking is that medical costs are higher for smokers, then why not apply the same logic to those who eat red meat, consume butter fat, drink alcoholic beverages, or refuse to exercise in the face of all the evidence that government epidemiologists are stacking up in each of those areas as well?

Much more is going on here than just the protection of public health. In the years since the Surgeon General's first report in 1964 focused attention on the tobacco companies, it has become customary to refer to them as a "vested interest"—a designation that is undoubtedly accurate. Often lost in these discussions, however, is the fact that the other side of the argument is a vested interest, too—and an increasingly large and powerful one at that. No longer a small band of true believers, the movement to stop tobacco is now large and well organized, and provides employment and social status to sizable numbers of people. Peter Berger argues that the ideological objective of the anti-smoking movement is nothing short of a total ban on smoking:

> The freely proclaimed agenda of the antismoking campaign is to stigmatize, segregate, and (at least partially) criminalize smoking. An often announced goal of the campaign is to reduce smoking to a socially unacceptable activity engaged in by consenting adults in private. Smoking, in other words, would then be an activity comparable to what at least in the past was seen as repulsive sexual practices, morally condemned by almost everyone, driven into secluded private spaces, and punished by law if it dared to emerge from these spaces—ideally in the imagination of antismoking activities, "the habit that dare not speak its name. (Berger, 1994: 83)

Berger goes on to wonder whether human communities do not require some kind of detestable activity to feel morally righteous about, such that if one is given up, another must take its place. Hence the well-known contradiction whereby people who are properly outraged by governmental attempts to control even demonstrably healthy sexual practices are often in the forefront of movements pushing for the criminalization of smoking. A prime example can be found in California, where resistance to AIDS prevention measures that might interfere with the rights of gays has been virtually institutionalized and, at the same time, anti-smoking laws are being vigorously enacted. Contradictions of this sort are well known in the history of the meddlesome impulse, for the belief systems that justify meddling commonly represent the triumph of ideology over any other considerations. Given the marriage of health morality and public policy, the power apparatus of the commonweal is now being used to promote and enforce certain matters that heretofore were clearly understood to be in the realm of personal choice.

The recent decision of the regional university at which one of the authors teaches (but it could be *any* university, for these actions now constitute a nationwide movement) to hop on the bandwagon and ban tobacco in all forms from its campus is one of many examples that are instructive about the basic organizational and institutional dimensions of the meddling impulse. Invoking the canard that smoking both is "hazardous" and causes "discomfort," the university now prohibits smoking in any building and within ten feet of the entrance to any building. In a question-and-answer format, the administration noted that it is departing from its original policy—which allowed smoking in private offices— because of "new information" about the hazards of smoking. In the absence of any statement as to what this "new information" is or by what authority it is being promulgated, the new policy essentially institutionalizes the hatred and vilification of its employees who choose to smoke. Rather than resisting the current cultural warfare on the issue, the university chose to join it. The Q-and-A was particularly revealing for it raised one straw man after another and then proceeded to demolish them. For example, it asked the question "Isn't there a right to smoke" and then stated that no such right has ever been found by the courts. (Apparently our lives are increasingly to be reduced only to those matters that the judiciary has proclaimed as "rights.") It never discussed smoking as a privilege, or asserted that the policy of the university is to oppose intolerance in all forms, including intolerance of smokers. This, incidentally, is a university that prides itself on pursuing an all-inclusive "multicultural" agenda and puts up with an astonishing array of behaviors that are offensive to someone, but apparently this does not include smokers. Moreover, by prohibiting smoking within ten feet of the entrance to any university building, the new policy has enacted a particularly vengeful decision inasmuch as smokers typically congregate around entrances to protect themselves from the weather since they've already been thrown out of every building on campus. One has only to notice the hateful expressions on nonsmokers' faces as they pass smokers engaged in their disgusting habit to discover what the source of the policy is or to understand that it is based on a certain moral revulsion at the dissipated health habits of these thoroughly stigmatized miscreants.

Furthermore, the paternalism that underlies the university's new policy tips its hand when its authors discuss how violators will be treated. There are two choices. One the one hand, they may adopt the role of innocent victim of the enslaving drug called tobacco and, having professed their sins, actually receive university benefits by opting for the Employee Assistance Program, which will counsel repentant smokers who "have difficulty in complying with the program." In other words, the university asserts that it will be magnanimous and understanding if people will admit their purulent condition and get on board with the program. On the other hand, if they don't, and their violations "persist," disciplinary responses "appropriate for the employee will be utilized."

The Q-and-A was immediately followed by a spiel about the many benefits available to supplicants, including up to $200 a year in Wellness Program emoluments such as nicotine patches and so on, available to employees "who choose to use this change in policy as an opportunity to quit smoking." So the actual goal of the program at last reveals itself. It is nothing less than to meddle into the lives of its employees who smoke in an effort to force them to stop doing so.

This example could be multiplied many thousands of times in America during the past five years—and in many cases the measures taken have been even more draconian. National Public Radio (NPR) recently reported that the Motorola Corporation, which had previously banned all smoking even in outdoor areas on its grounds, had begun to rethink its policy because it appeared to be "too harsh." As one spokesperson put it, "Our employees came to believe that the company was intruding too much on individual behavioral choices" (NPR, August 2, 1996).

The disingenuousness of the tobacco companies in denying the health risks of smoking is probably clear to almost everyone.[13] Tobacco is a carcinogen, and drawing particulate matter into the lungs as a regular habit cannot possibly be good for anyone's physical health. Yet the anti-tobacconists' thirty-year battle to establish such an obvious scientific truism against an intransigent industry with a vested interest obscures the fact that the anti-smoking movement and its powerful governmental allies have played fast and loose with the truth, too. As Berger argues:

> [T]hey too have all along been using scientific findings selectively and even misusing them in the service of their cause. For example, there are data showing cigarette-smoking to be far more hazardous than cigar- and pipe-smoking, but these data are ignored in the simple propagandistic slogan that smoking kills. Nor does the anti-smoking campaign differentiate the individual who smokes two packs of cigarettes a day from the one who smokes, say, two cigarettes a day. (Berger, 1994: 22)

Moreover, the magnitude of the problem seems overstated (as one would expect) by the ideological proponents of a ban on smoking. The number of smoking-related deaths keeps climbing at the very time that smoking is decreasing. (Berger cites governmental data that put the figure between 300,000 and 500,000 deaths.)[14] The fact that deaths of nonsmokers from environmental tobacco smoke are even more subject to question does not seem to concern the sources spewing out the data. John Luik, in a recent article in *Bostonia*, quotes a prominent epidemiologist on the EPA's misuse of data on smoking: "Yes, it's rotten science," he says. "but it's in a worthy cause. It will help us to get rid of cigarettes and to become a smoke-free society" (quoted in Berger, 1994: 22). So, bolstered by policy-driven science and unexamined premises about the nature of our relationship with one another, the war on passive smoking has become a trial run for a much larger program of meddling manipulation. Smoking is simply the most visible example of a slippery-slope viewpoint that is likely to lead to even more fascism in the name of various health and safety issues.

But there are others. The movement to make the world smoke-free has recently been joined by a movement to make it "fragrance-free" as well. (In America, the word *freedom*, we reiterate, is rapidly becoming a synonym for what heretofore was freedom's opposites—prohibitions and bans.)[15] Indeed, there are already workplace settings that, emboldened by their successful prohibition of tobacco, are now declaring themselves "fragrance-free" and banning perfumes, after-shave lotions, and deodorants as well. Their rationales for doing so follow directly from the logic of anti-smoking policies. There is surely some science somewhere that says the passive effects of such substances on nonwearers are not without hazards, and some people claim allergies and discomfort in the face of their noxious fumes. Hence the call to simply ban them. For example, a recent flyer announcing an academic conference has joined the meddling bandwagon by declaring itself "fragrance-free" and reminding conferees that "many of the attendees are sensitive to perfumes, colognes, recently dry-cleaned clothes, deodorants, etc.," and that they are not to be worn at the conference. It is not difficult to imagine that a cadre of fragrance police, specially trained to sniff out offenders, will be on hand to enforce the rules.[16]

Fat: The Next Meddling Crusade

Given the rapid cultural realignments that have occurred around the issue of tobacco, accompanied by the rise of health fascists who would control the lives of everyone under the banner of health and safety, it is not unreasonable to ask: What's next?" And given the slippery slope of meddlesome interventions, it would seem that the most likely candidate is fat. The same career line that occurred with tobacco and rapidly moved it from the preeminent icon of cultural coolness and virtue to the scourge of the age is already being set into motion around fat—which, interestingly enough, was formerly associated with wealth and prosperity.[17] The scientific basis for a strident anti-fat and -cholesterol movement appears to be taking shape and is becoming as documentable as the research findings about the dangers to both the individual and society resident in the use of alcohol and tobacco. Hypertension, diabetes, heart disease, and cancer (in fact, almost every disease on the smoking list) have been associated with obesity and a lipid-rich diet. Moreover, there are far more butterfat outlets than there are tobacco shops or taverns. And the effects of fat on others may, when all the data are in, be as great as those of to-bacco smoke. To be sure, butter doesn't jump off the plate of the health miscreant and into the arteries of the health paragon, but the hermetic-seal logic of "your behavior is interfering with my health" is wonderfully holistic and does apply. The clogged arteries of some *are* costly to others, and almost everyone's consumptive "excesses" can be associated with some kind of health risk that affects, at the very least, the insurance rates of someone else. Awareness of this interconnectedness between fat and money has led to the startling idea that fat should be taxed. Such an os-tensibly absurd idea has been seriously advanced by Dr. Kelly Brownell, professor of psychology and director of the Yale Center for Eating and Weight Disorders.

Dr. Brownell is to fat what C. Everett Koop was to smoking—a crusad-ing Savonarola[18] determined to stem the rising tide of obesity in America. Writing in so august a venue as the op-ed page of the *New York Times*, he urges that fat should be regulated by the government just as alcohol and tobacco are: "Fatty foods would be judged on their nutritive value per calorie or gram of fat; the least healthy would be given the highest tax rate" (quoted in Crawford, 1997: 34.) In other writings, Dr. Brownell says that the government should follow its own lead in imposing sin taxes on cigarettes and alcohol by taxing low-nutrition food and banning com-mercials for fatty snacks targeted at children: "As a culture, we get upset about Joe Camel, yet we tolerate our children seeing 10,000 commercials a year that promote foods that are every bit as unhealthy. . . . Junk food advertisements should be regulated and excise taxes imposed on highfat foods" (quoted in Reiland, 1998: 12).

Perhaps the group that has gotten the most attention from a credulous media system (which has found that everything it says sells well in the age of anxiety) is the Center for Science in the Public Interest, an organi-zation with only two "scientists" on staff. This is a group that began as an informational agency pushing a nutritional newsletter but has recently devolved into a grim-faced band of modern Savonarolas, sounding the alarm against virtually everything that tastes good—such as movie pop-corn and ethnic food. (For example, Fettucine Alfredo is labeled "Heart Attack on a Plate," Mexican food is dubbed "OILE!," and Chinese food is described as "A Wok on the Wild Side.") Playing fast and loose with the very science that presumably authorizes the Center's pronouncements in the first place, it is able to push more easily onto the consciousness of an anxiety-ridden public "[a] Puritanical agenda against alcohol, fat, desserts, caffeine, microwave ovens and even flatulence" (Glass, 1996: 17). Its members have become the meddling mothers of food. "They're really a misnomer," says Bernadine Healy, a former director of the National Institutes of Health. "It's not always science, and these mini-scares are not in the public interest." (quoted in Glass, 1996: 17).

The most recent campaign to sanitize the nation's eating habits launched by this Puritanical band of meddling media hounds is one directed against soda pop. Citing statistics suggesting that the average American is drinking twice as much soda as in 1974, and noting that ads target children, the group makes as many associations between soft drinks and tobacco as possible. Director Michael Jacobson urged states to tax soda sales in order to pay for health education campaigns and "linked soda consumption to obesity, kidney stones, heart disease and calcium deficiency in teenagers" (Schuman, 1998: 2).

As this latest manifestation of the new Puritanism continues apace, it is becoming clear that food is the new sex—with all the attendant sin and guilt that this equation implies.[19] Barbara Haber, the curator of books at the Schlesinger Library at Radcliffe College, has suggested in the *New York Times* that as sex has gotten more dangerous, people are freer with food—hence the new prohibitions and repressions. More to the point, perhaps, is the fact that the electronic and information age has created a seemingly insatiable appetite for advice about the self, and the postmodern subjectivism that drives these enterprises competes most effectively with the babble of advice-givers by making the warnings as stridently dire as possible. Thus, demonstrating a solemn asceticism in the face of the excesses of the cornucopia of dietary plenty is a way of showing fidelity to the Puritan spiritual strain that still runs deep in secular America. As Mark Twain saw it, a healthy man combines his meddling with a certain noblesse oblige: He is one who "eats what he doesn't want, drinks what he doesn't like, and does what he'd druther not, all the while smugly announcing himself to be energetic, joyful, and certain of long life, and exhorting his errant neighbor to reform."

As is usually the case in such matters, a backlash against all this morality-mongering in the name of health is brewing. An organization called "Diet Breakers," headquartered in Banbury, England, is dedicated to helping people kick diets and simply start eating again. They claim a membership in the thousands. A magazine called *Fat SO* celebrates the joys of guilt-free corpulence. A cola named *Jolt* advertises all the calories and *twice* the caffeine of standard brands. Sales at all-you-can-eat restaurants are up. And despite two decades of hectoring, the average weight of the average American is on the rise. It is apparent that some people are fed up with people telling them how, when, and what to eat in the name of health and fitness.

Such beliefs as those we have discussed in this chapter are typically offered, not in an open market, but in one patrolled by ideological bullies.

Fueled by a media system that has discovered that there are ratings points to be had by putting on the air two of the most strident proponents of banning this substance or that behavior and having them scream at each other for thirty minutes, ideological fanatics have indeed found a niche. Thomas Sowell notes some examples: "[e]mployees who are harangued and insulted by so-called "diversity counselors," demands for more resources by the "elderly" who have the highest average income of any segment of the population, affirmative action bullies who use race to their own political advantage. We could add to this list the aforementioned healthists and virtually every other proponent of the ideologies already discussed. The lesson of status politics in this country seems to be that moral intimidation is the way to get what one wants and that special interest tactics work, especially when a sacred symbol such as "the children,"[20] "God," or "health" can be invoked. Ideological bullies tend to listen only to themselves, for they act out of a postmodern idea that has been called "categorical representation"—the notion that the interests of particular groups can be articulated only by members of those groups. With identity politics now increasingly the law of the land, meddlers need not talk with anyone but themselves in order to obtain a license to meddle into the lives of those who "don't get it."

The Hermetic-Seal Conception of Life: Guarding Against Negative Experience

A primary implication of the health movement can be reduced to an idea we might call the "hermetic-seal conception of life." As the postmodern celebration of the self has continued to absorb American consciousness, individuals have become further insulated in their own cocoons. For contemporary Americans, the answer to the confusion that befogs the culture seems to be to wrap themselves in a hermetic bubble to fight off and control the polluting and toxic behaviors of others. Buick advertises its luxury Park Avenue model with a scene that shows a well-dressed executive driving home after work through the squalor of the city, car windows sealed. The voice-over offers the inducement that the Park Avenue "shuts out urban unpleasantness." Wall yourself off and look to the behavior of everyone else as the reason why you might get sick. In short, always guard against even the possibility of negative experience. Court cases have recently elevated the hermetic-seal conception of life to the status of legal precedent. In New York, for example, a couple recently sued the Rainbow Room for $1 million, claiming that while they dined there on their honeymoon, smoke from a nearby table "upset their expected right to conjugal happiness" (Shaw, 1996: 153). Similarly, courts in California, Ohio, and Georgia have held that exposing someone to sidestream smoke can constitute "battery." Even though the evidence for the detrimental environmental effects of secondary smoke are both slim and debatable (Viscusi, 1994: 33), many Americans have apparently decided that those who choose to smoke are spewing death out of their mouths and onto them.

The hermetic-seal conception of life may be seen in an almost literal form in the increasing number of lawsuits filed by those who allege that they have the new postmodern disease known as "multiple chemical sensitivity syndrome," whereby virtually all aspects of the environment make them sick. Although even the existence of this disease is questionable, courts take cases on behalf if its victims, physicians are called as expert witnesses, and settlements are made. These trends are clearly linked to the increasing subjectivism of the postmodern world, where anything a person believes is taken to be "real" and public policy bans are grounded in politically connected science or special-interest prejudices. A new sexual harassment policy—written by a new species of meddler, the "affirmative action intern" at the university where one of us teaches—expands the boundaries of meddling to a point where all professors who talk about human sexuality in the courses they teach now put their careers on the line. In addition to listing the usual types of conduct that constitute sexual harassment—touching, patting, pinching, attempted kissing or fondling, and coerced sexual activity (previously called rape)—the new policy asserts that sexual harassment can be based on "an individual's perception of the events in question." It goes on to say that "if conduct is unwelcome . . . [or] is offensive to someone complaining . . . then the conduct may constitute sexual harassment, even if it was not intended to be offensive." This latest policy also removes a warning found in an earlier version, which reminded people that the very charge of sexual harassment can destroy a person's career and, therefore, that unwarranted charges would not be tolerated. When we asked about the removal of that reminder, noting that it would be open season on faculty if students didn't like something about the faculty member or the course (their grade, for instance), we were told that people never charged anyone with sexual harassment unless it had occurred.

The idea of an "offensive environment" is merely the latest among the ever-expanding number of hermetic seals in which contemporary Americans have wrapped themselves. In the new ideology of meddlers, everyone has a right to only positive experiences—negative ones being the grounds for lawsuits, harassment charges, the convening of grand juries, or, at the very least, censure and opprobrium. And, in any case, with life itself being viewed more and more phenomenologically as merely a string of experiences, the view seems to be that since a person has only so many experiences, he or she has a proprietary right to exclusively *happy* ones.

Hermetic seals are everywhere. Indeed, they represent a sea change in the way Americans relate to themselves and each other. If the 1960s were a decade in which people believed they could actually save society, and the 1970s a time when, having given up on that project as hopeless, they sought to save themselves through exercise and other forms of virtuous living, the latter part of the millennium seems to have been a period in which people increasingly believe that in order for them to save themselves, others have to stop *their* wretched and impure practices. A certain social consciousness was thus replaced by a subjective consciousness, and that subjective consciousness has now turned outward to others as the source of *its* problems. Those others have come back from the preoccupations of the "Me" generation, but as a fearful impediment to the safety and security of the individual—dangerous and in need of control. Old-style meddlers at least had the saving grace of trying to rescue society from rack and ruin—Carry Nation actually believed that the United States would be a better place if its citizens would stop drinking and return to God. But contemporary meddlers do not seem the least bit interested in saving society; their concern is with saving themselves. They "imagine that they would be beautiful and virtuous and live forever, if only you would put out that cigar" (Morrow, 1991: 15).

Meddling in the Name of Safety

One of our spouses recently purchased a sunshade for her car. The device consists of two opaque screens that are placed in the windshield when the car is parked. The idea is to keep heat from building up in the summer sun. The screens work nicely. When in place they completely obscure any view through them (indeed, that is the idea), and yet a tag sewn into the corner contains a warning label: "Remove screens before driving car." Now it is doubtful that anywhere in America there is a driver stupid enough to try to drive a car with opaque sun screens in place, and yet the manufacturer's attorneys presumably insisted that stating the obvious in the form of a warning label was a good defensive measure to take.[21] Much as we might acknowledge that the history of human stupidity is a long and rich one (Tabori, 1959), it still represents a sign of the times that one should be warned against every conceivable hazard of modern living. Americans seem now to want to be protected from everything. Warning labels are so ubiquitous that they have become almost meaningless. A label glued to the side of a 59-cent butane lighter contains seventy-six words of warning:

- Warning! Keep away from children.
- Misuse may cause serious injury.
- Follow instructions.
- Ignite lighter away from face and clothing.
- Be sure flame is completely out after use.
- Contains flammable gas under pressure.
- Never expose to heat above 120 degrees or to prolonged sunlight.
- Never puncture or put in fire.
- Do not keep continuously lit for more than 30 seconds (it will burn you).

The lighter is, of course, "child-proof" (or, as someone has said, only a child can figure out how to work it), and in the spirit of multicultural correctness, the warnings are accompanied by various pictures for those users who cannot read English. And all this for an item that costs less than a dollar. As the scale of expense and complexity increases, so does that of the warnings. Indeed, modern aircraft, aside from having manuals whose pages number in the thousands, are festooned with placards, labels, and even automatic bells and sirens that alert the pilot to every possible hazard. The problem with all these cautions and safety-mongerings in aircraft is the same as in everyday life: They are becoming meaningless—even extinct—through saturation. Accidents are actually now being caused by the proliferation of warning bells, in two ways. First, pilots ignore them because they go off so often when they shouldn't; and second, to the extent that the pilots do try to rely on them, they may have an accident because they were relying on them and they didn't work. In moving from the smallest possible venue of safety, cigarette lighters, to the largest, aircraft, we can see the same attitude at work. Accidents are all avoidable, someone is responsible besides the person doing the lighting or the flying, and, therefore, no risk is acceptable.

Henry Fairlie has noted the debilitating effects of such an attitude:

> [T]he idea that our individual lives and the nation's life can and should be risk-free has grown to be an obsession, driven far and deep into American attitudes. Indeed, the desire for a risk-free society is one of the most debilitating influences in America today, progressively enfeebling the economy with a mass of safety regulations and a widespread fear of liability rulings, and threatening to create an unbuoyant and uninventive society. (Fairlie, 1989: 14)

Fairlie traces this prevalent refusal to accept virtually any risk at all as simply part of living to the early 1970s, when, in the wake of the debacle in Vietnam, Americans turned their attention to a totalitarian concern with the environment and with their own physical and mental well-being. Unsuccessful at protecting the rest of the world from the resident hazards of life, Americans felt sure that they could at least protect themselves. The massive tool for this project proved to be tort law, and the nation's morbid fear of risk has become a bonanza for meddling attorneys.

What's wrong with this emphasis on safety? Isn't the protection of human beings a proper regulatory function of government and institutions everywhere? The problem, of course, is that safety endeavors increase the incidence of meddling without necessarily increasing levels of safety and, as Aaron Wildavsky has shown, actually make the world more hazardous. "Just as governments imprison people in the name of liberty," says Wildavsky, "so they endanger people in the name of safety. The safety mania of the modern state is not merely expensive, disruptive, and coercive; it actually makes life more dangerous" (Wildavsky, 1988: 6). How does this happen? The answer has to do with the problem of trade-offs. The method that has been in place for a number of years is that governmental and other institutions identify a risk and ban it; identify another risk, ban it too; and so on. But, as Walter Olson (1992) has suggested, all the easy apples were plucked from the safety tree long ago. What remains are a series of choices between one risk and another, and the government, driven by a cacophony of differing political interests, typically chooses badly.

Some of these trade-offs are obvious, but others are not. It is obviously the case that if nuclear power is blocked, more wood and coal are burned—with all the hazards that mining and pollution entail. But not so obvious is the trade-off involved in the recent decision, under consumer watchdog group pressure, to require child-safety seats on airlines in order to prevent the handful of cases in which unrestrained children are killed in survivable crashes. Since compliance with such a law requires the purchase of a separate ticket (children under a certain age previously flew free and sat on the laps of their parents), the result, of course, is that more families with small children are forced to drive instead, and driving kills far more children than flying. It may be said, then, that the net effect of safety regulations requiring every child to be buckled into a restraint seat on the airlines actually kills more children. Hardly what the regulators envisioned.

Moreover, the actual levels of safety enjoyed by most Americans are not a function of regulation anyway. Olson suggests that "[o]n a graph of trends in workplace or household injuries, one cannot detect the influence of OSHA or the Consumer Product Safety Commission. But safety correlates extremely well with wealth, both individual and societal" (Olson, 1988: 52). As people grow more affluent, their environment changes for the better in a host of ways. Peter Huber points out that "[f]or a forty-five year old man working in manufacturing, a 15 percent increase in income has about the same risk-reducing value as eliminating all hazards—every one of them—from his workplace" (quoted in Olson, 1988: 52). Yet the ideology of risk is well established and growing. An ABC documentary titled "Are We Scaring Ourselves to Death?" (March 13, 1996) interviews a series of Americans who proclaim that no risk of any kind is acceptable. The goal of life, they say, is to eliminate as much risk from their lives as possible, especially where their children are concerned. The problem with this widely held view, of course, is that in attempting to eliminate all risk we further wrap ourselves in a prison of our own making as well as insufferably meddle into the lives of others perceived to be putting our lives at risk. Distinctions between statistical risk and actual risk, between what *could* happen versus what is most likely to happen, are largely absent from this discourse. The doctrine of strict liability that holds manufacturers liable for any damage that might be done with their products has replaced the legal concept of "negligence" that was in place prior to the late nineteenth century. Under these rules, one person can be held accountable for virtually anything that befalls another, even if the former was not involved in any way. As a result, insurance companies find themselves in a situation where paying off alleged victims is cheaper than fighting the drift of the times. The following account is instructive:

> Trainer Bill Shoemaker has reached an out-of-court settlement in his malpractice suit against Glendora Community Hospital and the physicians who treated him immediately after the April 8, 1991, car accident that left him a quadriplegic, according to yesterday's *Los Angeles Times*. The *Times* reported that Shoemaker would collect approximately $2.5 million from the Ford Motor Company, the manufacturers of the Bronco II he was driving at the time of the accident, but would receive no money from any other defendants. Shoemaker previously collected $1 million from Ford in a 1993 settlement and was guaranteed another $1.5 million from the auto manufacturer should he be unable to collect the amount from other parties. "I'm happy that it's all over," Shoemaker told the *Times*. "This is the way it should be. I don't think I wanted this to go all the way to a jury verdict." (Bloodstock Research, Inc., 1997)

Mr. Shoemaker, one of America's greatest sports figures, was injured in an accident when his Ford Bronco slammed into a ditch while he was driving home after an evening of drinking with friends. He had a blood alcohol level of .13 at the time of the accident. But even though this was well over California's legal limit of .08, Mr. Shoemaker seemed to blame everyone but himself. He sued Ford for the design of the Bronco, as well as the physicians who had treated him after emergency teams brought him to the hospital. In the world of safety, the one person who is immune from suit is the injured party himself. Legal meddling, of course, thrives on such contradictions. Olson reports that in the first trial of what was eventually a long series of litigations, a jury in Washington, D.C. awarded $50 million in punitive damages against Korean Air Lines for, as Olson puts it, "having the temerity to let its airliner be shot down by a Soviet fighter plane" (Olson, 1992: 310).

The avalanche of victims claiming to have been wronged by an unsafe environment is partly the legacy of no-fault legislation. When legislators in the 1970s decided that insurance companies should stop trying to figure out who was at fault and instead simply award damages to injured parties, the climate changed precipitously. No longer shackled by traditional notions of responsibility, victims of accidents could sue anyone with pockets deep enough to pay, regardless of their personal complicity in the incidents that occasioned the injuries in the first place.

"For the Sake of the Children"

The belief that children must be protected from a hostile world is the source of a host of meddling interventions that might be summarily quashed as rhetorical ruses if they were directed at adults. Sex is a prime example. The innocence of children must be shielded from the erotic passions of adults that spill over into the public discourse via the mass media and corrupt them. Obviously this means meddling into the lives of adults. Given the impossibility of keeping children away from the media in this postmodern age, the solution, from the standpoint of some meddlers, is to make certain that nothing is aired that doesn't have a G-rating. As children have gained greater access to the mass media via explosive technologies that are imperial in their impact, parents feel overwhelmed. If scientific technologies created the problem, as the argument goes, then science can solve the problem, too; for that reason parents are being offered technologies such as V-chips, Net Nanny™, and other means of surrogate parenting. As community has seemingly collapsed into a conflicting set of cultural icons often at war with one another, and as the family has broken up and scattered itself to the winds, children have been left in the care of the media. Hence the call for program censorship and control devices. But meddlesome interventions and greater technologies will never solve such problems. (Imagine the popularity of the kid in the neighborhood whose parents have *not* installed a V-chip.) Yet such solutions seem sensible to many. Meddling into the lives of others is almost a default position we take when the subject turns to children. No strategy is too extreme, no meddling unjustified when it comes to our kids. A call from the community for parents to tattoo children so that they can be identified in the event of crime is hailed in some quarters as a step forward.[22] It's "for the sake of the children."

Of course, much of this impulse to meddle in the name of "children" can be joined with other forms of meddling in order to secure conformity to somebody's preferred way of living. For example, if states decide that fetuses are people in the post–Roe versus Wade society that seems to be inching closer all the time, then it is not, as Lawrence Tribe has suggested, "altogether far-fetched to think about the state's prohibiting pregnant women—or even women who only may be pregnant, say, those of childbearing age—from smoking or drinking. Pregnant women could be prohibited from eating what they choose" (Tribe, 1992: 67). Already some bartenders, acting in what they consider to be the noble cause of child protection, have been reporting pregnant patrons to the authorities. Although this seems akin to casino employees reporting customers to Gambler's Anonymous (not so far-fetched an idea either), it is certainly consistent with interventions likely to be tolerated "for the sake of the children." Indeed, should we decide that fetuses are people, the stage will be set for one of the most profound interventionist stances ever sanctioned in American society. Every pregnancy that fails to come to term will involve, at least potentially, a police action to determine if the "rights" of the fetus have been violated. Not only the eating and drinking habits of the pregnant mother, but also her physical fitness behaviors and relationships with others, will come under scrutiny. At least theoretically, nothing would be spared (or tolerated) in the interest of protecting the life and well-being of unborn children.[23]

Popular sexual-purity campaigns also rationalize their meddling into the lives of everyone who disagrees with their ideology by asserting that their interventions are "for the sake of the children." Campaigns against pornography and obscenity use this argument as a trump card. Consider the following examples drawn from Murray Davis's (1983) study of the phenomenology of sexual ideologies.[24] The first is a statement made by a Los Angeles city councilman protesting nude beaches: "'When we send our children to the beaches, we have an obligation to see that they are fully protected. . . . [T]he display of private parts in public is offensive and harmful *to young persons*. Even though people are 'born nude and ignorant,' he said, 'they shouldn't stay that way'" (originally cited in *Los Angeles Times*, July 19, 1974, p. 19; emphasis added). Note that the councilman claims implicitly that he is trying to shield not adults (who presumably wouldn't faint away or find themselves hopelessly contaminated at the sight of a naked body) but, rather, *children* from the ghastly effects of nudity on their innocent and still-developing minds. Those who disagree are misguided at best or, at worst, perverts themselves. Furthermore, the entire fate of society is at stake if we don't do the right things (the things, of course, that the meddler wants done)—a point nicely articulated by Mayor Abraham Beame in discussing the scourge of child pornography: "We have not yet sunk to the level of savage animals, but if we don't draw the line against child pornography, we can kiss civilization as we know it . . . good-bye" (originally cited in *Los Angeles Times*, June 1, 1977, p. 7). Those who are motivated by religious ideologies tend also to combine their sacred beliefs about God with sacred beliefs about children to justify their meddling into the affairs of others. A potent combination, this merger of two arguments shuts the door tight.

Almost any kind of meddling is seen as justified in order to protect children from sexual predators. For example, Detective Lloyd Martin, the head of the Los Angeles Police Department's sexually exploited child unit, says that pedophilia is "the worst crime of all, worse than homicide or armed robbery or burglary. A crime against a child has no equal" (quoted in *Los Angeles Times*, May 3, 1981, p. 14). In addition, John Leonard argues that in the case of the most recent version of the film *Lolita*, a classic piece of fiction about a twelve-year-old seductress, "we seem to project onto the body of an imagined child—'innocent,' coveted, abused, eroticized, abandoned, commodified—our fear and rage" (Leonard, 1997: 12). The European film has been refused distribution in the United States because of its alleged offenses against the 1996 Child Pornography Act, which, in its meddling enthusiasm for protecting children, forbids "any visual depiction including any photography, film, video image or picture that appears to be of a minor engaging in sexually explicit conduct" (Leonard, 1997: 12). As a result of our thorough confusion about the issue of children and sex, America has become a nation where six-year-olds are run up on sexual harassment charges for kissing their classmates, and where police raid video stores and the home of a member of the ACLU, seizing copies of the movie *The Tin Drum*. The censors greeted the latter case with a full-court press, though it may be noted that depictions of children in sexual poses are still permissible as long as the subject is the moralistic denunciation of such crimes. Hence, television shows and documentaries can focus on "battered-child syndrome, rape-trauma syndrome, sexual-abuse syndrome, kiddie-porn sex rings, . . . cabalistic cults of pedophiles, sodomy, rape, group sex and Satanism" *ad infinitum* (Leonard, 1997: 15). By "alerting" us to the danger, the media can have it both ways—morally denouncing the horrible specter of sexual child abuse and depicting the crimes in a salacious, ratings-enhancing way. All of this is occurring at a time when the controversial notion of "repressed memory syndrome" is being exploited for all it's worth by therapists who have convinced some adults that their problems are due to sexual abuse in earlier years. Lawyers get rich suing everyone from the parents of those adults whose memory has recently been "recovered" as well as, on the other side, the therapists who talked them into it. Things have clearly gotten out of hand, and there is profit to be had for a raft of professional meddlers who cash in on our dis-ease about children and sex. But as Leonard argues:

> No one rational is saying there isn't any child abuse. Nor that there isn't any child sexuality. Nor that we don't in self-defense occasionally repress a painful memory except perhaps in upfront Berkeley. But . . . we also know that there is child *fantasy*, shape-changing and manipulated as much by advertisers of products and merchandisers of entertainment as by satanic therapists. Moreover, there is *adult* fantasy. We are so insecure and negligent in our parenthood and citizenship, caught between a public sphere (officialdom) that feels hollow and a private sphere (family) that feels besieged. . . . Caretakers become scapegoats, as do novels, movies, television, and Calvin Klein. (Leonard, 1997: 15)

In the Name of God

While meddling has been transformed over the past half-century into an increasingly secular enterprise, meddling in the name of God continues to be a popular activity and one that is currently resurgent. Religious fundamentalists from the Christian Coalition to Americans for Church and Families dot the landscape with evidence of their meddlesome attempts to alter the world in their own religious imagery. The otherworldy stance of traditional Christianity in this country now seems almost quaint; contemporary adherents are not nearly so interested in the hereafter as they are in meddling into the affairs of everyone who disagrees with them in the here-and-now. Surprisingly, groups who hold different religious beliefs are much less likely to be the targets for conversion than are secular groups whose behavior must be changed in order to make the world safe for Christians themselves. Numerous such groups are targeted for conversion. For example, "[g]ays can be changed into heterosexuals," says Jerry Falwell in a recent television interview. "I've personally seen many of them convert as a result of my ministry."[25] Addicts, abusers, alcoholics, even smokers and the obese who wish to turn over a new leaf, are now welcomed at church programs that may or may not have an overtly religious tone. The church, it seems, is in direct competition with secular clinicians of various stripes who want to cure the same constituencies through psychotherapeutic techniques. Such competition calls to mind the rationale of members of the Catholic church in the New World who believed that it was the duty of indigenous peoples to accept evangelization because they were children who did not know how bad their lives were. Since the missionaries who targeted them for conversion *did* know, their obligation was clear (Trujillo, 1996: 67).

So much meddling has been conducted in the name of the deity that, for some, it seems almost natural to equate religious experience with the effort to meddle into the lives of others. Historically, though, much of the meddling done in the name of God was actually an attempt to get others not to meddle into *their* religious affairs. Religionists meddled so that others would not. But although this form of meddling still lies behind many meddlesome interventions in the name of God, the playing field has changed considerably. Meddling in the name of God is now more often an attempt to create a hermetic seal around believers who see society—the very environment in which they live—being compromised by immoral ideologies that threaten to sweep them and their children away. As the meddlers increase their vigilance and their efforts to bend the community to their will, the backlash against them grows as well. Witness the reaction to the "Promise Keepers" organized by former University of Colorado football coach Dan McCartney. Vowing to renew their commitments to God and family, to commit themselves once again to fidelity and fatherhood, the members of this organization have nevertheless stirred deep resentments among such groups as the National Organization for Women. The latter has taken the position that because the Promise Keepers are traditionalists about the role of women, they threaten a political revolution that could sweep away the gains of feminism and return us to a time of sexual inequality.

Anxiety, Guilt, and Shame: New Uses

So, in a nation of meddlers, these are the fundamental ideologies that rationalize interventions into the lives of our fellow human beings. As such, they are the primary techniques of persuasion that people use to gain conformity to their ideals. At their best, they are bonding agents; at their worst, ideological blackmail. Health and safety meddlers intervene in the lives of others, confident that their ideology of security and eternal life comes from God himself. Wrapping themselves in a hermetic seal for protection against the impure behavior of their fellow man, which they see as threatening their lives, they are perhaps the preeminent busybodies of the current age. Those who meddle "for the sake of the children" invoke the myth of childhood innocence and argue that if ever a group needed the protection of a hermetic seal, it is children. Those who meddle in the name of God believe that they are in possession of the truth and only need to see that others are brought into line. What lies behind such notions is a certain view of emotional conformity, which then becomes the primary concept that enables meddling. Of course, anxiety, guilt, and shame have always been the traditional devices by which society has secured conformity from most of its members, but these tools have recently been joined by a series of dichotomies that further justify meddling into people's lives. Health is posed as a Manichaean choice between fitness and wellness versus disease and illness. Those who meddle in the name of God argue that the choice consists of virtue and holiness versus sin and immorality. Those who meddle in the name of "community" say that the issue is one of safety and security versus accidents, tragedies, and crime. Those who meddle "for the sake of the children" see the world as a series of choices with childhood innocence lining up on one side and corruption and defilement on the other. Those who argue for health as a mental state of mind see our identity choices as self-happiness, harmony, and self-fulfillment, on the one hand, versus misery, disharmony, and unrealized potential, on the other. Because these choices are offered in a passionately emotional context, each with appropriate atrocity stories emanating from sources as diverse as the evening news and scholarly articles in the human sciences, there is little to debate. Who, after all, can argue against the second half of each of these proffered choices? Accordingly, anxiety, guilt, and shame[26] are used to emotionally blackmail the person temeritous enough to argue against the entreaties of the meddlers. If these are indeed our choices, then the more meddling the better.

These ideologies are basically arguments—tools for conversational battle. They are employed in one fashion or another by all of the major types of meddlers, a lexicon of which is the topic of our next chapter.

Notes

1. This is not to say that people have *ever* felt they could afford them.

2. Some of these themes are also discussed in Edgley and Brissett (1990: 257–279).

3. Even the User's Guide for the Apple Macintosh computer, the word processor we are using to type this manuscript, now says that it contains not simply the usual information about setup, troubleshooting, and so on, but also "important health-related information" for Macintosh users.

4. Not that sex has taken a backseat altogether, but it has been transformed in this age of healthism from sin, pleasure, or duty (Puritan obsessions) to a health-related activity engaged in for the general welfare of the human body. As Alan Watts has observed: "Even sex is becoming acceptable for the same reason: it is good for you; 'it is a healthy, tension-reducing outlet'—to use Kinsey's statistical term for counting orgasms—and some wretched hygienist will soon figure out the average person's minimum daily requirement of outlets (0.428 would be three times a week) so that we can screw with a high sense of duty and freedom from guilt. Watch your outlet, count your orgasms, and keep a chart beside the bed" (Watts, 1970: 32–33).

5. The list of health behaviors is growing. It also changes frequently. Indeed, almost daily reports suggest yet another new health marker about which the properly concerned should worry, replacing old worries that should now be taken off the list.

6. As we showed in Chapter 2, the nineteenth century was full of health, purification, revitalization, and renewal movements of all kinds.

7. Comedian George Carlin was even less kind: "We have lost our souls, but are trying to save our bodies."

8. Traditional cosmetic surgery is not always sufficient to achieve the perfect body, for there is a nagging problem that has typically been associated with such procedures—changes in one part of the body often leave the rest of it in even greater need of improvement. (This is a common problem among people who buy furniture: The new piece makes the rest of the house look shabby.) The medicalized solution is "body sculpturing," whereby perfection is achieved by altering the entire body in proportion to the most important changes sought.

9. The pursuit of health by convicts seems to have its own problems, however. On March 23, 1994, Ohio Congresswoman Deborah Pryce brought a bill before the House Rules Committee banning weight training in federal prisons on the grounds that convicts were using their time in prison to bulk up so they would be in better shape to return to the criminal wars when they got out. For a discussion of this issue, see Todd, 1994.

10. It is useful to note, as does David Shaw, that the anti-smoking movement has also occasioned a considerable rewriting of history: "When the United States Postal Service issued a twenty-nine-cent stamp in 1994 honoring Robert Johnson, the legendary Delta bluesman, they made sure they removed the cigarette from his lips—a cigarette that was his trademark and that was present in the photograph on which their engraving was based. . . . [T]his reminds me of the publishers of history books in Communist China, who used to remove cigarettes from photos of Mao Tse-tung. Why does it remind me of Adolf Hitler, a rabid anti-smoker before his time who ordered cigarette smoke removed from a photo of Joseph Stalin shaking hands with Joachim von Ribbentrop, the Nazi foreign minister?" (Shaw, 1996: 152).

11. Traditionally, self-help groups have confined their treatment protocols to the individual. In recent years, however, they have fanned out to incorporate a widening circle of others who are "affected" by the despicable habits of the miscreant.

12. "Data dredging" is a methodological technique made possible by the availability of the enormous excess of cheap computing power. It consists of bypassing the usual careful business of epidemiological research in terms of postulating a theory and then testing it with evidence. Instead, data dredgers run computer correlations between ever more exotic sets of variables relating to disease and lifestyle choices, and, upon finding a cell that contains numbers more than likely to have been made by chance, claim that a "statistically significant" relationship exists between behavior x and disease y.

13. However, it is perhaps less clear than many people believe. The author of an article in the *Washington Post Weekly* interviewed executives at Phillip Morris on the question of how they could work in such a business. What they found was

a culture very different from that of cynical businesspeople concentrating on corporate profits: "[I]t becomes clear that the two sides in the cigarette wars are not just battling over facts or profits. This is a clash of moral systems. Phillip Morris people believe that they are fighting for something more than just life spans or cardiopulmonary health—something as deeply American as you can get: freedom" (Frankel, 1997: 8).

14. Data on smoking are now so numerous that they have engendered the satirical suggestion that a new warning label might read: "Warning: Smoking has been determined to be the cause of 95 percent of all statistics."

15. Few restaurants would have the temerity to follow the lead of the famous Arthur Bryant's of Kansas City, a century-old barbecue joint that displays a sign reading "Smokers and Non-Smokers Welcome. Separate Seating Not Available."

16. Eve Browning Cole, who reported this incident, notes that such a request creates in most people the "What next?" reaction, as each new area of forbidden behavior and language is fenced off. "I'm sure some daring renegades will attend the conference wearing coats that have been dry-cleaned or with hair smelling faintly of lavender or strawberry. But I picture the bulk of the conference attendees in a great scentless procession, wearing cloth or plastic shoes ("No products of animal exploitation!"), taking notes only on recycled paper, lunching on tofu sandwiches because the assassination of soybeans has not yet become a political issue" (Cole, 1993: A-5).

17. A delightful account of our culture's ongoing fascination with the meaning of fat may be found in *Never Satisfied* by Hillel Schwartz (1986), who notes this change: "[F]at is now regarded as an indiscretion, and almost as a crime."

18. A fifteenth-century Florentine priest, Girolama Savonarola was the Carry Nation of his time, leading symbolic crusades against various pleasures that he held accountable for the moral decline of the nation. Many contemporary healthists—especially those who combine healthful living with religious ideologies—would feel immensely comfortable in his presence.

19. Not that any of this is new. Farb and Armelagos, in their book on the anthropology of eating, point out that "[m]ore words from the lexicon of eating than from any other human activity have been used to describe sexual relations and organs." Women are "dishes," "pieces of meat," "hot tomatoes," and "good enough to eat." A woman's breasts are "melons," and her virginity is a "cherry." A man's testicles are "nuts," his penis is a "banana," and his buttocks are "buns." In many languages, moreover, the words for "hungry" and "horny" are identical.

20. As this is being written, an impeachment proceeding is being filed against President Bill Clinton. Among the more prominent arguments being made in support of such an extreme measure is the idea that he must be removed from office "for the sake of the children."

21. A warning label sewn into a Batman™ cape solemnly intones "WARNING: CAPE DOES NOT ALLOW WEARER TO FLY."

22. In effect, what such a proposal tells children is "Mommy and Daddy are tattooing you so that if you are kidnapped or even killed, the police can identify your body"—a sobering thought for a small child.

23. Such a turn of events would, perhaps, be the ultimate triumph of those who meddle in the name of health and safety; for if fetuses are accorded human status,

as William Saletan has pointed out, the implications would be staggering. For example: "Four weeks after the Supreme Court reinstated a Missouri statute declaring that life begins at conception, Kansas City attorney Michael Box filed a federal lawsuit against Missouri's attorney general, governor, and five other state officials for jailing the fetus of a female prison inmate without due process. 'The state of Missouri says that fetuses are persons,' Box argued. 'You've got somebody in prison for the crime of another person. The 13th Amendment says you can't do that'" (Saletan, 1989: 18). Other lawyers have tried similar tactics, including the notion that if life begins at conception, then nine months should be added to the life of every citizen. If that were the case, the cost to society in additional Medicare and social security benefits alone would be massive, for the instant a citizen turns sixty-one years and three months old by present methods of counting, he or she would automatically be sixty-two and eligible for social security.

24. Davis's work represents a watershed in our understanding of how religious and social ideologies come to be used as levers to meddle into the lives of everyone else. Dividing sexual ideologies into three camps—Jehovanists (the Judeo-Christian tradition), Naturalists (the tradition derived from scientific, literary, and intellectual views of sex), and Gnostics (the tradition that traces its lineage to de Sade)—these differing views constitute the battleground over which America's sexual conflicts are fought. The Jehovanists believe that sex is a powerful force that has to be kept in check lest it overwhelm us and destroy society. The Naturalists spend their time insisting that sex is "no big deal." And the Gnostics feel that the dirtiness of sex is what makes it interesting and are always looking to the Jahovanists for rules they can violate and sacred categories they can defile. Each group represents its own brand of meddling in the name of sex, and each uses children and God arguments as either points or counterpoints to its own ideological preferences.

25. This statement must come as an enormous surprise to psychologists and psychiatrists who for some time have insisted that sexual orientation is not exactly a "preference."

26. For a classic discussion of shame as a conceptual enabler, see Helen Merrell Lynd's *On Shame and the Search for Identity* (1965). It is Lynd's contention that although contemporary society is focused on guilt, shame rituals continue to be far more significant, especially in a culture where identity is ever more problematic. In short, those who don't know who they are meddle into the lives of others in an effort to engage some kind of communal meaning in a world increasingly bereft of connection.

5

Types of Meddlers

[D]o not meddle in the affairs of wizards for they are subtle and quick to anger.
—J.R.R. Tolkien

Wizards may be able to avoid meddlers, but most of the rest of us cannot.[1] A lexicon of meddlers, like that of sports, shows two broad categories: amateurs and professionals. Amateur meddlers meddle for a variety of personal, social, and even idiosyncratic reasons, but professionals are distinguished by the fact that they do it primarily for the money. Although amateur meddlers are more common, they are also, for the most part, less powerful in shaping the lives of the people with whom they meddle. They are generally more of an annoyance than a threat. Amateur meddlers tend to be those in the community who single themselves out as the watchdogs over other people's behavior. In previous eras they would have been called bluenoses, prudes, busybodies, or candlesnuffers. H. L. Mencken earned an international reputation denouncing them. Perhaps because their own lives are so boring and uneventful, they live vicariously by meddling into the lives of their neighbors, primarily through talk (Brissett and Snow, 1993). Gossip is the primary vehicle of this kind of meddling—a safe way to feed on activities that, for reasons of safety and security, we do not normally engage in ourselves (Spacks, 1985). Meddlers of all types seem to enjoy the power that meddling gives them. They are sufficiently self-centered that the "good" they seek to impose on others seems far more important than any good they may have determined for themselves. This chapter develops and examines a typology of modern meddlers. But we must confess that its major divisions, the line that separates amateur meddlers from professional ones, is slim indeed. Food and nutrition meddlers, for example, encompass both categories. But because of the increasing presence of professional meddlers and their potential for doing harm, much of our discussion is devoted to a consideration of governmental meddling and the "service" efforts of lawyers, psychiatrists, social workers, psychologists, and the medical and divorce industries, all examples of professional meddlers—those who, by definition, meddle without heart.[2]

A Caveat

A typology of meddlers must proceed cautiously, for meddling needs to be differentiated from such necessary concepts as social control, benevolent altruism, and valuable activism. When we talk about meddlers we are not talking about those things. The difference lies in the character of the person or persons engaged in the activity in question, the consequences to which it leads, and the rationale that supports the activity. These factors are also interrelated. Even if one is armed with impeccable rationales and sterling characters, the consequences of the activity may not work out. And even if they do, the motives of the individual may be suspect and therefore cast doubt on the presumed good results. Thus, as Plato argued in *The Republic*, although justice requires social control and all forms of social control constitute a type of meddling, justice may still be defined in terms of performing one's own task and "not meddling with that of others." Plato also explained that one part of the soul and one part of the polis has the task of meddling with others in the sense of controlling their activities, so some meddling on the part of both the individual and the state is justified. This is not to say, however, that Plato didn't mean it when he defined justice in terms of, among other things, an absence of meddling.[3] Plato presumed what modern Americans seem to have lost: a sense of perspective and balance about when to meddle and when to leave well enough alone. Figuring out ways of getting that sense of perspective back is one of the most formidable tasks of our time. Some suggestions for doing so are to be found in the concluding chapter, where we attempt to tie the interpersonal and the social back together in a postmodern world that has rent them asunder.

Motives for Meddling

Meddlers of all stripes typically engage their craft without recognizing themselves as meddling at all. Few meddlers are likely to discern themselves in the lexicon we are constructing, though most anyone will recognize others whom they know. Meddling, after all, is almost universally regarded as a bad thing, and few people see themselves in such a light. Instead, they see the typical justifications for meddling as a license to transform what would be meddling into something else. Sometimes they are right; the nub of meddling hangs on the consequences to which it leads and, to a lesser extent, on the heart of the meddler. It is all a matter of interpretation. Borrowing heavily from a framework first offered by literary critic Kenneth Burke, C. Wright Mills (1940) described the terminologies through which the interpretation of conduct proceeds as "vocabularies of motive." Believing that the fundamental human situation is talk, and departing from the Freudian convention of seeing motives as lying "deeper," Mills identified motives as "unquestioned answers to questions concerning social and lingual conduct." They typically arise in the context of a challenge, he said, since "men live in immediate acts of experience and their attentions are directed outside themselves until acts are in some way frustrated. It is then that awareness of self and of motive occur" (Mills, 1940: 208). Motives take two primary forms: *excuses*, which involve acceptance of the charge that what one did was wrong but denial of full responsibility for having done it, and *justifications*, which involve acceptance of responsibility for having done the act in question but denial that it was wrong (Scott and Lyman, 1968). Illness, accident, and bodily infirmities fall into the former category; and autonomy, denial of the victim, and the good of the commonweal, into the latter. When called on to account for their meddling, meddlers almost always choose to justify rather than excuse themselves. Indeed, they are likely to supply such justifications as these:

- "It affects me, too."
- "It's best for everyone involved."
- "It's for your own good."
- "He doesn't know better."
- "I'm your friend."
- "People have a right to know." (This is a common media response.)
- "You don't know what you're doing."
- "Because I love you."
- "I'm just trying to help."
- "I'm your _____ (mother, father, etc.)."
- "I care about you."
- "It's not good for you."

The utterance of such words is an attempt to overcome the problematic introduced by the very presumption of meddling in the first place. I am intervening in the life of another, asserts the meddler, but for sterling reasons and with sound motives, not simply to be troublesome, nosy, or the like.

Before we turn to the topic of the meddling professionals, it will be well to spend some time on the amateurs who are all around us and who have always made such a nuisance of themselves.

Amateur Meddlers

Gossips, Snoops, and the Specter of Big Brother

If you can't say anything good about someone, sit right here by me.

—Alice Roosevelt Longworth

Gossips, snoops and rumor-mongers are among the most ubiquitous of the amateur meddlers. They represent a common, everyday, taken-for-granted constituent of seemingly every community, and most everyone has joined their ranks at one time or another. Gossip is so common that Pascal's aphorism—"If all men knew what others say of them, there would not be four friends in the world"—certainly has the ring of truth. Much has been written about gossip and rumor[4] (Bergmann, 1993; Goodman and Ben-Ze'ev, 1994), and most of this literature echoes Sissela Bok's definition, which is now standard: "Gossip is informal personal communication about other people who are either absent or treated as absent" (Bok, 1983: 91). Gossip has also been described as "news in a red silk dress"[5] (Spacks, 1985) and as "conversational embroidery" (Thomas, 1994). Alternatively, Walter Winchell called it "the art of saying nothing in a way that leaves practically nothing unsaid." Gossips meddle primarily through talk ("pick-a-little, talk-a-little, pick-a-little, talk-a-little, cheep-cheep, cheep, pick-a-little, talk-a-lot," as the small-town characters in Meredith Wilson's *The Music Man* sing), but not all gossip is particularly meddlesome. Consider, for example, the constant chatter one hears about who is marrying whom, who might be moving to another town or taking a different job, or who was seen where or with whom. Most of this kind of talk is relatively innocent and gotten from clearly public sources that do not involve overt intrusions into a person's life. Such talk is also useful and even positive to the extent that it gives people the kind of information they need to avoid awkward situations. ("Don't mention her to him—it was a nasty divorce, you know.") This kind of gossip is meddlesome only to the degree that it represents a kind of informal rule-enforcement police, the very presence of which makes it certain that everyone knows they are being watched. On the other hand, there are forms of gossip that are clearly reprehensible because they meddle into persons' lives with at least the potential for dire consequences. These forms of gossip constitute a kind of nonviolent aggression that can and often does destroy lives, both reputationally and, on occasion, physically. Bok (1983) singles out three forms that are particularly despicable: gossip that breaches a confidence, gossip that the speaker knows to be false, and gossip that is "unduly invasive." In the first category is the gossip of doctors who speak about confidential matters involving their patients at cocktail parties; in the second is gossip implying that person x who was seen with person y might be having an affair, when the speaker knows that the meeting was innocent; and in the third is gossip that plants a rumor about a person's sex life that the speaker knows will have the effect of destroying that person's reputation. In some instances this latter form of pernicious gossip may destroy even a person's life, as when the FBI planted the rumor that actress Jean Seberg had had an affair with a member of the Black Panther Party and had born him a child—a rumor that subsequently led to her suicide, and that the FBI knew to be false.

It must also be noted that those who are gossiped about tend to gossip themselves (as a Spanish proverb puts it, "Whoever gossips to you will gossip of you"), so a kind of co-conspiracy exists between gossiper and gossipee. Intimates who gossip with one another share the sweet guilt of knowing that they are engaging in an activity from which they are not themselves immune. It is also the case that being talked about may not be altogether negative. In an age when informal information can be exceedingly useful to both sides, Oscar Wilde's assertion that "there is only one thing in the world worse than being talked about, and that is not being talked about" is more poignant than ever. Taken together, these observations indicate that gossip is for the most part benign and may well have gotten a worse press than it deserves. As Robert Goodman and Aaron Ben-Ze'ev suggest, the typical gossipmonger is "intelligent, with a good memory and an ability to discern connections between events. Gossips are quite realistic people; their extensive knowledge of embarrassing events prevents them from being naive. Gossips are often quite sensitive, curious, social-minded, and involved" (1994: 19). Put this person up against a nongossiper, and you may discover that the latter is self-absorbed, with no interest in other people—no interest in the intimate details of their personal lives nor in other matters as well. Which should we prefer? The answer to that question depends, of course, on the nature of the gossip as well as the motivation underlying it, on the person it reaches, and on the consequences it brings about. But faced with a choice between a world with no gossip and a world with too much, we would almost surely select the latter as the more interesting place in which to live.

Nevertheless, gossip *does* constitute meddling, and in this age of information, its potential for doing harm may well be escalating. There is little doubt that a press obsessed with celebrity gossip and the worldwide culture that feeds on it may have had some complicity in the recent death of Lady Diana, since a photograph of her commanded hundreds of thousands of dollars. Whatever else the paparazzi were doing (engaging in freedom of the press, just trying to make a living, and so on—the traditional media motives), or however much others may have played a role in the accident, the press was certainly meddling into her life at the moment of her calamitous death. And it is to that mournful consequence that people directed their wrath at a meddling world that adjudged her fame and fortune to be sufficient justification for allowing her little if any personal freedom.[6]

As surveys regularly report, privacy issues are a major concern of the contemporary American, and they are directly related to the technology of snooping. A century ago, in an age of low technology, the inclination of snoops to spy on the private lives of others was severely limited by their relative inability to do so. Things have changed considerably. Audio tape recorders, video camcorders, and various kinds of telescopic devices have not only increased our ability to look into the lives of those we wish to know about but have also inured us to many of these intrusions. Laws that used to prevent phone conversations from being tape-recorded at all have been altered to allow taping as long as one party knows that he or she is being taped. This change has effectively rendered the surreptitious taping of phone conversations entirely legal. Big Brotherism abounds in the nation of meddlers, and the computer has become a prime source of concern and attention. The largest commercial data base company in the country, Lexis-Nexis, recently received near-universal denunciation when the media revealed that a new product, P-track—a Lexis-Nexis master file that the company sells to anyone who wants it—has personal information on some 250 million Americans. The computer revolution, the source of so much concern about invasions of privacy, could, ironically, also be the source of a backlash against meddling. That is because the information "snooperhighway," as it is now being called, is so rampant with stories of anonymous and malevolent busybodies monitoring every click of the mouse that something like a consumer boycott could frustrate the interactive marketing pretensions of companies that have embraced the Internet as the new frontier of product merchandising. A recent Harris poll found that 84 percent of all consumers worry about threats to their personal privacy, compared to only 54 percent in 1970 (Cyr, 1995: 2). Other surveys are even more ominous for on-line marketers, indicating that as many as 80 percent of consumers wouldn't shop on-line due to security worries. The consumer fear that credit-card numbers trustingly given through a keyboard will wind up in the hands of cyberthieves capable of engaging in large-scale theft without ever leaving their homes is giving many potential consumers second thoughts about using this information technology. Since consumers who are afraid to buy often won't, and since fears of new technologies are more powerful than the familiar risks one takes daily in making credit-card purchases, venders are in the position of having to cool out the public by showing that they are capable of protecting them from bandits on the information superhighway. But whatever transaction security is offered by marketers on the Internet, it settles only part of the privacy dilemma. "Think of it this way," says Diane Cyr, writing in *Catalog Age:*

> Years back, in the sunny burg of Mayberry, "online" transactions, so to speak, were always routed through Sara, the town phone operator and busybody. So, if Andy Taylor picked up the phone to call Floyd the Barber, Sara at the switchboard might first remark that, yes, Andy's hair is getting a little long, and by the way, Floyd's using this new shave lotion Andy will just love, especially since he's taking Ellie to the dance Saturday night.

Now, 30 years later and cybermiles away . . . the Internet threatens to turn the marketing universe into the world's biggest and nosiest switchboard. Potentially, anybody can be monitored by some ill-meaning Sara bent on snooping into everybody's business. (Cyr, 1995: 3)

Another privacy concern stems from a source that is less technological and has more to do with the culture of our interaction rituals. Americans are less likely to exercise the kind of civil inattention that Asian countries are noted for. They refrain from invading the lives of others even when the situation renders it possible to do so. For example, living in a ground-floor apartment in Manhattan is tantamount to offering others visual entrée to one's life. An article in the *New York Times* reported on the dilemma as follows:

"Your private life is very public," says Mary Fitzgerald, a writer and film producer who shares a 600 square foot ground-floor duplex in Greenwich Village with Nick Smith, a film director. Simultaneously blessed and cursed with huge front windows that sometimes double as front doors, the two explain how they sometimes hide in the kitchen or skulk behind the couch to avoid passers-by who try to spy on them through the glass. (*New York Times*, November 9, 1997)

This account suggests that gazes themselves can be meddlesome—and, indeed, the lengths to which the people in the above example were forced to go in an attempt to shield themselves from the prying eyes of others offer us insight into the problem. As a result of these changes, privacy issues now constitute one of the most important topics of conversation in American life.[7] The explosion in information technologies promises only to make the problem worse.

Because ideological snooping into the private affairs of people tends to follow technological advances in our ability to do so, concerns over a Big Brother government have become more pronounced. Writer Greg Bear envisions in his science-fiction novel *Slant* a fanciful future in which every home is monitored via the bathroom. In this scene, for instance, a guest enters a man's home and asks where the washroom is:

"The bathroom is over there," the man says. Alice follows his finger toward a door barely visible against the velvety grayness of a far wall. The door opens as she approaches and a light shines brightly within, white marble and cold fixtures. . . .

The toilet is simple and elegant, gracefully curved like an upside-down seashell, the seat low-slung, incorporating a bidet. It is a diagnostic toilet, common in many homes these days—and ubiquitous in public lavatories,

where your deposits—though guaranteed anonymous—are quickly analyzed and become part of public health records. (Bear, 1997: 81)

Should such a device be introduced (perhaps not such a fanciful notion
given our previous discussion of the triumph of the health police), the rationale offered by whatever government agency/private business part-
nership was promoting it would be predictably appealing. Early detec-
tion of diseases, better control of epidemics, the welfare of our
children—these arguments would all be broached and would be compelling to many people. The argument that the resulting data could be
forwarded to one's physician for routine lab work to catch developing
diseases in their earliest stages would also be difficult to counter. Those
who argued against it on the grounds of invasion of privacy and the potential for abuse would be dismissed as paranoid. Once established as
precedent, court cases would be filed by insurance companies to get the
results from individual clients and/or applicants to see if they had conditions that would prevent them from qualifying for insurance. Government agencies would find the information simply too good a source for
apprehending miscreants not to press for its revelation—to "appropriate
law enforcement agencies," of course. Bear's novel, in fact, ends with a
revolt against such totalitarian scenarios.

If the specter of "Big Brother" were not enough, there is also what
William Staples calls the procession of "Tiny Brothers," which are increasingly present in our daily lives and whose technological ability to snoop
is expanding. Unlike large institutional challenges to privacy, which are
ushered in with dramatic displays of state power, Tiny Brothers are the
more subtle tactics used by both governmental and private organizations
to monitor our performance, gather evidence, and exact penalties when
we get out of line (Staples, 1997). They involve such techniques as video
cameras on school buses, pagers and other monitoring devices, computers that count the number of key strokes per minute, random drug testing, and the creation of genetic data banks. Staples contends that we are
moving rapidly toward a "disciplinary" society—one that is increasingly
lacking in personal privacy, individual trust, and a viable public life that
supports and maintains democratic values and practices.

"Friends" and Neighbors

It is somewhat ironic that as Americans have become more geographically intimate because of advances in transportation and communication,
they have simultaneously become more isolated from the very people
around whom they live. Like other circumstances in which isolation
breeds a certain anxious resentment and hostility, living close to someone

seems now to be less an exercise in the sort of neighborliness characteristic of other times than one characterized by isolation and the contempt for others that it breeds. The transformation of friendship into "friendly relationships" has made it all the more difficult to simply be friends.

Bereft of a firm sense of identity, postmodern Americans are more likely than ever to engage in what Rob Shields calls "lifestyle shopping"—the relentless search for a way to live. With so many alternatives available, the angst-ridden are prime targets of those who offer a behavioral road map (Shields, 1992). Part of this process seems to involve a thorough trashing of our neighbors' choices. Friends and neighbors simply do not know how to live. Confronted with a vast shopping mall of choices, we conflict with our neighbors over fundamental moral questions of how to deal with the vicissitudes of life. Problems in our neighbors' lives get our immediate attention, usually in a way that differentiates how they are living from what we are doing. We sometimes even revel in their problems since the moral dialectic increasingly defines us in terms of what we don't do and what we are against. The Germans actually have a word for this phenomenon: *schadenfreude,* which means "pleasure in the unhappiness of others."[8] Absent a distinct label, critical Americans simply trash their neighbors' lifestyle. Such suspicion of our neighbors also denies the fundamental fact that all people's lives are a yet-to-be completed process, a point made nicely by a character in Anita Brookner's *Hotel du Lac:* "'Harold,' said Edith, 'I simply do not know anyone who has a lifestyle. What does it mean? It implies that everything you own was bought at exactly the same time, about five years ago, at the most'" (Brookner, 1995). Professional meddlers, as we shall see, thrive on such uncertainty, for if a person is looking for a "lifestyle" and someone claims to have one, it can be packaged, advertised, marketed, and sold—often at high prices.

Friends also represent an ambiguous category of meddling. They are entitled to meddle by virtue of their close personal relationship with the meddlee, yet good friendship is defined in terms of knowing when to meddle and when to refrain. Friends have a license to meddle but often don't exercise it (Brissett and Oldenburg, 1982).

Parents and Relatives

Ironically, the very people who have the most clear-cut license to meddle are often the ones least likely to use it. Parents and close relatives, those who are charged with the responsibility of caring for young people and seeing to it that they are raised correctly, seem increasingly reluctant to exercise their traditional prerogative to meddle. Owing perhaps to the welter of conflicting possibilities, the absence of commonly agreed upon standards, the lack of time, or, more likely, the confusions created by professional meddlers who compete for the same territory, parents often find themselves in situations with their children where they do not exercise their right to meddle. Hence we discover situations in which parents discover to their horror that their children have been using drugs, often for long periods of time, and they didn't even suspect it. Couple this with the fact that parental meddling is a touchy issue even under optimal circumstances because much of it is ineffective or even promotes the very problems it seeks to alleviate, and we begin to understand why parents might adopt the reluctant stances that they do.

As families are increasingly seen as the foundation of pathology and parents are blamed for more and more of the most vexing problems in living, it is little wonder that they are confused about how to proceed. To see why parents might take a more hands-off approach to child rearing, we need only look at the number of pathologies and personal problems that now have labels pointing to the family as their root cause: "toxic families," "dysfunctional families," "co-dependency," "sick relationships"—all of these terms aimed at the people who gave us life.

Moreover, there have been those highly publicized cases where meddling into the lives of your children may get you killed, as it did the wealthy parents of Lyle and Erik Menendez, who shot-gunned their parents to death in their Southern California home in order to get their money. But when caught and tried, they claimed they were victims of sexual abuse at the hands of their father. Therapists and legal representatives of the therapeutic state lined up to defend them, the focus having been successfully shifted from the question of what they did to why they did it (a ground on which both therapists and lawyers are quite comfortable). "What they did is not the issue," said their attorney Leslie Abramson "It's why they did it. These boys were not responsible for who they turned out to be. They were just little children being molded" (quoted in Hughes, 1993: 13). The use of the "abuse excuse" (Dershowitz, 1995) is not only growing in popularity but also seems inevitable given the assumptions of the therapeutic mentality. There are no actions, only happenings. And there is no sin, unless it is the sin of parents who abuse their children. If we think we remember something, then it happened— or so say the repressed-memory therapists who can also be brought in for a fee to testify at trial. As Robert Hughes has observed, "Under the sign of vulgar therapeutics, the moral buck is endlessly passed back to people who, being dead or absent, can't reply" (1993: 98).

Because meddling into family life is so common these days, it is difficult for us to believe that this form of meddling was almost unheard of in earlier times. Historically, notwithstanding the meddling "villages" in which "my child was your child," people have been very reluctant to meddle into the affairs of families. Feminists have made much of this issue in the current controversy over spousal abuse, yet it is difficult to see how things have been improved through the constant surveillance of family life and the increasing mistrust that family life inspires. Teachers who are compelled by the state to report any suspicious marks on children have surely contributed to this breakdown of trust, which, in many families, has had consequences at least as devastating as the cases of abuse that it occasionally uncovers. Innocent parents who are apprehended by authorities after being turned in by teachers are unlikely ever to view school officials, or their community, in the same way again.

Work Associates

As work has become home life, and home life increasingly work, colleagues on the job have come to believe they know more and more about us—as well they may—and boldly act on this presumption by meddling into the lives of their fellow workers. Sometimes their interventions are expected or even welcome, as common problems are discussed; but here again we observe a circumstance whereby people are likely to meddle with little precise understanding of either motive or outcome. David Riesman's comment that, in the postindustrial consumer society, the office has become a ranch house seems to fit many of the circumstances we see around us. Now that best friends and even spouses belong to the same work setting, companies tout themselves as "families," and it is almost impossible to keep one's problems from one's nosy work associates, meddling has become the response that expresses "concern" regardless of how badly motivated or misguided it might be. In the category of "badly motivated," we might note that because co-workers are often involved in competition with one another for the spoils of economic warfare, knowledge of a colleague's problems and "helpful" attempts to direct him or her to therapy might as easily be seen as neutralizing the competition. In this easy climate of victim hustling, disease-mongering, quick fixes, and pharmaceutical miracles, meddling—even when it is well motivated, often puts people in a position of knowing things about their fellow workers that inevitably, if not unwittingly, place them in a conflicted position. If they use the information to help, their colleagues are in their debt. If they use it to destroy them, they are obviously guilty of reprehensible ethics. When workers meddle, they run the risk of all of these negative things. If they don't, they are accused of "not caring."

Social Action and Advocacy Groups

As the postmodern culture has become ever more Balkanized into a babble of competing interests, social action and advocacy groups have likewise enjoyed a favorable climate for the production of their wares. Led by people who claim to be the victims of other people's bad habits, health and safety crusades have set the standard; but other meddling movements from child welfare advocates to animal rights movements have also enjoyed a renaissance. The social action/advocacy format has become a socially sanctioned way of demonstrating one's "concern" for others while at the same time allowing one to appropriate a license to meddle into the affairs of anyone who disagrees. David Shaw envisions a fanciful but instructive future: Determined to protect Americans from the dangers of cigarette smoking, he says, an umbrella organization called "Americans Stop Smoking Happily or Lose Everything Suddenly (ASSHOLES)" is eventually formed. Its members persuade the government to pass laws that prohibit growing tobacco or making, selling, or advertising cigarettes. As a result:

> Supplies plummet. Demand soars. A black market quickly develops to fill the void. Prices skyrocket. As with Prohibition, people start making their own illicit cigarettes, growing small tobacco plants in the backyard or on isolated plots of vacant land not likely to be discovered by authorities. Some of the tobacco is grown—and some of the cigarettes made—under unsanitary conditions. People get sick and die from the toxic, bootleg product. Meanwhile, gangs fight for control of the small patches of suddenly converted tobacco-growing land and for the increasingly valuable crops they produce. Kids—and adults—start stealing cigarettes and hijacking shipments of cigarettes. Latter-day Al Capones use modern terrorist tactics in a battle to control the illicit tobacco trade. Suddenly, Joe Camel looks pretty benign by comparison. (Shaw, 1996: 176)

Social-action meddlers also juggle and combine various ideologies in order to effect the optimum public response to their issues. Clever with words, they symbolically reconstruct a reality conducive to their interests. In the abortion debate, for example, a handbook for members of the radical Operation Rescue—a group that received worldwide attention when one of its members murdered an abortion doctor in Wichita, Kansas—urges members to use language strategically. One never talks about *abortion;* the preferred term is *murder.* The word *fetus* is not to be used; one should always say babies. Doctors are *murderers, assassins,* and *merchants of death.* There is to be no talk about a joint decision between a woman and her doctor; rather, the phrase to use is *conspiracy to commit murder.* Pro-choice advocates, of course, do the same thing. They avoid the word *abortion.* They talk about a medical *procedure,* a D-and-C. They discuss not *babies* but *fetuses,* and *abortion* is not abortion, killing, or ending a life but a *woman's right to choose.*

Even more interesting, perhaps, is the fact that opponents of the National Rifle Association (NRA) have recently recast their opposition to guns by switching from the traditional rubric of "gun control," which sounds fascist, to "gun safety," which presumably no sane person can be against. They have discovered that this language ties in with the ideology of safety and gets them more support. The NRA will presumably follow suit by claiming that the opposition is in favor of "gun confiscation" and attempt to reclaim the territory of "gun safety" by arguing that this is what they have always stood for. Once again we see that health and safety have emerged as the unchallengeable ideologies in the nation of meddlers.

Safety- and health-mongering, like other moral and religious crusades, also run the risk of generating a backlash to the very righteousness they seek to enforce. A campus newspaper columnist, observing the wave of fascist actions taken in the name of health, suggests the following counterstrategy:

> This passive thing has to stop. It's time for you to bum-rush all those health freaks with their low-fat yogurt and their homogenized minds and stub your cigarette out in their caffeine-free Diet Coke. This nation is brain-washing the masses into a bunch of tofu-sprouting sissies. Before long, it's going to be impossible to smoke anywhere except prison, and we all know what will happen then. (Kurtz, 1997: 4)

Whether social action and advocacy groups are amateur or professional forms of meddling is an open question. In recent years, groups such as those organized against smoking take on quasi-professional status. Moreover, many social-action groups have paid lobbyists in Washington to advance their causes. Indeed, in an age when organized meddling without money is as inconceivable as it would be ineffective, we have seen these groups grow more powerful each year.

Feminists

No book on meddling would be complete without noting the meddling excesses of the women's movement. The modest demands by women for equal treatment under the law, which arose in the mid-1800s,[9] has now developed into a full-scale social movement that asserts a license to meddle into just about everything in the name of gender equality. This movement and its leaders, which Rene Denfeld (1995) has labeled the "New Victorians" because of their stridently Puritan view of women,[10] has joined with the postmodern tendency to treat every problem in a person's life as a public issue requiring a policy statement and an advocacy group. No longer are the demands modest or solely confined to legal questions of equal treatment. Indeed, under the banner of women's rights, some contemporary feminists[11] have made the following claims:

- Heterosexuality is the institutionalization of an inherently violent and invasive act and is the root of all female oppression. One must abolish intercourse if one is to defeat oppression (Rich, 1980).
- All sexual intercourse is rape. "Physically, the woman in intercourse is a space inhabited, a literal territory occupied literally: occupied even if there has been no resistance, no force; even if the occupied person said, yes please, yes hurry, yes more" (Dworkin, 1987: 181).
- "Forced" heterosexuality and cosmetic surgery are part of a conspiracy—a "reign of sexist terror comparable in magnitude, intensity, and intent to the persecution, torture, and annihilation of women as witches from the 14th to the 17th centuries in Europe" (Caputi and Russell, 1990: 35).
- Only lesbians can be true feminists because they are the only women not dependent on men. Heterosexual feminists are thus "crippled feminists." A 1991 issue of the San Francisco *NOW Times* suggests that "[e]mbracing lesbianism, or lesbian-feminist theory, is pivotal to the feminist movement, which works to change society through the elimination of gender-defined roles. . . . [H]eterosexism and male supremacy reinforce one another in maintaining our oppression. Both must be eliminated for any women to be free."
- Musicologist Susan McClary claims that Beethoven's Ninth Symphony is actually a celebration of rape: "The point of recapitulation in the first movement of the Ninth is one of the most horrifying moments in music, as the carefully prepared cadence is frustrated, damming up energy which finally explodes in the throttling, murderous rage of a rapist incapable of attaining release" (McClary, 1987).
- Women are being secretly controlled by a backlash against feminist gains (Faludi, 1991) and by their own internalization of the "beauty myth" (Wolf, 1992).

Such fatuous nonsense fuels the meddling impulse by arming the meddler with ideological ammunition and phony data under the imprimatur of scholarship. Reinforced by such notions, feminists' sense of "empowerment" has resulted in wholesale meddling into everything from university curricula to court cases when their sisters are charged with felonies. In the latter category, for example, feminists nationwide, orchestrated by the National Organization of Women, rallied around the trial of Lorena Bobbitt, the Virginia woman who responded to the troubles of her turbulent marriage by severing her husband's penis while he slept and later throwing it into the street from the window of a moving car. To "Bobbitt" a man thus became part of the angry language of feminism. The facts of the case were irrelevant; the response broke down along gender lines, with hordes of women who knew nothing about the details of the incident shouting their way into the Manassas County Court House to champion the cause of their latest feminist hero. Blurring the line between tragedy and entertainment, venders hawked T-shirts with a picture of a bloody knife and the slogan: "Manassas County—A Cut Above the Rest."

Obviously not all feminists agree with such ideas and tactics or endorse their enforcement. Nevertheless, the collective weight of such a movement, unable to maintain boundaries separating the extremes of its left and right wings, has provided the license to meddle into most everything in the name of gender equality. In their enthusiasm for attacking patriarchy on every front, feminists have targeted men as the antagonists, and women not interested in joining this anti-phallic campaign have routinely been dismissed as traitors who are sleeping with the enemy. Not surprisingly, fewer and fewer women of the current generation are willing to identify themselves as feminists. The unkind perceptions of feminists that have emerged among younger women include that of Esther Pettibone, a twenty-five-year old welder from the state of Washington interviewed by Rene Denfeld:

> Male bashing. Like I said, hairy armpits, no makeup, no lingerie—almost asexual, if that's the right word. Not sexual beings, because that would be "objectification." Wearing dumpy clothes, because if you were to wear a miniskirt or a skimpy top, you would be "objectifying" yourself. . . . [J]ust being really defensive toward men and maybe even going so far as not to have relations with men, sexual, romantic relationships. On the extreme end, feminists are lesbians. (Denfeld, 1995: 56)

Some contemporary feminists, far from being sympathetic to the lives of women, meddle into them regularly and with an alarming sense of certainty for their own ideological purposes. Like other meddlers with whom they share a common bond, they know, or allege to know, what is wrong with the lives of women. They have located the enemy and it is men. And bent on eradicating the evils of a male-dominated world, they have instituted

> a new set of confining rules for women, many of which smell suspiciously like the same repressive sexual mores that our mothers fought to escape. We are told that sex with men is dangerous and morally wrong, resulting not only in our own oppression and shame but the oppression of all women. We are told that lesbian relationships are the only form of acceptable sexuality,

and while this might seem radical and liberating, it is, in fact, based on the same Victoriansque belief that male sexuality defiles the purity of unsullied womanhood. We are told that regardless of our orientation, the acceptance of sexuality we learned from the sexual revolution was a huge mistake and that the woman who pursues sexual freedom cannot consider herself a feminist. (Denfeld, 1995: 57)

Yet in the midst of all these warnings and cautions, advice-givings and intrusions, feminists have offered surprisingly little wise council on how to conduct male/female relationships. Few of their treatises propose anything other than handbooks on damage control for those women foolish enough to love men. They have politicized the bedroom to the point where fewer relationships are likely to work, carrying, as they do, the burden of centuries of male oppression to bed with them each night. Indeed, says Denfeld, "with the exception of a few fringe works written primarily by lesbians (such as Susie Bright) and reprints of *Our Bodies, Our Selves*, there hasn't been a celebratory book on female sexuality written by a feminist since the mid-seventies" (1995: 94).

Moreover, the Puritan and Victorian sources of the contemporary women's movement can be seen in the many ways that feminists have chosen to advise women on how to deal with a world they allege is organized against them. The message is that they are fragile creatures in constant need of protection, and its underlying theme is not new:

Earlier in this century, many households still had smelling salts on hand in the event that "delicate" women reacted to displays of male vulgarity by fainting. Today, women of delicacy have a new way to demonstrate their exquisitely fragile sensibilities: by explaining to anyone who will listen how they have been blighted and violated by some male's offensive coarseness. If nothing of a telling nature has recently happened to us, we can tell about how we felt on hearing what happened to others. We faint, "discursively" and publicly, at our humiliations at the hands of men. (Sommers, 1994: 29)

As a result of this new/old delicacy, feminists have taken on the role of what Christina Hoff Sommers, in one of the most thoughtful and devastating critiques of the excesses of contemporary feminism yet written, calls "gender wardens." These vociferous meddlers find offense in any statements or activities that do not hold to the party line of patriarchal victimage, a position that puts them at odds not only with other women but, often, with reason itself. The gender wardens of the feminist movement have a difficult time, however, coming to grips with the fact that many women, both within and outside of the academy, have found such propagandistic nonsense too much to bear—"[w]omen as diverse as

Camille Paglia, Betty Friedan, Katie Roiphe, Midge Decter, Mary Lefko-witz, Cathy Young, Erica Jong . . . , and Wendy Kaminer, women who are not fazed by being denounced as traitors and backlashers" (Sommers, 1994: 274–275). Just as Dr. Martin Luther King, who led the movement to secure civil rights for blacks in the 1960s, must be differentiated from contemporary race meddlers such as the Reverend Al Sharpton who seek personal gain and celebrity status through the tactic of racial division, so must feminism be split into classical and contemporary forms. In its classical incarnation, feminism concerned itself with central questions of gender equality in the eyes of the law and, in doing so, created a revolution that has made it possible for women to achieve their individual destinies on a par with men. Fairness and the refusal to accept discrimination were the hallmarks of classical feminism. "We very much need that concern and energy," says Sommers, "but we decidedly do not need their militant gynocentrism and misandrism. It's too bad that in the case of the gender feminists we can't have the concern without the rest of the baggage" (1994: 275).

Cassandras

Meddling Cassandras, named after the daughter of Priam in Greek mythology who was always going around prophesying some disaster or another, seem universal. But whatever their historical status—they seem to have always been around in some capacity or another—their potential for making such colossal nuisances of themselves is enhanced by the burgeoning technologies of alarm-sounding. The media love them, so much so that there is hardly a television station left that does not have the obligatory "Health Check" segment that communicates to a rapt audience the latest news on health and illness. But since no one knows for sure what health even is, stories of palpable dangers are far more interesting than the dull language of ordinary health, and they certainly lure larger ratings (see Figure 5.1). It is virtually impossible to watch television or read a magazine or newspaper without being warned by these meddling Cassandras about the disease of the day, the health danger of the week, or the threat to humankind posed by this practice or that substance. "The march of stories is remarkably rapid and fickle. Today's hazard tends to obliterate yesterday's," says Marcia Angell (1996: 154). As we watch these shows and note the public's attraction to them, we almost have to conclude that we enjoy scaring ourselves to death about issues of health and safety. Indeed, the contemporary fascination with "frightening" news suggests that we watch these shows for the same reason that people read Stephen King novels: We enjoy being horrified. But unlike fiction, such shows allow us to quote knowledgeable sources in our con-

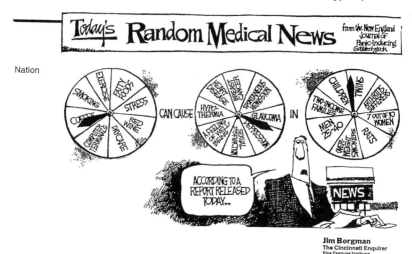

FIGURE 5.1   Health Check
Reprinted with permission from King Features Syndicate.

versations the next day with our friends and co-workers and to spread
the news of imminent doom. In this game of "sound the alarm" the latest
fear is always the one with the most currency:

> The fear that asbestos insulation causes lung cancer yields to the fear that
> exposure to lead causes mental retardation, which in turn gives way to con-
> cern that electro-magnetic fields from household appliances and power lines
> generate leukemia and brain cancer. It is, after all, difficult to worry about
> everything at once. . . . And so on: Alar on apples, radon in their basement,
> alcohol, estrogen, cigarette smoke, and hot dogs—all said to cause cancer.
> (Angell, 1996: 155)

Moreover, some groups are even more vulnerable than others. If you are
pregnant, the list of cautions will be endless. If you have children, a dedicated *60 Minutes/Dateline* segment will soon be devoted to the latest caution about them. It is a wonder anyone ever survived childhood. Our
personal favorites are the television weather Cassandras who warn us in
ever more strident terms about storms. Although knowledge of what the
weather is going to be the next day is a useful service (for which we pay
billions of dollars in taxes to the National Weather Service), what local
television weather stations do with this information—in their pursuit of
their roles as pseudo-family members—borders on the ludicrous. We are
told gravely that there is a "Winter Weather Alert" (it is going to get cold)
and that we should stay tuned for advice in the event that it is upgraded
to a "Winter Weather Emergency." We are given point-by-point instruc-

tions about what to do if we have to go outside: "Get out your winter coat, wear heavy clothing, put on extra layers, bundle up, bring in your household pets, cover your head," and so on. Before the era of television weather, presumably, people, not realizing these dangers, wandered naked into the streets and froze to death in snowbanks.

Henry Fairlie (1989) places the responsibility for this preoccupation with risk aversion on the members of a new privileged class who work, not in the manufacturing industries, but in the burgeoning service sector—including, not insignificantly, government and corporate bureaucracies, which create nothing except rules and meddling perspectives on everyone else's business. Since these groups have an interest in expanding their own domain of influence, they have encouraged the growth of government regulatory agencies that likewise shuffle paper and meddle into the lives of everyone else. Certainly this, too, is the stuff of which a meddling society is made, for much meddling these days occurs in the name of rules and regulations, health and safety; and whereas one would not want to argue that rules are unnecessary in a society, it does not take long to see that they can become ends in themselves for the ever-expanding group of people who meddle as a way of making a living.[12] No longer a nation stressing personal responsibility and trust, we resort to monitoring and accountability as ways of securing conformity.

Food and Nutrition Meddlers

It has recently been discovered that, after thousands of years of occupying this planet, human beings do not know how to eat—at least according to the food and nutrition meddler, for whom the American diet is a license to coerce those whose diet is unsatisfactory relative to their true and righteous standards. Those who meddle in the name of food and nutrition are a subspecies of those who meddle in the name of health. Many of their tactics are the same, but the main strategy of food and nutrition meddlers is to take the most basic element of life and turn it into a call for yet another revitalization movement. In this case, the movement is the latest incarnation of a very old theme: "Food kills." Their meddling may be mainstream, as is true of those who peddle the standard line of the governmental food and nutrition bureaucracies; or it may have a "natural health" counterculture flavor to it. Either way—and the two trends seem to be moving closer together—these meddlers are firm in their conviction that ignorant Americans are chewing themselves into an early grave and that this national tragedy can be averted if only people will listen to their caviling and follow instructions.

Nutrition meddlers are alarmed by the conventional American diet. Too high in fat and sugar, too low in complex carbohydrates, the diet of the average citizen in this country is to them a disaster that breeds not only obesity but also cancer and heart disease, in addition to sapping the energy and strength from a vital and healthy society. Adopting the line taken by the Natural Health Food Movement in both its historical and recent forms, officials in private as well as governmental nutrition agencies agree that the future has been seen and there is no fat in it. As Richard Klein observes:

> [L]et's be clear. In our culture, fat is poison. Whether it's the fat on your hips or the fat in your food, being fat or eating fat is seen as a ticket to disease and early death: heart attacks or cancer, diabetes or stroke, to name a few. Obesity itself is widely considered to be a disease, both physical and psychiatric. Doctors everywhere discriminate against the fat, blaming and shaming them, holding them morally responsible, because of their fat, for any signs of ill health. (Klein, 1996: 21)

The fat are obvious examples of people who are either nutritionally illiterate (at best) or nutritionally derelict (at worst). Fat as a substance is routinely labeled a killer. But there are other deadly substances as well. Refined flour and sugar have reemerged as major candidates for the title of Public Enemy #1. Writing in the late 1970s, J. I. Rodale would have made Sylvester Graham proud as he railed against the evils of sugar. Rodale saw juvenile delinquency, suicide, unhappy marriages, criminals, and even counterculture hippies as possible "sugar drunkards" whose plight is due to the intemperate consumption of sugar. His most notorious example? Adolph Hitler himself:

> Hitler was a typical example of sugar addiction relating to a tendency toward crime. Hitler was a "sugar drunkard," and a criminal. Was his love for sugar the most important factor that contributed to his being a shouting, trigger-brained, rabble-rousing maniac? Did it cause him to lose his sense of values? The evidence is there. There can be no doubt about it. Hitler must have suffered from low blood sugar due to an overconsumption of sugar. (Rodale, 1966: 142)

Furthermore, food meddlers see trouble everywhere. As Dennis Brissett and Lionel Lewis have shown in their study of the natural health food movement, the most insidious of all food eaten by Americans is ice cream. "In fact," they note, "the Good Humor Man would appear to be something of a wolf in sheep's clothing." For, according to one author they quote who sounds the alarm about this commonplace treat, the consequences of eating ice cream are grave indeed:

> [L]ike the melting glaciers of the past, which in releasing from their frigid storages the long-preserved tissues of animal life, surrendering them to ele-

mental dissolution and decay—so the ice cream melting in the body of the individual frees the carcasses of the ice cream and milk cells, to lay them open to the restless attack of swarming and festering bacteria—through the evidence of the ghostly carnival of putrefaction escapes the taste. (quoted in Brissett and Lewis, 1978: 65)

Armed with the latest science, certain that reality can be apprehended only through their advantaged eyes, and seemingly not the least bit concerned about dubious connections or unwarranted conclusions, food and nutrition meddlers reduce eating to chemistry, as shown in the following analysis of what ice cream may contain:

Piperonal is used in place of vanilla. This is a chemical used to treat lice. Diethyl glucol, a cheap chemical, is used as an emulsifier instead of eggs. Diethyl glucol is the same chemical used in anti-freeze and paint removers. Butyraidehyde is used in nut-flavored ice cream. It is one of the ingredients in rubber cement. Amylacetate is used for its banana flavor. It is also used as an oil paint solvent. Ethyl acetate is used to give ice cream a pineapple flavor. It is also used as a cleaner for leather and textiles and its vapors have been known to cause chronic lung, liver, and heart damage. Aldehyde c17 is used to flavor cherry ice cream. It is a flammable liquid which is used in aniline dyes, plastic and rubber. (Hanson and Roth, 1971: 8)

Bon appetite.

Americans, according to this dour view advanced by the food and nutrition meddler, are caught in a downward spiral of nutritional deficiencies and appalling ignorance. The problems of society are all somehow related to poor eating habits, which undermine people's health and destroy their well-being. We are fat, unhealthy, mentally sluggish, and morally bankrupt. Moreover, the pathological interactions caused by fertilizers, chemicals, preservatives, appearance enhancers, and artificial substances designed to improve the texture, smell, and taste of food products all combine to produce a diet that might as well be coming from the outlet of an industrial waste plant, for all its carcinogenic potential. The effluvia called the American diet are thus seen as the cause of numerous problems that heretofore had been understood as the result of other factors. Hence the nutrition meddler plays into an age-old theme: We are what we eat, and if we don't like what we are, we need only change our diet. As noted in Chapter 2, the roots of such ideas go back a long way; all we have to do is consult the work of the nineteenth-century social reformer John Harvey Kellogg to discover that his reborn dietary philosophy is predicated on the view that the kind of foods Americans eat are virtually poison. Meat was the critical item in Kellogg's time, and it still has a long list of detractors who trace the dyspepsia of the contemporary American to the consumption of too much red meat. As argued by Kellogg, the problem with meat is that it is so high in protein that it encourages the growth of putrefactive bacteria in the colon. As the microbes began to work on undigested flesh, the body, he asserted, is "flooded with the most horrible and loathsome poisons," and will surely suffer headaches, depression, skin problems, chronic fatigue, and damage to the liver, kidneys, and blood vessels as well as a host of other injuries. An "enormous mischief," as he put it. Given the view of contemporary food and nutrition meddlers, his conclusions sound as fresh now as they must have then: "[T]he marvel is not that human life is so short and so full of miseries, mental, moral and physical, but that civilized human beings are able to live at all" (Kellogg, 1919: 131).

Cashing in on contemporary Americans' obsession with personal appearance, one author suggests that those who may doubt his dreary forecasts need only play the "supermarket game":

> I enjoy playing a "supermarket game." While I am waiting in line to have my items checked out I usually inventory the contents of the shopping carts ahead of me. I try to discover if the contents of the carts match the physical appearance of the shoppers. For example, recently one cart contained a sack of bleached white flour, refined white sugar, spaghetti, cookies, cola drinks and a can of spaghetti sauce. Everything in the cart was white, refined, or "dead," no enzymes. Sure enough! The woman herself was pasty white, slightly sallow and pudgy with unwholesome-looking fat. She also gave the impression of being worn-out. On the other hand, I have observed that the people who generally have their carts laden with fresh fruits, vegetables, cheeses, meat and fish look quite different. They are apt to be the ones whose skin glows; their hair is full of life and luster, and they themselves look as if they had vitality. (quoted in Brissett and Lewis, 1978: 65)

Few meddlers are absent a remedy for the alleged evils they identify— and so it is with food and nutrition interventionists, who happily set about righting the toxic condition of those fortunate enough to read their books and listen to their advice. Using terms like *joy, cheer, magic, the new you, vitality, revitalized, good looks, youth,* and, of course, *health,* these meddlers extrapolate the benefits of healthy eating to the whole society. As one proponent puts it: "I would say that in one generation we could produce a race of youth of unusual intelligence, strength and health: we could then turn many prisons into universities; we would be able to walk safely in our parks at night. Our taxes would be lower; there would be more honesty in the land" (quoted in Brissett and Lewis, p. 66). All because of food and nutrition. With outcomes like these, who can be against them?

Advocates of "Political Correctness"

It is to much of the political left that we owe the absurdities of that meddlesome movement called "political correctness" (PC). Revealing their Puritan roots to be as deep as those growing from the political right, the devotees of the movements for women's rights, racial equality, and economic justice began in the 1960s to systematically deconstruct the "split between the public life of 'politics' and the 'private' life of sexual, cultural, and familial life" (Wagner, 1997: 138). The idea that there had ever been a split in the first place was passed off as a legacy of patriarchy and a tool of repression. People's personal lives were no longer their own but, rather, were to be seen as a reflection of hegemonic power structures and, thus, as public property available to be meddled with as the occasion required. "Who rules America?" was the burning question. And the answer was what it had always been: the same old gang of rich white males who have regularly determined everyone else's lives—the "power elite," as C. Wright Mills (1956) called them. To correct such an intolerable condition, the advocates of the liberal democratic movement known as political correctness called for an analysis of everyone's personal lives. Like Queen Victoria herself, the Puritan spirit of these movements was utterly devoid of humor. Jokes became prime vehicles for communicating one's political correctness (or incorrectness) along with virtually everything else that one did or said in matters ranging from personal appearance to university relations and curricula. "The personal is political" became the totalitarian by-word of the postmodern left, effectively opening up everyone's life for criticism about whether it did or did not fit the standards of the new PC police. These scenes from the PC zeitgeist are probably all too familiar:

1. Joseph Epstein, editor of the *American Scholar*, made the mistake of repeating in an article on the essential lack of humor of feminist critics and professors a joke about a Manhattan couple who cannot decide whether to get a revolver or a pit bull dog in order to protect themselves against burglars. They compromise by hiring a feminist. The joke provoked so much wrath within the university community where feminist faculty reside that he was compelled to write a *mea culpa* to the *New York Times* in which he lamented that he had to pay such a high price for a response that made his point exactly (reported in Lapham, 1991: 12).
2. Two faculty members at the University of Minnesota–Duluth posed for pictures with a Roman sword and pistol, thinking they were helping to publicize the campus history club in an amusing and offbeat way. University officials seized the photos after the administration received complaints that they were "insensitive"

and "inappropriate." The head of the school's Commission on Women complained that the pictures "contributed to a climate of fear on campus." (The University of Minnesota–Duluth is one of the safest campuses in the nation.)

3. At the University of Connecticut, the President's Policy on Harassment defines as "harassment" any remarks that offend women or minorities. These include "inconsiderate jokes," "misdirected laughter," and "conspicuous exclusion from conversation." Sanctions for these new crimes against the political order range from reprimand to expulsion.

4. PC lexicons, many of which are standard fare in newspaper editorial rooms, alert writers to substitute *person* for *man*—as in *postperson* and *mailperson*—to appease the gender sensitivities of female readers. Further, they should never use terms like *qualified minority* because they suggest that some minorities might be unqualified. Words like *mafia* must be avoided because they are offensive to Italians. No one can be described as being *gypped* anymore because gypsies might complain.[13] The handicapped should be referred to as *physically challenged, differently abled*, or *handi-capables*. To speak otherwise is to reveal one's *ablism*. More radical voices do not urge the adoption of new terms for the formerly "disabled" but, rather, incorporate the rubric of *temporarily abled* to refer to everyone else. Broken homes are *dysfunctional families*, and cheating in school, according to these new dictionaries, is to be linguistically transformed into *academic dishonesty*. Most astonishingly, the word *community* is no longer acceptable because it implies "a monolithic culture in which people act, think, and vote in the same way" (Goodman, 1991: 32).

5. Even the fictional "Camp Swampy" of the Beetle Bailey comic strip has surrendered to the humorless PC police by having a contrite General Amos Halftrack issue an apology to Miss Buxley for his insensitive sexual remarks and leering poses over the years. Mort Walker, the cartoon's creator, avows that he can't fight the army of feminist groups who have challenged his characterization of Ms. Buxley as an empty-headed blond and charged him with creating a climate conducive to the sexual harassment of women. His comic strip was, in other words, no longer a source of amusement but a vortex of fate in which readers were unwitting co-conspirators in the oppression of women. Furthermore, these groups have charged, his caricature of Mrs. Halftrack as a battle-axe and a crone caused homemakers to suffer further from their already low self-esteem.

6. The university curriculum has become a prime battleground for revisionists intent on establishing a new world order of rectitude. The literary canon is denounced as the product of "dead white males" and a "tool of oppression." The standards for classical status in literature are arbitrary, it is charged, and they discriminate against non-Western traditions and practices. Anyone who defends the established canon of Shakespeare, Chaucer, and Milton is denounced as a racist and a sexist. *Huck Finn* is removed from libraries because of its "racist" dialogue by enlightened and well-educated members of the community who would have been the first to show up to testify as ACLU witnesses when right-wing groups tried to ban the novels of Henry Miller or D. H. Lawrence. Discussions of curriculum seem less akin to idea-centered faculty meetings than to political rallies concerned with people's "feelings" and "sensitivities." And *Principia Mathematica* is described by some feminist groups as "Newton's Rape Manual" (Ellis, 1997).

7. As Generation X'ers enroll in college—fresh from eighteen years of being pampered and fed a steady diet of electronic entertainment—even teaching itself has begun to reevaluate its mandate to the young along politically correct lines. Speaking at a national conference in Washington, Houston Baker of the University of Pennsylvania argued that the American university suffers from a crisis of too much reading and writing. "Reading and writing are merely technologies of control," Baker alleged. Universities should instead be "listening to the voices of emerging peoples." He suggested rap music and popular rock-and-roll groups as more suited to teaching the new generation than the traditional practice of having students read, write, and speak (quoted in D'Souza, 1992: 6–7).

These examples demonstrate that those who meddle in the name of "political correctness" have been particularly effective at changing the landscape of universities, if not the whole society, through their brand of intolerance. Not usually known for shutting off debate, universities are now places where discussions of a wide variety of topics are hemmed in by the requirements of "sensitivity," thereby effectively preventing any further consideration. Thus one finds that discourse on topics such as race and gender have the boring flavor of disingenuousness to them. Women and minorities are "oppressed" victims of white male patriarchy; discrimination and victimage account for most of the differences between human beings. The issue is not that the relative "truth" of any of these statements is under question; it is that the discourse is closed. "I wouldn't dream of teaching a course on race relations," says a colleague. "It is impossible to approach the subject with anything resembling intellectual integrity. The whole area is patrolled by ideological bullies. I don't need that kind of grief." The real problem with PC, says critic Robert Hughes, isn't that it is "post-Marxist" but that it is "post-Puritan":

> Its repressive weight does not fall upon campus conservatives, who are flourishing, delighted that the PC fold give some drunken creep of a student who bellows "nigger" and "dyke" into the campus night the opportunity to posture as a martyr to speech-repression. The students it harms are the kids who would like to find a way of setting forth their dissatisfactions with the way America has gone and is going, but now find they can't speak so freely about them in case they use the wrong word and thus set off flares of complaints and little airbursts of contempt from those on their left. (Hughes, 1993: 30)

Indeed, the trouble with political correctness and those who advocate it, under whatever rubric and vocabulary of motives, is the same as that pointed out by Nietzsche: "Of necessity, the party man becomes a liar, . . . wishing not to see something that one does see; wishing not to see something *as* one sees it." That institutions committed to free inquiry and the politically unaccountable pursuit of truth should be the site of such censorious meddling is especially paradoxical.

Professional Meddlers

The meddling trades that have arguably had the single most profound impact on life in American society are those burgeoning groups who meddle for money. In this category we include a raft of professional and quasi-professional groups from lawyers and social workers to psychiatrists and counselors. These groups are to be found everywhere, and they constitute an entirely new approach to meddling, for they do so in the name of human conflicts that they themselves typically have had a hand in shaping (see Box 5.1).

Governmental Meddlers

Year after year, reform after reform is enacted with the high purpose of empowering the people, yet the people grow more hostile and suspicious and frustrated and disillusioned and snappish.

—**Paul Greenberg**

Meddling, as we have shown, proceeds from a multiplicity of sources. But perhaps no derivation is as easy to identify as the wave of meddling

BOX 5.1
Law, Medicine, the Media, and Greed:
The Case of Silicone Breast Implants

There exists perhaps no better example of the success of a coalition of professional meddlers using their power and influence to enrich themselves at the expense of a public who bought them and a company who manufactured them than the case of silicone breast implants. These devices—implanted for both cosmetic and reconstructive reasons in millions of women worldwide (the exact number is unknown but the best estimate in the United States is 2 million), the majority of whom by all accounts are extremely satisfied—were nevertheless banned in 1992 by David Kessler, the commissioner of the Food and Drug Administration (FDA), on the grounds that they had not been proven safe. (The ban exempted implants used for "reconstructive purposes," concentrating on those being installed for merely "cosmetic" reasons.) Documented by Dr. Marcia Angell, executive editor of the *New England Journal of Medicine,* in a book titled *Science on Trial: The Clash of Medical Evidence and the Law in the Breast Implant Case* (1996), the case demonstrates that the FDA's action was taken as a sign that the relatively few claims that the implants caused various kind of diseases and other complications were probably correct. The press and the media, smelling a story about greedy corporations putting profit above safety—a sort of cosmetic version of the Ford Pinto case—quickly adopted the FDA view that whereas no scientific evidence had yet been discovered linking the implants to the diseases they were alleged to cause, the implants were undoubtedly the cause of the complaints. The action by Mr. Kessler set off a wave of lawsuits, including a class action suit that eventually required the manufacturer, Dow Corning, to set aside a total of $4.25 billion for women who were sick or who might get sick from the implants. Dr. Angell's analysis of the disparity between the scientific evidence in the case and the verdict in the courts centers on how a penurious network of lawyers, doctors, feminist groups, consultants, expert witnesses, and consumer advocates got rich driving Dow Corning out of business. The portrait she paints is one of passion and greed overwhelming the legal system's requirement of justice and fair play. Each of these groups, spearheaded by a professional organization representing a specific group of meddlers waiting in the wings, sought to use the case to advance its own agenda. Lawyers got rich filing the suits; doctors got rich as expert witnesses advocating on behalf of their patients who claimed to be sick (motivated in part by their jealousy of cosmetic surgeons who, even by the lofty standards of medicine, are highly compensated for their popular work). Feminist groups, seeing another opportunity to push the idea that women are victims of patriarchal medicine, rushed to the fore, advancing an agenda that included the idea that cos-

(continues)

(continued)

metic enhancement of breasts was preposterous anyway and played into male fantasies about what women should look like. Expert witnesses did what they have been doing for years—hiring themselves out to say whatever their benefactors wanted them to say. Members of the burgeoning-consulting trades found a rich and fertile ground for their intervention strategies, and consumer advocate groups saw the entire matter as an opportunity to enhance their status and role as the guardians of the consuming public.

This case represents a kind of meddling zenith—and one all the more interesting now that it is clear, as Angell clearly documents, *that there was never any credible scientific evidence that silicone-gel breast implants were responsible for any diseases at all.* A report published in the fall of 1997 in the *Journal of the National Cancer Institute* gives silicone breast implants a "clean bill of health." In fact, there is some evidence suggesting that women with implants are *less* likely to get breast cancer (Brown, 1997). Be that as it may, the earlier ban (which, as of this writing, is yet to be lifted) proved to be a bonanza for a kaleidoscope of meddling interests seeking to gain from their intrusions into the lives and choices of others. Attorneys, government officials, feminist groups, "expert witnesses," victim advocacy organizations, and the courts themselves all clamored to get aboard. Despite the complete lack of any scientific basis for these claims, the media fed the public's quenchless thirst for news of yet another health scare. When the amount of money available in the Dow Corning settlement became known ($4.25 billion), even perfectly healthy women with implants considered having them removed simply because the money was so good.[1] Lawyers were ingenious in advising their clients whom to sue. They urged them to go after the manufacturer rather than the doctor because Dow Corning had deeper pockets. And, besides, they could employ an old legal trick: Sue them both initially, and then drop the charges against the doctor in exchange for his or her cooperation in testifying at trial. It worked. Plaintiffs were awarded as much as $25 million apiece, even though they never proved that the implants were responsible for any diseases at all. The courts awarded the money on the basis of their attorneys' argument that the implants could be responsible for *future* diseases. In fact, the strategy worked so well that the attorney for the recipients of the $25 million put out an instructional video teaching other lawyers how to win a lawsuit involving silicone breast implants by keeping the jury's mind off the question of whether or not the implants caused his client's illness.

This tale of meddling greed, medical mendacity, and journalistic irresponsibility shows that meddling is escalating because it is so profitable. Dow Corning filed for bankruptcy in the spring of 1995. Lawyers hauled away billions. Angell suggests that the "peculiar" incentives of the legal professions were the most obvious problem in this case. The present body

(continues)

(continued)

of tort law enables lawyers "to prey on people's fears, to destroy thriving companies, and, in the breast implant case, even to threaten an entire industry (medical devices) and an important area of medical research (epidemiological studies)—and at the same time to make huge amounts of money in fees" (1996: 203). She also suggests several remedies: getting rid of contingency fees except for the poor, arranging for judicial appointment of expert witnesses, and holding accountable those doctors who collect fees for making dubious and nonexistent diagnoses. None of these reforms are likely to succeed, however, simply because those who specialize in tort cases (like those who oppose radical IRS reforms) stand to lose so much money if they did succeed. As this is being written, the diet drug "Fen-Phen" is giving rise to a similar pattern of events, as may be expected for any future drugs that hold out the possibility of weight loss.

Note

1. The following exchange, quoted by Marcia Angell (1996), took place on October 10, 1994, in an interview aired on Houston's KHOU-TV featuring a healthy woman with breast implants who was considering having them removed. *Question:* "Your family wants you to take the money and run?" *Answer:* "I think so."

interventions stemming from the kind of government Americans have developed since World War II. Centralized government, long a source of concern to those advocates of small government that trace their roots to the nation's founding fathers and principles, has essentially won the argument. *Boston Globe* columnist Jeff Jacoby describes this state of affairs clearly:

> Today, Washington decides what medicines we may buy. Washington decides how long new mothers stay in the hospital. Washington decides how we may prepare for our retirement. Washington decides what our children shall cover in school, what labels must appear on wine, how many gallons of water our toilets may flush. Washington decides whether office-supply companies can merge, whether tobacco billboards may go up in ballparks, whether cars may be sold without airbags. Soon . . . the federal government will start operating a computerized directory showing every person newly hired by every employer in the country. (Jacoby, 1997: A-13)

The meddling government that Hamilton and Jefferson feared has largely materialized. Their concern was that more government inevitably equals less liberty. Things seem to be working out pretty much that way. A cursory Internet search on the term *meddling* brings up almost 3,000 items, most of them having to do with complaints about governmental meddling. Politicians who would verge on a call to arms if other countries meddled into the affairs of ours, routinely urge that American power be used to meddle into theirs. A colleague, one admittedly prone to choleric outbursts of suspicion, maintains that "someday soon a bar-code will be tattooed onto the wrist of every newborn that will determine every aspect of their lives." Paranoid, perhaps—but then that, too, is a term that meddlers have dreamed up to describe those who do not share their sense of "reason."

Health and safety meddlers routinely use the power of government to impose their views on the rest of the citizenry. A satirical letter to a local newspaper suggests that things have gone far enough:

> Citizens owe a thank you to state Senator Ben Brown for sponsoring the new mandatory seat-belt law. He realizes we ignorant subjects can't function without the decrees of our all-knowing government. There are some other important areas he should go to work on immediately, one of which is to out-law tobacco, which is responsible for much death and disease. Also, I believe liquor is responsible for more traffic deaths than not using seat-belts.
>
> We might even deal with the terrible proliferation of pizza, hamburger and other fast-food outlets, which cause heart disease, diabetes and other debilitating illnesses. While we're at it, bacon and sausage should be abolished along with countless other known perils. People shouldn't be allowed to do things that will affect them negatively. After all, personal freedom is an out-of-date concept. When people don't make the right choices, government must step in and do it for them." (*Daily Oklahoman*, November 7, 1997, p. 8)

As the American government in all its forms has grown, so has its capacity and appetite for meddling into the lives of its citizens. Little wonder. Meddling, it can be argued, is what governments do—and, indeed, part of the legitimate function of government is proper meddling. But even as the government struggles to find the money to perform legitimate functions such as keeping the streets safe, running the park service, and issuing passports and visas, it has found the wherewithal to meddle into the lives of its citizens in increasingly innovative ways. For example, the Department of Agriculture and the Department of Health and Human Services have combined their bureaucratic energies to issue the latest version of their "Dietary Guidelines for Americans," complete with height and weight charts and proper warnings about drinking in moderation, partaking sparingly of animal products, getting precisely the government-approved quantity of fiber in our diets, and policing fat. Yet in spite of all this meddling attention—or perhaps because of it—the average American gets fatter ever year. Corpulence and obesity are said to be a national crisis, especially among children. We are alleged to be living off the "fat of the land." And heart disease (rates are actually down) continues to be the *sine qua non* of the national dialogue, with medical Cassandras issuing daily warnings about the dire health consequences of the way we live. Middle-class people either exercise to keep fit (assured as they are that fitness will protect them from the dreaded perils of modern life) or worry about it if they don't.

Furthermore, meddling government agency *A* competes with meddling private agency *B* for a piece of a pie worthy of Savonarola. As the average weight of the average American increases, there are those who actually want the federal government to do more, not less—those who, as Jonathan Yardley puts it, "want to turn the food police into the Food Gestapo" (Yardley, 1996: B-2). One such individual is Michael Jacobson, current director of the aforementioned Center for Science in the Public Interest, who has been quoted as saying, "The dietary guidelines should be telling the public what is the best possible diet. The [current] guidelines don't. I don't see any motivational language in these guidelines. They should have urged diets much lower in saturated fat, . . . cholesterol, sodium and sugar." As Yardley sums up the matter: "If Michael Jacobson and his minions were running the show, we'd all be strapped to our Exercycles and force-fed rice cakes garnished with wheat germ. . . . Uncle [Sam] can't find the cash to pay his bills, yet here he is preaching at us like a latter-day incarnation of Sylvester Graham" (Yardley, 1996: B-2).

Advocating health, it seems, puts the government on the side of the angels; but the fact that the government also has the power to enforce anything it endorses places the entire matter in another sphere—the sphere of governmental control. What this means politically, of course, is that the progressive left, long a staunch advocate of civil liberties and protections from a leviathan government, now finds itself labeled by its opponents on the right as an advocate of "big government." The urge to meddle by employing the formidable array of instruments of the state is a powerful one, and because this can often be done through the faceless regulations of bureaucracy, even those who are otherwise disinclined to support government intervention in personal matters may find themselves reluctant to object when the issue is framed in terms of health, fitness, safety, and the like.

The Regulatory Dilemma

Winston Churchill observed that "if you have ten thousand regulations you destroy all respect for the law." Nothing could describe our current situation better, except that the number he chose is an absurdly conservative one. We have regulations on everything, and they seem to be propagating themselves exponentially. When the government decided to regulate flying in 1927, there were ten simple rules for pilots to observe, including such common-sense ones as "Before taking the plane off the ground, make certain it will fly," "Make sure there is enough gas on board to complete the trip," and "When prop-starting a plane, be sure to get out of the way." Today, the Federal Aviation Regulations cover thirty-seven feet of shelf space in the library and are so complicated that no one can really say for sure what they are (though if you should have an accident, you can rest assured that you broke one or more of them). The same can be said for the tax code (it is doubtful that anyone actually files a correct tax return in any given year), the regulations for which are often so contradictory that in complying with one you violate another. The regulatory muddle is itself a grand source of meddling, for if regulations are unclear or contradictory, we then need other regulations to interpret them, along with legions of lawyers, accountants, counselors, and others beneficiaries to sort out the inevitable conflicts and collisions between them.

Moreover, if we regulate one thing in the name of a popular ideology— for instance, drinking—then logically and consistently the call will be made to regulate others as well. If drinking causes the deaths of innocents on the highway and pregnant females must to be meddled with because their drinking may (*may* is a huge word among meddlers who meddle in the name of health and safety) lead to fetal alcohol syndrome, then surely the epidemiological data dredge applied to the passive "victims" of, say, smoking may lead to still other regulations. In fact, the concern for the unborn child has extended to parental health practices even *before* conception, and we are told that the prospective mother must alter her health habits at least twenty-eight days before even attempting to get pregnant. Furthermore, the prospective father, heretofore thought to be immune from fetal health concerns, is now urged to take special precautions before conception, for, as *American Health Magazine* warns, "don't forget, 'smoke gets in your sperm': so watch out for 'steamed semen'" (quoted in Barsky, 1988b: 160). As we have seen with other meddling interventions, if this is good advice, someone will eventually call for regulations making it mandatory and for more police to enforce the rules against such health miscreants.

There is also a cycle at work when regulators regulate. Rules create ways around rules. Ways around rules create the call for more rules. More rules create new ways around them, and so on, *ad infinitum.* Lawyers, the experts on rules and getting around rules, get rich in this regulatory game. Whether it serves the interests of anyone else is debatable, and what it means for a society enamored with litigation and short on trust is certainly a subject that should occupy our attention.

Teachers and Teaching: Education as a Meddling Trade

Education is a business that thrives on meddling. In this society, where education is an enormous business employing millions of people, it is a primary source for a host of meddlesome interventions. In some ways, of course, education cannot proceed without interventionist meddling. Engaging the minds of students with new ideas is instrumental to both good and bad teaching, and we cannot imagine an educational process that did not occasionally meddle into the affairs of those who spend their days in the company of teachers. Once again, however, we may note that proper distinctions are largely absent, such that entire programs are being built in schools around busybody assumptions. In the name of health, safety, a therapeutic agenda, and a host of other meddling ideologies, public education has become considerably more than a matter of teaching students basic skills. For example, John Leo notes that a health curriculum called "Here's Looking at You, 2000" is being used in several thousand public schools. This program involves a toucan named Miranda who encourages children to check the family cupboards for "poisons"—including alcohol and tobacco. "The busybody curriculum also urges them to confess 'problems at home' by writing secret messages to the teacher" (Leo, 1997: 2). Getting parents in trouble is thus a route to getting A's and being regarded as a "good student."

Such spying and reporting by children on their parents takes many forms. It is becoming standard fare in some schools, says Leo, to use students to "re-educate" their parents. "Adults commonly joke about being 'turned in' by their children for such crimes as drinking a glass of wine with dinner or failing to recycle a soda can." In a ninth-grade class in Petaluma, California, students in a "human interaction" program were sent home with worksheets assessing whether their families interacted according to an "open, democratic" model or a "closed, authoritarian" model. In other classrooms, students are asked how many of them hate their parents. In a sex education handbook entitled *Changing Bodies, Changing Lives*, parents are hermeneutically deconstructed to become merely one of many "voices" that students must evaluate. They are regarded either as problems to contend with or as examples of what to avoid. If many parents are "not doing their job," a complaint frequently heard in many quarters, it is little wonder: Their authority is being systematically undermined by classrooms that are less instructive than they are meddlesome.

It is not just a matter of students spying on their families; families also encourage the schools to spy on their children. The following news report has a familiar ring:

> The Salina (Ks.) school board, determined to discourage underage drinking, has approved random breathalyzer testing at high school dances ... The district has acquired a portable testing machine for each of its four high schools and teachers were authorized to test any student entering a school

function. Students suspected of drinking during normal school hours could also be tested.

Some students complained that testing violated their trust and constituted an unlawful search, but others thought it would improve the atmosphere at school. Any student caught is automatically suspended for five days. (*Reuters*, November 2, 1997)

Such blatant and controversial interventions aside, education, it can be said, has become a vast staging area for meddlers of all stripes. Recognizing the power of ideas and ardently adhering to the doctrine of "molding minds," virtually every educational venue is now a rich and fertile field for meddlers. Fundamentalist religious groups meddle into the work of teachers so much these days that it is only novel when they don't. In the name of political correctness, as we have pointed out, the university's traditional commitment to academic freedom has been compromised to the point where classes in which controversial topics are taught are just a complaint, a newspaper article, or an internal investigation away from being sanctioned into submission. The *London Times* educational supplement of January 31, 1997, commenting on a teacher's union election in Britain, finds that the manifesto asks for "more money and less meddling." But, alas, with money comes meddling, and the political ideologies of both the left and the right have discovered what religious fundamentalism has already found—that mobilizing Puritan jihads against sex, religious sanctity, and free speech can be effective ideological instruments to promote social and culture agendas as well.

Medical Meddlers

As medicine has increased its moral scope (Szasz, 1977), medical moral entrepreneurs have found a fertile field in which to sell their wares. We are talking here not simply about the marketing of meddling interventions—a topic that we will deal with comprehensively in the next chapter—but, rather, about the selling of a certain moral framework that makes these wares attractive in the first place. The "medicalization of society" (Conrad and Schneider, 1992) that America has witnessed over the past century has been brought about through adoption of the techniques of what Howard S. Becker (1963) has called "moral entrepreneurship." Moral entrepreneurs are those people who are involved in the merchandising and selling of morality. They are meddlers by their very nature. Leaders of reform movements such as child welfare advocates, leaders of temperance movements, and those who crusade against pornography and indecency are obvious examples. But as Eliot Friedson notes, because medicine is not a scholarly or scientific profession but a practicing

one committed to seeking out and defining illnesses as bad, these meddlers take an activist orientation that puts them in the same camp as
other reformers.[14] Such a juxtaposition is not readily accepted:

> At first thought it may seem peculiar to include the medical man with
> bluenoses, reformers and others who are more obviously moral entrepre-
> neurs. The physician's job is not generally seen to be moral; he is supposed
> to treat illness without judging. There is, however, an irreducible moral
> judgment in the designation of illness as such, a judgment the character of
> which is frequently over-looked because of the virtually universal consen-
> sus that exists about the undesirability of much of what is labeled illness.
> Cancer is so obviously undesirable to everyone that its status as an illness
> seems objective and self-evident rather than what it is—a social valuation on
> which most people happen to agree. (Friedson, 1970: 252)

So when a physician claims that alcoholism is a disease, he or she is
just as much a moral entrepreneur as the fundamentalist who says it's a
sin. There does, however, seem to be a major division of labor among
medical meddlers who lead crusades against various infirmities of mind,
body, and spirit. Friedson notes three such types, though in the years
since he conducted his research in the 1970s, the Surgeon General of the
United States has also grown into enormous prominence from the standpoint of meddling.

1. First are those representatives of the medical profession who seek to influence public policy by realigning public opinion around the core of their
interests. Here we have public spokespersons for organized professions and
specialties, such as the Surgeon General of the United States. The Surgeon
General, whose job, technically speaking, is merely to administer the public
health service, has changed to the point where he or she occupies one of the
most political positions in the nation. Health is now more clearly seen as a
moral issue; hence the difficulty in confirming recent incumbents of the office. (Joycelyn Elders was dismissed for suggesting that we might want to
look into teaching masturbation in the public schools;[15] and nominee Henry
Foster was skewered and ultimately rejected when he admitted that, as a
physician, he had performed abortions.) Since former incumbent C. Everett
Koop's campaign against tobacco, anyone can see that the stage was set for
this role to be the meddling nanny for all Americans, hectoring them into
being good and doing the right things in the name of health. Sermonizing
from the "bully pulpit" of their office, recent Surgeon Generals have taken
on not only tobacco but also fat, sedentary lifestyles, sex education, teen
pregnancy, and a host of moral issues. Since bodies are connected to all
morality, these Surgeon Generals have seen themselves as having a license
to meddle into the lives of everyone in the name of health.

2. Second are the major moral entrepreneurs of medicine itself who are typically associated as spokespersons for major institutions such as hospitals, clinics, medical schools, health departments, and the like. They seek political power by having more and more of human life subsumed under the banner of medicine. These are the groups that have lobbied to extend the domain of medicine to such problems as drug addiction, mental illness, alcoholism, obesity and other "eating disorders," and even crime and juvenile delinquency. Seeking to remove many of these problems from the jurisdiction of the courts, they have argued that such problems constitute "illnesses" that should be treated clinically rather than punatively.

3. Third are the special lay groups, growing in number, that seek to sell us new medical moralities built around their favorite disabilities. Here, as Friedson puts it, "untrammeled by professional dignity, are the most flamboyant moral entrepreneurs in health, each concerned with arousing the public to give it the attention and resources that can only be gained at the expense of the other, each trying to create in the public mind profound pity and horror at its own specially chosen human failing" (Friedson, 1973: 254). In this category we find aligned a curious mixture of celebrities and political figures who use their visibility and prestige to lobby for some and (in a zero-sum game) inevitably against others. Hollywood celebrities such as Barbra Streisand, Jerry Lewis, and Carroll O'-Conner are but a few of the luminaries who have sought to use their public personas to gain adherence to their medical causes. And among political figures we may note that almost every First Lady has used her position to lobby on behalf of some "cause" or another—many of them medical, and most of them meddlesome. Roselyn Carter urged us to "ring the bell for mental health," Nancy Reagan urged teens to "just say no to drugs," Betty Ford helped create a series of centers to help further medicalize alcoholism. Current First Lady Hillary Clinton campaigns on behalf of pediatric issues. She *has* to meddle, because the alternative, as she put it in response to critics of her role in the national health care debate, is to "just stay home and bake cookies." But this need not be so. In sharp contrast to these First Lady meddling cheerleaders for the moral entrepreneurs of medicine was Lady Bird Johnson, who spent her time sowing wild flowers in the medians of interstate highways.

Mental Health Professionals and the
Rise of Meddling Service Industries

Although systematic data are difficult to gather, the best estimates are that professional meddlers constitute a multibillion-dollar industry. For example, if we consider only mental health and treatment services, we note that from 1975 to 1990—a short fifteen years—psychiatrists increased in number from 26,000 to 36,000, clinical psychologists from 15,000 to 42,000, psychiatric social workers from 25,000 to 80,000, and marriage and family counselors from 6,000 to 40,000. The total increase over these years was from 72,000 to 198,000 professionals in just the four professions (Goleman, 1990). Moreover, H. C. Schulberg and R. W. Manderscheid reported in 1989 that the number of personnel in NIMH-surveyed psychiatric facilities ballooned from 375,000 in 1976 to 441,000 in 1984 (Schulberg and Manderscheid, 1989). And although there are no reliable figures on the total cost of mental health care in America, 1991 figures from the NIMH suggest a direct economic cost of about $55 billion. The growth of private mental health facilities has been no less spectacular. In the same fifteen years as mentioned above, the number of private psychiatric hospitals grew by 47 percent. The fact that 75 percent of all private psychiatric treatment is on an outpatient basis puts the total even higher (Schulberg and Manderscheid, 1989). In the past four decades, the mental health trade has changed from a relatively few large public facilities to what Stuart Kirk and Herb Kutchins call

> an array of public, not-for-profit, and for-profit inpatient facilities and an explosion of clinics and private psychotherapists from many disciplines. From a system in which the majority of treatment facilities were public institutions of last resort for the impoverished, elderly, and mentally disabled, where admission was by involuntary civil commitment and resulted in lengthy stays at public expense, we now have a fragmented, multitiered, diversely sponsored and financed array of services for less impaired clients who voluntarily seek help from those who dispense what has been dubbed the "popular psychotherapies." (Kirk and Kutchins, 1992: 75)

If we add to these imposing statistics the growing number of treatment facilities spawned by the medicalization of addiction and the government's war on drugs, as well as the marital discord industry produced by and now dependent on the culture of divorce, we may begin to appreciate just how many people are financially dependent on meddling into other people's lives for the maintenance of their own. Each of these therapeutic enterprises has a vested economic interest in generating more of the very problems they claim to cure. For example, despite an official posture of therapeutic neutrality, as well as protestations to the contrary, there is every reason to believe that marriage counseling actually has a bias toward the cult of the individual—which means, in many cases, toward divorce. In *One Man, Hurt*, a personal account of his own divorce, an anonymous author recounts how, as a young husband and father of four young boys, he entered therapy in the hopes of salvaging his marriage. Instead, he discovered that therapy actually encourages it:

The counseling itself pulled us further apart rather than bringing us closer together. Yes, it did put us in touch with ourselves, it did enable us to see our needs better, and it did encourage us to fulfill them. But that is what is dreadfully wrong. . . . [T]he tragic result is that people caught in the emotional chaos and upheaval of marital crisis can seldom look beyond the tough, unpalatable, excruciating steps of rebuilding the relationship. It is easier to say that no basis for the rebuilding exists or that it is not his or her need. (quoted in Whitehead, 1997: 71)

When he explained to the marriage therapist that he really wanted to save his marriage, he was told that "[w]e are in the business of saving individuals, not marriages" (Whitehead, 1997: 71). If we also take into account the additional money that accrues to the therapeutic and counseling trades when people divorce, it is not difficult to see the conflict of interest. In divorce situations, especially when children are involved, a whole host of additional meddlers are brought into the picture—child psychologists, financial counselors, social workers, and lawyers, to name but a few of those whose interests are better served by people divorcing than by their staying together.

The bible of victimage for both professionals and increasingly large numbers of amateur meddlers who have acquired its language from the media is the *Diagnostic and Statistical Manual of the American Psychiatric Association,* now in its fourth edition. The *DSM-IV* is a monumental project, trying as it does to catalog the entire human experience in symptomatic terms. As L. J. Davis prosaically puts it:

For roughly five thousand years, poets, playwrights, philosophers and cranks have incinerated untold quantities of olive oil, beeswax and fossil fuel in pursuit of this maddeningly elusive goal; all have failed, sometimes heroically. . . . Despite the best efforts of minds great, small and sometimes insane, the riddle of the human condition has remained utterly impervious to solution. Until now. According to . . . the *DSM-IV,* human life is a form of mental illness. (Davis, 1997: 61)

The *DSM-IV* is now almost 900 pages in length, and it grows with every subsequent new edition. The first edition in 1952 was less than 100 pages long, but each edition since has increased the range and variety of human experience and behavior that it sought to classify under the rubric of scientific psychiatric nosology. Having gotten at the sick roots of almost everything, the disease metaphor has become a way of life in this country for amateur and professional meddlers alike. But the issue is not just that everyone is sick and that everything is now alleged to be evidence of psychological illness; it is that a central and unifying theme of the meddling trades is that everyone and everything can be treated. The meddlers do not offer diagnosis without the possibility of treatment. "Here on a staggering scale," writes Davis, "are gathered together all the known mental disturbances of humankind, the illnesses of mind and spirit that cry out for the therapeutic touch of—are you ready for this?—the very people who wrote the book" (Davis, 1997: 62). Virtually every problem known to the human condition has now been translated into a disease. From the trivial (coffee nerves, snoring, and bad writing) to the profound (psychotic breaks with reality, necrophilia, and debilitating depression), the *DSM-IV* offers a compendium of human problems great and small, all neatly medicalized and packaged ready for treatment. That this form of professional meddling is big business may be seen in the fact that each diagnosis is accompanied by a billing code number, making it easy for insurance companies and accountants to know what the treatment is for. For example, the billing code for one of the current favorites—attention deficit/hyperactivity disorder—is 314.01.

The problem with the *DSM-IV* (among other things, of course) is that if everything is an illness, nothing is an illness (Szasz, 1961). Unlike ordinary medical illnesses that, like AIDS, are only incidentally political, those listed in the *DSM-IV* are almost wholly political. The decision to include (or exclude) any number of behaviors from the list of mental diseases, psychiatric syndromes, psychoses, and neuroses is often the result of intense lobbying and political pressure—on the part of both psychiatrists who need its contents to justify their interventions and groups whose members believe they will gain or lose by their inclusion. A prime example is homosexuality. Long seen as a moral weakness, homosexuality made its way into the lexicon of human psychological disorders via the *Diagnostic and Statistical Manual.* At first, homosexuals embraced this new definition, thinking it would be a way of tempering the prejudices afflicting them. After all, if homosexuality was a disease, it wasn't their fault. On closer reflection, and bolstered by the civil rights movement of the 1960s, homosexuals began to see that labeling their lifestyle a "disease" actually demeaned and further stigmatized what they considered to be a perfectly normal, though alternate, way of living. Organizing themselves politically, they put pressure on the American Psychiatric Association to remove homosexuality from the list of psychiatric disorders. In 1973 they succeeded. By a narrow plurality, homosexuality was no longer considered an illness except under specialized conditions in which the person was conflicted by his or her homosexuality. Homosexuality was thus "cured"—not by a drug or a new medical procedure, but by the simple political expedient of dropping it from the official list (Bayer, 1987).

The Panoptic Vision of Life

What many of these different types of meddlers, both amateur and professional, have in common is their obsession with and use of the technologies of what the late French philosopher Michel Foucault called the Panopticon. Related to the rise of the prison system in the eighteenth century, Foucault explained, the Panopticon is a system that allows officials the possibility of complete observation of people under their sphere of control. Since control presumes visibility, and visibility is the essence of control, many types of meddling are dependent on some way of seeing. Indeed, as Foucault suggested, constant visibility traps people "in so many cages, so many small theatres, in which each actor is alone, perfectly individualized and constantly visible" (Foucault, 1975: 200). This theme is similar to one echoed by Erving Goffman, who notes in *Asylums* that the toll exacted on individuals who live in what he calls "total institutions" is the result not so much of being isolated as of being constantly available for inspection. Given such a technology of observation, no officials are even necessary. The mere existence of such a system is often enough to ensure conformity. More important, Foucault saw the Panopticon as a virtual laboratory for the development of the human sciences. Social science techniques for gathering information about people connect them to institutional sources of meddling control. It has been asserted, for example, that sociology is the technological arm of the welfare state because of its ability to fix its gaze on people in the round (Gouldner, 1980). The Panopticon, then, is not just about prisons but about "a whole type of society"—a disciplinary society based on the principle of surveillance[16] (Foucault, 1975: 216). Medicine's gaze has become increasingly inclusionary, an all-encompassing desire to see human behavior as a series of diseases.

Even more important, in a nation of meddlers the government need not even be the agent of meddlesome interventions. As illustrated by the examples we have assessed in this chapter, the interpersonal vehicle of meddling is often enough. It is as though human beings have become their own Panopticon, watching, talking, and employing the highly effective interpersonal tactics of harassment, intimidation, and stigma to secure conformity. The triumph of the therapeutic is, by the same token, the triumph of the Panoptic principle.

These examples of types of meddlers must be concluded with a note about mixed types. To be one type of meddler does not preclude being another as well. Indeed, they often go hand-in-hand. Thus, those who meddle in the name of the various ideologies discussed in Chapter 4 may find compatibilities with more than one of the types we have discussed. Feminists who meddle in the name of political correctness may also meddle "for the sake of the children" or in the name of health or any number of other popular meddling ideologies. On the other end of the political spectrum we find that those who meddle in the name of God also meddle "for the sake of the children," as do parents. (Poor children—they are the object of everyone's meddlesome interventions.) Governmental meddlers, teachers, parents, co-workers, nutritionists, and medical meddlers all find league with each other as well as with other types on specific issues. Indeed, once people indulge the impulse to meddle as a result of having the license offered by one type, they often find that they have much in common with other meddlers as well.

Notes

1. Unless one is very rude or very rich, meddlers of one kind or another are likely to make their way into one's life sooner or later. The rude avoid meddlers by simply telling people to mind their own business. The rich use their money to shield themselves from such pests. Sometimes the rich are also rude, which is likewise helpful.

2. By "meddle without heart" we mean meddling without connection to, or concern for, the meddlee beyond his or her significance as one of hundreds of patients, clients, or cases.

3. I am grateful to my colleague Edward G. Lawry for this insight into Plato's thinking on meddlesome interventions.

4. The Bible is an especially fertile source of cautions about the evil of gossip, which ties into what we would today call *boredom:* "And withal they learn to be idle, wandering about from house to house; and not only idle, but tattlers also and busybodies, speaking things which they ought not" (Timothy 3:15).

5. Patricia Spacks reports that when she was discovered to be writing a book about gossip, a friend slid under her apartment door a newspaper clipping about the Academy Awards, containing this definition: "A red silk dress: A slattern's dress, making the news tawdry, claiming false seductiveness? Or an assertively feminine garment focusing attention on details that might otherwise go unnoticed? The ambiguities, the perplexities, associated with gossip appear endless."

6. Ironically, but not surprisingly, when Diana called a press conference earlier to announce that she was scaling back her schedule of public appearances to spend more time as a private citizen with her children, the price of photographs of her went up.

7. Steven Nock (1993) has argued that surveillance is the cost of privacy we now pay in a society where people no longer know each other. If we are to have any privacy at all, it will only be because we have meddling technologies that can check out our reputations.

8. *Schadenfreude* is a bit different from the French word *ressentiment*, which Norman Denzin sees as the self-poisoning loathing that arises from the systematic repression of certain emotions and, in his view, has become the "predominant postmodernist form of emotionality." In our sense, *schadenfreude* is the response to the

other that comes from a culture of *ressentiment*. For an enlightening discussion of this issue, see Denzin (1991: 54–55).

9. On July 14, 1848, the following notice appeared in the *Seneca County Courier:* "A convention to discuss the social, civil, and religious condition and rights of women will be held in the Wesleyan Chapel, at Seneca Falls, N.Y., on Wednesday and Thursday, the 19th and 20th of July current; commencing at 10:30 A.M." (quoted in Rossi, 1993: 413).

10. Robert Hughes also connects many of the excesses of contemporary feminism to an "anile priggishness of the Puritan marm, lips pursed, seeking nits to pick" (1993: 28).

11. It is obviously quite impossible to talk about feminism as a unitary social movement when writers as diverse as Andrea Dworkin and Camille Paglia both appropriate the term *feminist* to characterize their widely disparate views. The contrast between Dworkin, Adrienne Rich, and Catherine MacKinnon, on the one hand, and Paglia, Rene Denfeld, and Christina Hoff Sommers, on the other, is but one of literally hundreds that could be cited to document the diversity and disarray that distinguish contemporary feminism.

12. It should not be inferred that only government is responsible for the rise of professional meddling. Many people *want* to be meddled with, and, in any case, regulatory agencies are under as much pressure to write more rules as to write fewer ones.

13. As Robert Hughes has observed, in an academic world where an administrator at the University of California at Santa Cruz could campaign against the words in phrases like "a nip in the air" and "a chink in one's armor" on the grounds that such words have expressed racial disparagement in other contexts, anything is possible. "How about banning 'fruit-tree' as disparaging to homosexuals?" (Hughes, 1993: 30).

14. The root of the word *illness* is Scandinavian and means "bad."

15. On that point, though Elders might not have known it, she was on solid psychoanalytic ground. Freud wrote in 1938 that "the ultimate ground of all intellectual inhibitions and all inhibitions of work seems to be the inhibition of masturbation in childhood" (p. 138).

16. Computers offer the latest extension of the Panoptic principle, giving those in charge a powerful tool for surveillance. See Zuboff (1988) for an analysis of this connection.

6

Marketing Meddling

Selling the Meddling Impulse

As the postmodern culture of consumerism ascended, the impulse to meddle, by now so firmly entrenched that few questions were any longer even being raised about it, joined the marketing revolution to create a climate in which meddling was for sale. "Therapeutics," said Philip Rieff, "need no doctrines, only opportunities" (1987: 18). The culture of ontological doubt, as it turned out, provided plenty of them, and proved to be a commercial bonanza for those who wished to make money selling new ways to meddle into the lives of Americans who were increasingly restless with the way those lives were going. The appeals no longer even had to traverse the pretenses of seduction. We know your life is defective, said the meddlers, and we have a regime that will fix it.[1] Consider, for example, the text of the advertisements reprinted in Box 6.1 (for a personal-injury attorney) and Box 6.2 (for three medically supervised weight-loss programs).

Several themes characteristic of the professional meddler's pitch tie these otherwise disparate ads together. Among them are the following.

Caring and Sensitivity

Ads with this theme, like many others of its kind, are designed to make professionals look caring and sensitive. The implied text says "Your

---

BOX 6.1
Advertisement for a Personal Injury Lawyer

Serious Injury & Accident Claims
GET THE MAXIMUM POSSIBLE RECOVERY!

FREE CONSULTATION

- All Injury Claims
- Auto Accidents
- Death Cases
- Defective Products
- Worker's Compensation
- Medical Negligence
  Brain Damage, Surgery,
  Birth Injury, Other
- Serious Injuries
  Paraplegic Injuries
  Amputation
  Permanent Disabilities
  Paralysis
- Fire
- Explosions
- Dog Bites

Mr. Self is a trial attorney practicing in the area of personal injury and wrongful death claims. He is a member of the American Trial Lawyers Association. During his career, Mr. Self has handled cases of both local and national interest. He has given media interviews in an effort to warn the public and bring attention to unsafe conditions and defective products.

Mr. Self concentrates his practice in the area of significant personal injury and wrongful death claims involving motor vehicles, defective products, and the negligence of others.

Self & Associates
Personal Injury Law
"We Get Results ... Period."

---

problem is our problem," and "We care" is a frequent and reassuring line. These ads give the impression that their sponsors care so much about your individual situation that they won't rest until the case is settled to your advantage. This is accomplished in part by offering free services until results are seen. Personal-injury attorneys routinely work on a contingency basis so that individual cases become the raw material out of which their practice makes money regardless of the individual merits of the cases. Add the thousands upon thousands of such cases together and you have an industry with a vested interest in human misery. Phrases such as "No fee if no recovery" and "Free consultation" suggest that the attorneys are working out of the goodness of their hearts.

Victims with Rights

The advertisements in this category make readers feel that they are victims who have certain "rights." Attorneys advertise that they can get vic-

BOX 6.2
Advertisments for Three Weight Loss Programs

tims the money they deserve. "You have rights," says one. "We specialize in getting you your rights," says another. The person who answers such ads is a victim of someone else's negligence, and the sensitive, caring professional will secure his or her rights in the form of a settlement. Even weight-loss and fitness programs refer occasionally to the "right" to be thin, and they are rich in the language of victimage.

Expertise and Special Knowledge

Meddlers are made to appear as experts through a listing of their qualifications, degrees, and specialty areas. The implication is that they have special knowledge not available to ordinary people and that, as a result of this special knowledge, they can cure anyone if only their clients will turn their lives over to them. Note, in Box 6.2, that the second weight-loss program takes a shot at the others by criticizing diet pills and "programs that don't work."

Helplessness and Confusion

These ads play on the emotional aspects of problems, making the readers feel helpless to solve them on their own. For example, specialists in weight loss—especially those who practice it as a medical specialty—routinely indicate that victims cannot lose weight by themselves.[2] The implication of such weight-loss ads is that we need the assistance of a physician if we are going to succeed at losing weight. Helpless, confused by the sheer magnitude of the problem, and reassured by the medical patina of the helper, many people find that these ads have a powerful appeal.

Reaching the Public

Contrast these enthusiastic sales pitches with times past. Less than a century ago, a common street scene in any American town would have included a few discreet signs indicating the locations of the offices of the community's dentists, doctors, lawyers. The signs were low-key, tasteful, and reserved. If one was good at one's profession, satisfied clients spread the word and the professional's work grew. The idea that professionals might actually *solicit* business was unheard of, and aside from being regarded as unethical, the advertising of professional services was illegal. Attorneys were (and still are) technically "officers of the court" whose role was to assist in securing justice as opposed to merely winning cases. But such circumspect helpers of the past have been replaced by an army of highly specialized professionals who have made it their business not only to acquaint the American public with their therapeutic specialties but also to provide us with new diseases, disorders, and complaints that require their services. They run the gamut from legal and medical professionals and paraprofessionals to the soul doctors of psychiatry and psychology to the practitioners in social service organizations and agencies. In the case of the first of these categories, the sea change occurred in the 1970s following a series of court decisions that allowed the previously forbidden helping professions of law and medicine to advertise their services. Since then, the marketing of meddling has sky-rocketed in the legal profession as well as in other meddling trades. In the legal arena alone, the number of lawsuits filed in the past thirty years has tripled (Glendon, 1996: 53). The Supreme Court decision that freed the legal profession from its traditional reticence about advertising its services flew in the face of Abraham Lincoln's advice that lawyers should discourage their clients from suing as often as possible: "Persuade your neighbors to compromise whenever you can. Point out to them how the nominal winner is often a real loser—in fees, expenses, and waste of time. As a peacemaker the lawyer has a superior opportunity of being a good man. There will still be business enough" (Lincoln, 1850/1957: 33). Compare this modest stance with the aforementioned advertisements and it is apparent how far professionals have devolved into the practitioners of simply another trade, hustling their wares before a hectored and confused public. Physicians, like attorneys, found the climate hospitable to their business interests as well. Those reticent about joining the new "dirtier" climate were cast in a no-win situation—the public readily patronized the competition, which had no such qualms, and it seemed that the more flamboyant the marketing strategies, the more successful and profitable they became.

In keeping with this new climate, meddlers of all stripes now hustle business by marketing their services in the same ways as those who have commodities to sell. They advertise through print media such as newspapers, magazines, and the yellow pages of phone books, and through the electronic media of television, radio, and, increasingly, the Internet. They reach us through the distribution of flyers and direct mail, through both audio- and videotape recordings, and even, occasionally, through face-to-face encounters. They are masters at adopting new technologies. A 1993 issue of *Home Office Computing* profiles attorney Cheryl Mead, who sells legal advice through a 900 number called "Law Line" that operates twenty-four hours a day. The magazine certainly sees the advantages of this method:

> For any consultant who sells services or advice, setting up a 900 number can be a way to expand the business. Because callers are automatically charged when they call, there's no need to bill or collect fees. Professionals can serve

a large area, since 900 calls can be made from anywhere in the country. (*Home Office Computing,* March 1993, p. 38)

Such a technology decentralizes professional meddling, thereby offering an innovative remedy to the age-old problem of the professional—having to actually see and talk with clients. Says Ms. Meade, "You can be anywhere and do this—in the mountains, on a deserted beach."

Even more startling is the fact that marketers have discovered that they can meddle into the lives of people without even being directly intrusive. The new technologies of meddling such as computers, data banks, and automated telephone dialers allow people to meddle into the lives of others in essentially invisible ways. New mothers, for example, often find themselves on mailing lists for neonatal products shortly after their pregnancy has been medically confirmed. The new technologies employed by meddlers are so efficient that sometimes we don't even know we've been meddled with until after the fact. Consider the title of a recent Public Broadcasting System special that documented how direct-mail advertisers target the people they want to reach: "We Know Where You Live."

If the meddling industry in question is nonprofit,[3] it may be able to market its services without cost through free "community service" ads in local newspapers. Such ads range from the sublime to the ridiculous, as can be seen from the names of the following groups listed in a local newspaper's "Health Calendar" lineup for the week:

Art of Creative Living
Coping with Urinary Problems During Menopause
Free Hearing Tests
Free Blood Pressure and Blood Sugar Checks
Holiday Survival Class
Irritable Bowel Syndrome Symposium
Preventing and Managing Osteoporosis
Preventing Diabetic Retinopathy
Sports Injury Clinics
Stroke Outreach Training Programs
TOPS (Take Off Pounds Sensibly)
WeighDown Workshop
Singles Network

The sheer power of the therapeutic can be detected in the juxtaposition of the conditions these earnest servants of mankind treat. They range from the profoundly medical (Stroke Outreach Training, which helps families whose members have suffered strokes) to the absurdly medical (Irritable Bowel Syndrome Symposium: Does anyone really need a group for that?) to the highly specialized medical (Coping with Urinary Problems During Menopause) to the questionably medical— (WeighDown Workshop) to the medical by one's own hand (Sports Injury Clinics;) to the not medical at all (Art of Creative Living and Singles Network). The fact that they are all on the same page under the general rubric of "health" shows what a pastiche the therapeutic has become—as well as a bonanza for the huckster with a program or a pitch to sell. Nor are all of these programs actually free. Some charge a modest fee, and most refer sufferers to commercial interests that charge much more.

Whatever the method of reaching the public, all such meddlers attempt to create a market for their products and services by exploiting the vulnerabilities brought on by life in the postmodern culture of discontent. They often succeed in making us believe that without their services, we will remain helpless and confused victims of our own muddled plight. Their announcements are typically accompanied by an array of testimonials from those who suffered before and reached the transcendent state of perfection after. In the case of weight loss, the endless pursuit of the nirvana of sveltness is all the more amazing when one considers that there is no evidence that *any* weight-loss product or service produces lasting results. The success rate for all diets, both commercial and medically supervised, is extremely low. As Michael F. Jacobson and Laurie Ann Mazur (1995) report, for example, researchers at the National Institutes of Health have concluded that nine out of every ten dieters regain most or all of the weight they have lost—and that they do so within five years of losing it.

Solutions for Pandora's Box

Given the raft of problems plaguing Americans in the new culture of anxiety, there weren't many of life's dilemmas that couldn't be translated into profit for the meddler with an advertising budget and a product to hawk. The never-satisfied citizen, in a perpetual state of annoyance over his plight and ready to snarl at anyone who could be viewed as the source of his predicament, was an easy target for marketers who used their basic strategy of "segmentation" to divide and conquer.[4] The whole of life was now regarded as a shopping mall of consumer desires. Whatever one's life consisted of, it could be improved. Thus, not only the perennial problem of weight—too fat, too thin, not the right composition—could be solved but also the age-old quandaries of imperfect children, flawed marriages, emotional distress, and even anxiety itself. Added to this ever-lengthening list was a plethora of substances from alcohol and drugs to tobacco and food that were fodder for the grist mills of marketers now armed with technologies that would have put nineteenth-century snake-oil salesmen to shame. Everything that could be meddled with could be sold, often in the name of caring—a sentiment that still had appeal even as the traditional sources of its realization were being systematically stripped away by changes that most Americans were either unaware of or understood only vaguely.

The work of these new persuaders was aided by two key assumptions, deeply rooted in American culture, that committed us to the desirability of personal, if not social, change. Both have the consequence of feeding the marketplace of the meddler. The first and more significant assumption is that people should always be prepared to change when they are not as competent or as healthy or as happy as they could be. Weight-loss programs frequently advertise their wares with questions beginning "Isn't it about time?" The second assumption is that there are few limits to the changes people can make, and that such changes are relatively easy to effect if only they will follow the right procedure, call on the right experts, or purchase the right products. The promises of personal transformation—radiant health, peace of mind, better communication and relationships, more satisfying sex, development of potentials, an end to addiction and bad feelings, and, in essence, happiness itself—are unshakable. All of these promises and more can be found among the efforts of marketers who convince us that we should listen to those who make a living meddling into the lives of others. Many social critics interested in this matter have mistakenly concluded that the advertising and marketing apparatus of postmodern society is based on the most blatant kinds of self-indulgence. But as Christopher Lasch points out, modern advertising seeks to promote not so much self-indulgence as self-doubt:

> [I]t seeks to create needs, not to fulfill them; to generate new anxieties instead of allaying old ones. By surrounding the consumer with images of the good life, and by associating them with the glamour of celebrity and success, mass culture encourages the ordinary man to cultivate extraordinary tastes, to identify himself with the privileged minority against the rest, and to join them, in his fantasies, in a life of exquisite comfort and sensual refinement. Yet the propaganda of commodities simultaneously makes him acutely unhappy with his lot. By fostering grandiose aspirations, it also fosters self-denigration and self-contempt. (Lasch, 1979: 180–181)

So, the solutions offered to the Pandora's box of problems that assail Americans reduce themselves to an endless squirrel cage of buying and selling. Given the worldview of the entrepreneur selling solutions, no one can ever be satisfied because once the market for one solution is saturated, another will have to be created to take its place. Disease and cures are thus part of a never-ending cycle, and the issue may not be so much one of coming up with cures for every disease as one of coming up with a disease for every cure—a point made nicely by Barbara Ehrenreich:

> We may not have a cure for every disease, alas, but there's no reason we can't have a disease for every cure. With silicone implants, small breasts become micromastia. With injectable growth hormone, short kids become treatable dwarves. Plastic surgeons can now cure sagging jowls and chins, droopy eyelids and insufficiently imposing male chests and calves. So we can expect to hear soon about the menace of new diseases like saggy jowlitis, prolapsed eyelid, and hypopectoralis. (Ehrenreich, 1995: 58)

The servicing of this cycle is one reason why American medicine has a long and storied history of this year's cure being next year's disease and vice versa.[5] Markets do thrive not on real solutions but on illusory ones that can be constantly recycled as restless consumers move from one promise to the next. And what are they promised? Perfection in every realm of life.

Perfection for Sale: Minds, Bodies, Selves, and Souls

Besieged by self-doubt and willing to accept nothing less than the best, Americans respond to the market for perfection with characteristic enthusiasm. The hucksters who meddle into our lives find a fertile field: Promises relating to minds, bodies, selves, and souls are pitched from all sides, and we empty our pockets as we rush to buy the latest. In the case of bodies, the pitch resembles a national stampede. Convinced by the drumbeat of gloom about the deteriorating state of the nation's fitness, Americans have hurried to join fitness centers with such names as Body Works™, Fitness Revolution™, Absolute Aerobics™, Contours™, Figure Firm™, Jazzercise™, and Physical Edge™. Even death itself is no longer an impediment to fitness; on the contrary, it can be evoked as a marketing inducement to make the postmodern consumer even more determined to achieve bodily perfection. On the Web page of Summum, an organization that offers modern mummification as an alternative to burial, there is a lengthy sales pitch designed to appeal to those who have spent their lives pursuing fitness:

> Unlike the mummification techniques used by ancient Egyptians, which left the dead shriveled, discolored, and ugly, Summum's method is designed to keep you looking healthy and robust for millennia. The appeal may be to anyone who has labored to stay in shape. Why spend thousands of dollars in health club fees while you're alive, then let everything go to pot just because you've died?" (quoted in Newman, 1997: 67)

The idea that a person's body is not simply a biological given but something that can be transformed into a social ideal is not new. As Foucault points out, this notion came about during the seventeenth and eighteenth centuries as a military imperative when armies discovered that instead of looking to recruit certain kinds of body types, they could create one by forcing on soldiers a particular regimen. "Over the intervening centuries," however, more and more people—from shop clerks to executive trainees to television newscasters—found themselves called upon to alter their bodies for the sake of their social status or their careers. Now, late in the 20th century, millions of civilians of both sexes voluntarily subject themselves to the rigors of physical discipline" (Glassner, 1988: 199). Once marketers had established the ethic that almost anyone could meet the social standards of fitness given the proper regime of diet, exercise, and right living, all they had to do was sell the game to a ready public who not only purchased the manifold products of fitness but also imposed them on others. Diet and fitness programs, wellness centers, and workout "clinics" all became a familiar part of the scene, and participation in them was not always voluntary. Businesses that had purchased wellness because it was "good for the bottom line" (in terms of lower health insurance premiums and greater productivity) quickly made them mandatory parts of the company routine. Thus, as soon as health was cut loose from disease-based definitions of science and medicine, it became a commodity—and like all commodities, it was available in the marketplace for a price. The pursuit of perfection in every sphere became a national pastime. Troubles were everywhere, but so were answers. This index to a catalog of available videos from Fanlight Productions in Boston suggests that a vast array of scientific answers were available for the asking:

Adolescent troubles
Aging and sexuality
Aging and gerontology
AIDS: caregivers
AIDS: clinical issues
Brain disorders
Chronic illness
Death and dying
Depression and manic depression
Eating disorders
Elder abuse
Epilepsy
Genetics
Grief and recovery

Long-term care
Nursing
Psychiatry and mental health
Waste management
Women's health
Alzheimer's

In most cases, the scenarios follow those we have already discussed. As Hillel Schwartz has observed:

> [T]he plot is remarkably standard across most cultures: anguish and false hope, climatic fevers and false dawns, then recovery. For life-threatening illnesses, the plot and the pathos are even more pronounced: first symptoms, evanescent but disturbing, irregular, then persistent pain or fatigue and a desperate search for a diagnosis; treatments, themselves often a torment; the crisis, in which one hallucinates and arrives at a new vision of life, or in which one becomes reconciled to some awful truth; convalescence, frequently underscored by religious conversion. Or, if no convalescence, then a well-sung diminuendo and death. (Schwartz, 1996: C-3)

Not everyone, of course, jumped on the bandwagon, but the refusal of those who didn't merely redoubled the efforts of those who did to stigmatize and harass them. Some, such as Florence King, were passed off as cranks:

> [T]hose who have lost their characters have nothing left but their bodies to make them feel like good people. Intense, obsessive interest in health, nutrition, and exercise arouses my suspicions. I distrust anybody who worries too much about such things. I take my leaf from Seneca: "Scorn pain. Either it will go away or you will." (quoted in Winokur, 1992: 209)

But there were not many who failed to get the message and follow the trail to perfection. Indeed, by the time this explosion had occurred, experts were firmly in charge of the culture, and most had lost their sense of perspective, as Morris Chafetz suggests:

> Despite all our research, all our knowledge, and all our technology, life and death are still a gamble. Some people will do everything right and die young; Adele Davis, the first proponent of "miracle foods," died of cancer in her fifties; Robert Rodale, founder of the health-oriented Rodale Press and of the popular bible of the wellness movement, *Prevention* magazine, died of heart disease at sixty. Yet Winston Churchill, an obese, cigar-smoking harddrinking, meat-eating workaholic, lived to age ninety-one with his faculties and his physical stamina intact. (Chafetz, 1996: 21)

Such sage advice was largely lost on the hordes of yearning Americans responding to the call of the marketers, as they continued their quest for perfection.

The Selling of Dependency on Experts

Selling the meddling impulse depends on convincing people that a class of experts exists who possess special knowledge that ordinary people do not have. That is not difficult to do given the basic justificatory framework that professional meddlers have successfully established, as discussed in previous chapters. Indeed, now that the ideology that undergirds meddling has been firmly incorporated, the impulse enjoys free reign. Consider, for example, the advertisement reprinted in Box 6.3 for a traveling series of workshops called "The Health Show."®

What this workshop program banks on is the assumption that experts must be consulted because there is simply too much to know. And knowledge that every woman must possess centers on common fears such as aging, cancer, obesity, menopause, and osteoporosis. The program has legitimacy because it is run by the nation's "top doctors, researchers, and health experts." It is current. It is *free*. It is, moreover, fun. Promotional come-ons lend the entire enterprise a carnival atmosphere. In addition to the aforementioned promises of better living through knowledge, one can win cash, free vacations, and the like. The pitch has all the trappings of a traveling road show of nostrums offered by the nineteenth-century snake-oil salesman—but with a difference. These people can hardly be called charlatans; they are *experts* on health and living who will share their knowledge. Their credentials immunize them from the charge of scamming. Readers are left wondering how they would feel if they nearly died from one of the terrible scourges of our time not knowing that help was just a workshop away.

Such ads are invariably cast in similar ways. A program to stop smoking and lose weight is accompanied by "hypnosis therapy"—offered, of course, by a licensed psychologist. Because the professionals behind these ads are now certified experts and not merely hucksters, because they wrap themselves in the legitimacy afforded by the medical model of life, and because they have our trust, they are free to work outside many of the usual restraints of the marketplace. Questions of truth in advertising can be skirted by means of professional opinions. And if many professionals are following the same pattern, it can be regarded as "ordinary practice." Indeed, the foregoing seems to explain how the public was sucked in by thousands of physicians who prescribed the weight-loss magic bullet "Fen-Phen," which, at least for some, proved to have disastrous consequences.

BOX 6.3
Advertisement for a Traveling Series of Workshops

What Women MUST Know About . . .

- Sex, love and intimacy
- Anti-aging miracles
- Cancer prevention
- Weight-loss breakthroughs
- Menopause and osteoporosis
- Mind–body connection
- And MORE!

Attend America's Greatest 3–Day Health Conference FREE!

THE HEALTH SHOW®

- Over 70 of today's top doctors, researchers, and health experts!
- More than 150 exciting exhibits!
- Over 100 in-depth workshops!
- A spirited debate on the healthiest diet
- Panel discussions with top experts on sex . . . anti-aging strategies . . . alternative medicine, and much more!
- Win up to $15,000 in cash, **FREE** vacations, and valuable merchandise!
- And much more!

The Packaging and Distribution of the Therapeutic

The marketing of products and services has been called the "genius of American society." If that is so, then the genius of most recent incarnation is the expansion of this technology to the mental health and social services industries. If the new climate of mass marketing could create a profit explosion in the previously staid and reticent professions of law and medicine, imagine what it could do for the newer therapeutics of human behavior offered by the ideologies of social science. Consider the advertisement reprinted in Box 6.4 for psychological counseling.

Typical of the genre, this ad casts a broad net that has the possibly of catching most everyone. The question is no longer who is sick but, rather, who might conceivably be well, given this inclusive definition of things.[6] Since medical screenings typically find what the screeners are looking for, especially in the arena of behavioral and mental disorders, the mar-

---

BOX 6.4
Advertisement for Psychological Counseling

Do You Have Mood Swings?

You may have Manic Depressive (Bipolar) tendencies

Have you experienced:	**Do you currently have:**
periods of feeling unusually high	feelings of hopelessness
too much energy	decreased energy
little need for sleep	poor concentration
talking more than usual	a change in sleeping habits
racing thoughts	a change in eating habits
spending sprees	decreased interest in things
excessive irritability	crying spells

Call 214-371-6026 for a Free Screening

Advertisement from the Dallas Morning News

---

ketplace is rich with possibilities.[7] Add to that the institutionalization of the languages of deficit and deficiency and we have a cornucopia of commercial services offered by meddlers with a therapeutic program. Says Bernard Zilbergeld, "It is a basic tenet of therapeutic ideology that people are not okay as they are; that's why they need therapy" (1983: 89). He goes on to describe a four-step process employed by the therapeutic culture:

- Continue the psychologization of life.
- Make problems out of difficulties and spread the alarm.
- Make it acceptable to have a problem and to be unable to handle it.
- Offer salvation.

"The truth," Zilbergeld concludes, "is that mental health researchers and clinicians see problems and not strengths because that is what they are trained to see and because it is in their interest to do so. The more pathology, the greater the need for more studies, more therapists, and more therapy" (Zilbergeld, 1983: 19; quoted in Sykes, 1992: 39).

No one has captured the basis of the marketing genius of the mental health industry better than Charles Sykes, who observes the symbolic transformation characteristic of this meddling trade: "Practitioners have been zealous in crafting new maladies from the raw material of daily life. Fears become phobias, concerns become complexes, anxieties become compulsions. Smoking can be transmuted into 'Tobacco Use Disorder,' shyness into 'Social Phobia,' and lousy grades into 'Academic Achievement Disorder'" (Sykes, 1992: 39). Once behavior is recast in the analogical terminologies of medicine, virtually everything is fair game. If all of life is seen as a disease, then whatever the seller is offering can be billed as "therapy." And once it is packaged in this guise of remedial treatment, it can be bought, sold, and even deducted from one's income taxes.[8] Thus, as Sykes tells us, we have in the therapeutic marketplace "jogging therapy, dance therapy, scream therapy, creative-art therapy, camping therapy, skydiving therapy, thumb therapy ('just gently rub your thumb for diversion from minor pressures and tension'), sailing therapy, guided imagery, . . . and movement therapy" (Sykes, 1992: 40).

Not surprisingly, a rich source of therapeutic marketing can be found in the classified ad section of the magazine *Psychology Today*. Linking ads to articles is a standard marketing strategy used to sell products and services. So, while *Psychology Today* tells us in its articles about the great strides being made in the discovery of new mental illnesses and psychological disorders, on the back page we find helpful advertisements to cure the very same problems. Under the heading "Better Health" we find ads for penile enlargement techniques, dizziness ("Doctors can't help! For cure send $20"), and a do-it-yourself remedy for nearsightedness billed as a "Radical New Breakthrough." Under the heading "Books" we find *A Revolutionary View of Mental Illness, Poems of Depression and Recovery,* and *The Angel Files* (this last is a monthly publication all about angels: "sightings, encounters, letters, collectibles, and more"). Personal counselors also find an outlet for their wares: "Relationship problems? Anxious? Depressed? Call 'Therapy Line,' professional counseling by telephone. Credit cards accepted." Instant results are even guaranteed: "Eliminate fear, shyness, heartbreak, anxiety in one telephone session— guaranteed. Visa/Mastercard." The 1960s guru Arthur Janov, propagator of "scream therapy," has moved on to organize a "Therapy Growth Center," which he advertises in the same pages: "Primal therapy, under Dr. Arthur Janov's personal supervision, with clinical scientific controls as outlined in *Why You Get Sick, How You Get Well.* Available only at Dr. Janov's Therapy Growth Center."

Even the "winter blues," it turns out, can be translated into a disease. Now called "seasonal affective disorder," this condition yields to a surprising solution, as evidenced by the advertisement reprinted in Box 6.5. (The text of this ad wraps around a picture of a light bulb in a bottle).

BOX 6.5
Advertisement for "Winter Blues" Cure

Chase those
dark and gloomy
days of
winter
away ......

With
Ott-Lites®
Natural Light Supplment

If you could bottle the vibrant
feelings you get on a sunny
spring day, you'd never leave
home without it.

Ott-Lites® bring you the
closest thing to natural
daylight, indoors . . . all year
long!

Nature's Perfect Light.

Great for everywhere in your
home or office, and ideal for
reading, too. Available in
tubes, bulbs, desk and floor
lamps.

Marketing Self-Help

The trend toward self-help, discussed in Chapter 3, constituted a recognition that everyone's life was capable of change—that no matter how disordered, one could take charge of it at least enough to seek out both services and helpers on one's own. Formal sources of helping made possible by the rise of the meddling professions thus spawned an entire industry of informal self-helpers who used techniques drawn from the professionals to run programs that they marketed and merchandised through the means we discussed earlier. This phenomenon is the result of a process we might call the AA-ing of America, otherwise known as the "recovery movement"—a movement that is now estimated to have more Americans recovering from something than there are actual Americans (since many people are recovering from more than one thing at a time). It would seem that the helping professions have constructed so many ailments for which Americans now *need* help that they are now overwhelmed to the point where they need a wide variety of assistant helpers to care for the overflow. The efforts to deploy such assistance have been vastly successful. Drawing on the technologies of a new area of research called "social marketing" (Fine, 1990; Goldberg et al., 1997), the helping professions rapidly expanded their domain.[9] As Marvin Berkowitz notes in a textbook on social marketing:

> The marketing of a social organization consists of both social (idea) marketing and the marketing of services. The prospective joiner of an organization intends not only to purchase the services offered by the group, but also to "buy" the idea itself that the group has value and is an acceptable entity with which to become associated. Even if the main product offering is a leisure time service, it is by and large an *ideational* product that is being sought. Moreover, the nature of the research to be conducted is quite the same for services and ideas. The same demographic and psychographic data need to be gathered for strategic planning purposes. (quoted in Fine, 1990: 215; emphasis added)

The "ideational" product had already been created by professional meddlers who had assembled a language and a vocabulary much more likely to encumber the self than to liberate it. In this connection, Kenneth Gergen (1991) asks us to consider the following labels:

low self-Esteem
authoritarian
externally controlled
repressed
depressed
burn-out (now fashionably called "compassion fatigue")
schizoid
stressed
paranoid
obsessive-compulsive
bulimic
sadomasochistic
midlife crisis
identity crisis
anxious
antisocial personality
anorexic
seasonal affective disorder
kleptomaniac
self-alienated
homophobic
post-traumatic stress syndrome
voyeuristic

These are all common terms used by mental health professionals, as well as by members of the population at large, to make sense of people. Two features of this list stand out. First, most of these terms have come into common usage only within the present century—and several of these, only within the past couple of decades. Second, they are all terms of deficit.[10] They serve to discredit the individual in one way or another, drawing attention to shortcomings, problems, or incapacities (Gergen, 1991). To put it another way, the vocabulary of human deficit has undergone enormous expansion within the present century, whereas the vocabulary of human praise has not. We now have countless ways of locating deficiencies in ourselves and others that were simply not available to previous generations. Self-help is typically packaged by homing in on these deficiencies and using the common languages of deficit and therapeutic relief in order to sell a service, product, or ideology. The culture may not lavish praise on citizens in general, but meddlers most definitely do.

At a recent conference in New Orleans, the authors took a quick look at the Yellow Pages under "Marriage, Family, Child, and Individual Counselors" and found no fewer than 125 such persons and organizations with their shingles out, offering to give help. Masters and Johnson, for example, market a "relational therapy program" that advertises help for

marital/premarital counseling
gender confusion
sexual therapy
adolescent trauma
eating disorders
sexual compulsion
separation and divorce counseling
homosexual dissatisfaction

This program is offered in an upscale area of New Orleans near the river district, has a director and two co-directors, and provides short-term treatments as well as complete diagnostic and evaluation clinical services. It also takes major credit cards. A quick perusal of the phone book for any large city would show a similar collection of professional helpers with an expansive list of problems, concerns, and difficulties for which they offer help.

These groups create a market for their services in large part by creating languages of deficit. And because the "deficit industry" needs raw material to stay in business, it is unlikely to deal with clients in anything other than sympathetic ways—a practice that often encourages excuse-mongering and victimage of the sort we have already discussed. One gets, for one's money, a ready-made series of excuses and justifications (Scott and Lyman, 1968) with which to account for the problems in one's life. Indeed, it is becoming characteristic of this society that no one is to blame for anything anymore—and the talk of the for-fee helpers is one reason why.

Self-help groups encourage the same kind of instant intimacy and openness that television does, and their members quickly get into the spirit of the kind of talk that is required there. It is testifying talk, victim-overcoming talk, transcendent talk, workshopping talk. Indeed, the talk at self-help groups follows a format as predictable as a church liturgy, proceeding from a statement of need (powerlessness over something, such as alcohol, food, drugs, sex, shopping, gambling, religion) to vows of group allegiance. Moreover, in the world of self-help groups, sickness and problems become stable sources of identity, creating pseudo-communities for their members, each with a permanent quality about it that people can depend on in a world falling around them. The "diseases" these groups treat tend to be conceived as chronic ones. Alcoholism is said to be a disease people have for life. Victims of child molestation, it is said, will never fully recover. The members of these groups are thus always in "recovery" or "remission." They are "Ex-er's," bound together by their having been one thing at one time in their lives and now thoroughly committing themselves to being something else. At their best, self-help groups save lives by offering social support to redirect members away from self-destructive habits. At their worst, they are meddling intrusions and trendy clichés that build a consumer culture around drugs, disease, deficits, and infirmities. They offer new selves with which people can identify. They speak clearly to a fundamental dilemma of the postmodern condition: We can't identify with our jobs because we might lose them. We can't identify with families because they are divorced and scattered to the winds and are the problem in any case. We can't identify with community because that seems long gone. So we identify with problems and sicknesses, and the gurus, books, workshops, and tapes that promote them.[11] The situation is, in many ways, the antithesis of self-help. And because openness is a rule enforced by group sanctions, one can never tell for sure whether it is the kind of honest candor you get from a good friend or simply a required facade necessary to be accepted and engaged in for the good of the order. Indeed, the spirit of openness also appeals to the meddling impulse, which allays its own boredom by asking others to spread their troubles out for all to see; but one really does have to wonder how much of it is manufactured for the sake of the collective ecstasies of the moment.

Because the kind of talk that characterizes the groups involved in the self-help movement has not confined itself to those groups alone, help talk is now also a virtually distinct media form. *Geraldo, Sally Jesse, Oprah*—one cannot turn on a television set or a radio without being besieged by the language of self-help. The informal intimacy of these media has led to an eruption of electronic help talk. Radio and television talk shows blanket the airwaves with advice and counsel on myriad troubles. CNBC, for example, carries a late-night sex-advice program entitled *Real Personal* that features sex therapists and other experts, moderated by a an earnest and candid host who interviews people about their sexual interests and difficulties. But the guests seem more like carnival freaks than recipients of real advice for real people. Amid the transsexuals, necrophiles, and toe-licking fetishists, the viewer is left to wonder where the show finds these people. But each case is discussed with a weighty seriousness that converts it into a generalized problem facing the country.[12]

In their usual oblique way, psychiatrists and other members of the meddling trades talk about talk as "therapy," as though that were what it was basically about. Talk may be helpful or unhelpful, high quality or low, relevant or tangential, but we would have difficulty seeing it as "therapeutic" without vastly expanding the domain of the word. It is, after, all, just talk. But expanding the domain is what the marketing efforts of meddlers is about; and since talk is the most basic thing we as human beings have to offer each other, it is somewhat sad, but not surprising, that as we have become more distant from one another, we reach out to those who meddle into our lives in the interests of selling talk.

Although it is not the purpose of this chapter—or this book—to construct a formal analysis of self-help movements, it is worth noting that the self-help tradition that these organizations represent as well as the flood of books they market have always been more authoritarian and conformist than personal and autonomous. For although the notion of "self" help would seem to imply a certain kind of independent self-reliance (taking responsibility for one's own actions and destiny, etc.), such organizations in fact rely on a mystique of expertise and encourage people to look outside themselves for standardized instructions on how to live. Watching the we/we orientation of self-help groups, one quickly realizes that self-help is usually a euphemism for "how-to" programs in identity formation. Indeed, as Wendy Kaminer has pointed out, these books are now famous for their mindless circularity:

The books [that such programs] inspire and are inspired by have a fatuousness about them that is funny because its sounds almost satirical. For example, in *Addicted to Misery*, Robert Becker says that "the first step in overcoming misery is to identify "miserable thoughts." . . . In the best-selling *Secrets*

About Men Every Woman Should Know, author Beverly DeAngelis clears up the mystery of why men don't like to talk and have sex at the same time. The answer, she says, is that "men have a more difficult time expressing themselves and simultaneously performing a task than women do. (quoted in Kaminer, 1992: 88)

In this sense, self-help is akin to the step-by-step "how-to" craft kits and magazines that say, in essence, "because we know you aren't creative, we're here to help you—just follow the directions and the pattern provided and you too can make lovely decorations for home and family." Self-help gurus are, in this vein, the Martha Stewarts of personal transformation.

Informal Help Talk

What is the antidote to the hucksters who market the meddling trades? In sharp contrast to formalized psychiatry, psychology, and the organized self-help movements that catch their overflow is what we might call informal help talk. This is the sort of talk that tends to deal with a category Erving Goffman (1975) has termed "ordinary troubles." These are difficulties that people have in framing the ambiguities of life. Informal talk helps us frame them in ways that are useful and encouraging, and that do not lead to formal labels or hold one up to media ridicule (Edelman, 1984). "Ordinary troubles," then, are an expression of the fact that we act more out of doubt than out of certainty—and they tie and bond us together. Their venues range from the office water-cooler to the "third places" of pure sociability discussed by Ray Oldenburg (1989). Their form and content are both highly informal. They make no demands—not even the demand that one accept the suggestion of the giver. They usually arise voluntarily and take such forms as "Have you considered . . . ?" and "Have you thought of . . . ?" and "I know a person who. . . . "

Goffman refers collectively to these expressions as "autobiographical address" in which an assertion, request, or piece of advice is prefaced by a self-reference such as "In my opinion," "Since you asked," and "In my experience." He notes that "what follows the self-referential connective is to be placed in parentheses, a voice slightly different from the one the speaker had been using, one which presumably allows the speaker and his listeners to align themselves together over and against the figure to whom the remarks are to be attributed" (Goffman, 1975: 531). In other words, one can offer help with another person's problems without conceding even conversationally that one is talking about the person to whom help is being offered—thus not only protecting the self of the person being helped but also immunizing the helper from the nascent charge of meddling.

Such forms of talk and the moments that constitute them have many advantages over professional, self-help, or media help talk. Some of these advantages are listed below:

- It is free.
- It is spontaneous.
- It can be disregarded with no reprisals.
- It is often genuine and stems from experience or at least from observation.
- It bonds the talkers.
- It usually takes place in a relaxed atmosphere.
- It seldom deals in stigmatizing labels.
- Because it doesn't depend on your business for its livelihood, it can "kick us in the butt" when needed.
- It constitutes subordination without victimhood. In other words, we are leveled in help talk because so much of it is reciprocal. That is, much of it consists of our telling others about our problems while trying to help them with theirs.

Note that each of these advantages of help talk offsets a disadvantage of professional help talk that tends to be expensive, based on theory rather than experience, constrained by professional ethics such that it is less likely to be open, and objective as opposed to rooted in the experience of the helper. Finally, the act of going for professional help may lead to stigmatizing labels[13]—no small matter in an "identity society" (Glasser, 1972) where publicly established identities may find a life of their own.

Finally, we may summarize the usefulness of help talk by giving a short list of those things it accomplishes for both the helper and the person being helped alike. (1) Help talk provides comfort. (Such phrases as "It'll be OK" and "It could happen to anyone" give comfort and solace in a world that is often devoid of both.) (2) Help talk provides for emotional check-offs. (When people respond to our problems by saying "You're not crazy," "It's perfectly normal to feel that way," or "When I went through that I was even worse," they place our feelings in a normalized context that answers feelings with feelings as opposed to facts. In the deficit society, where shortcomings are an industry, such talk gives reassurances that what we are going through is to be expected.) (3) Help talk forges social bonds. (Phrases like "You're not the only one" and "The same thing happened to me" help overcome the loneliness we frequently feel when caught up in a problem.) (4) Help talk provides acceptable solutions. (If what we call "mental illness" is really an unacceptable means of solving problems in living (Szasz, 1961), then informal help talk helps us understand the range of acceptable alternatives available to us. When someone says, "If that happened to me, I'd . . ." we see a way of handling a problem that is personalized, endorsed by someone else, and has, at least ostensibly, the imprimatur of practical personal experience.

So there does indeed exist an alternative to the meddling interventions of the marketers of the meddling trades. It is this intrinsically social nature of talk in general—a process that, in *Frame Analysis*, Erving Goffman has summarized in the following way:

> What the individual spends most of his spoken moments doing is providing evidence for the fairness or unfairness of his current situation and other grounds for sympathy, approval, exoneration, understanding, or amusement. And what his listeners are obliged to do is to show some kind of audience appreciation. (Goffman, 1975: 503)

The fact that such appreciation is sometimes for sale is not to say that it always is. The complaint that Americans don't care about each other anymore, now heard from many quarters, may be countered by the very existence of such talk. And although it is said that we are increasingly callous to the plight of our fellow human beings, hardened to other people's problems and difficulties, self-centered and myopic in our views of the world, the occasions we have pointed to belie that charge and offer an antithesis to all those instances of formal marketing of the meddling trades. Whereas meddling is often destructive to the social bond, these kinds of relationships cement it.

Notes

1. Jean-Paul Baudrillard, in his typically blunt and provocative way, says that the age of hidden persuasion is over: "[T]hose who govern us now resort unapologetically to arm-twisting pure and simple" (1990: 73). Powered by shamelessness and lust, by a strategic logic of violation and anxiety, advertising is like the postmodern suitor who seduces a woman "with the words, 'I am interested in your cunt'" (1990: 73).

2. A letter arrived at one of our homes a few weeks ago with the following message stamped across the front in bold letters: "IT'S NOT YOUR FAULT." We opened it to discover that the writer knew we were overweight, struggling with fat, and, furthermore, that medical science had discovered that this wasn't our fault. For $29.95 we could, of course, receive a miracle weight-loss product that would speed up our metabolism and "melt" the fat off.

3. *Nonprofit* means, of course, that no matter how much money the industry takes in, or how many people it supports with salaries ranging from janitorial to professional, it does not have to pay either stockholders or the IRS.

4. Segmentation is the basic principle of marketing. It entails dividing people into segments and categories; distinguishing them from one another along demographic, racial, ethnic, gender, or lifestyle lines; and then promoting products that

stress these differences. Segmented markets create segmented people. For further elaboration of this point, see Featherstone et al. (1991).

5. Drugs are a prime example. Hailed as a medical miracle, heroin was initially synthesized as a cure for morphine addiction. Later demonized as an illness—the "ultimate pharmacological heresy," as Szasz puts it—heroin addiction was treated by a new drug, methadone. Now, of course, there are methadone addicts on the streets being treated for *their* illness. For a discussion of this curious cycle, see Szasz (1985).

6. Comedian Jackie Mason says that it is no longer a question of being well but of finding a disease you can live with.

7. Even when dealing with organic disorders about which there is wide medical agreement, studies have repeatedly shown that physicians tend to find what they are looking for. Thomas Scheff calls this tendency a "medical decision-rule." For a review of these studies as well as an enlightening discussion of their implications, see Friedson (1970: 255–261).

8. Home spas, trips to nude beaches, visits to sex clinics where clients are taught to masturbate (a therapy for women who have difficulty reaching orgasm), and even the services of "sex surrogates" (a.k.a. prostitutes) have been certified as tax deductible.

9. According to Marvin Berkowitz, self-help groups in the United States date back to colonial days. By the latter part of the nineteenth century they were concerned with mobilizing resources to address such social problems as homeless children, the poor, the mentally ill, and the like. In the early 1900s, a variety of neighborhood- and community-based movements, such as settlement houses, provided social services and led to the development of social work as a formal profession. The National Association for the Advancement of Colored People was established in 1909, and in the 1920s the union movement set off a chain of events that culminated in the formation of various voluntary-action groups aimed at dealing with such problems as those of minorities, the aged, blind, welfare mothers, and so on. It is worth noting, however, that these groups were aimed at dealing with special populations. None of them were specifically mobilized for the purpose of dealing with individuals. That was to come later. For an account of these developments, see Berkowitz (1990: 217).

10. It comes as no surprise, perhaps, to find that marketers have traded on the spoils of this "deficit industry," which converts life and its difficulties into problems and their solutions. This industry ranges from formal psychiatric services and a wide variety of clinical and social services to self-help groups and their minions.

11. "A more sobering thought about self-help books," Wendy Kaminer suggests, "is that millions of people do seem to take them seriously. . . . [B]umper-sticker books such as Robert Fulghum's *All I Really Needed to Know I Learned in Kindergarten* turn existential questions into packaged clichés. After all, only people who die very young really learn all they need to know in kindergarten" (Kaminer, 1992: 44).

12. A recent show featured a thirty-minute discussion about men who carry the terrible burden of maintaining an erection longer than their partner wants them to. They suffer, the guest therapist said somberly, from "post-mature

orgasms"—an identifiable disease that is wrecking the lives of thousands of men everywhere.

13. The proposition that formal help often comes at an enormous price is now well established and documented. This form of helping places one's self and one's problems in a political context with enormous implications of power, control, and their stigmatizing potential. One of the best discussions of the consequences of such professionalized talk is to be found in the work of Murray Edelman (1984).

7

Meddling and the Social Bond

[J]ustice is to perform one's own task and not to meddle with that of others.
—**Plato**

The observations we have made in this book pose inevitable questions about the proper relationship between the individual and others. When should people meddle, and when should they not? What is the difference between good meddling and bad? What should one do to cope with the increasing onslaught of meddlers? How should one moderate these tendencies in oneself? The rights revolution has answered these questions in one way; we believe they are more appropriately answered in another. In this chapter we examine the idea of meddling in a more philosophical context. Our primary emphasis is on the status of meddling with respect to individual liberty and social control. In the end, our effort to propose a less meddlesome, but also more civil, society yields a more congenial view of social constraint.

Proper Distinctions

The seeming inability of many Americans—some in positions of authority—to make subtle distinctions among the plethora of problems facing our society is one of several hallmarks of the meddler. Are smoking and drinking really on a par with child molestation? To hear the discourse of those who meddle in the name of a smoke-free continent, one would think so. Is the lack of proper nutrition really the worst problem facing the republic? Such a sweeping generalization has been asserted. Are drugs really destroying the moral fiber of our nation? In the midst of this language of crisis and doom so frequently resorted to by meddlers, it is important to remember what is problematic about meddling in the first place. In the absence of a measured understanding of when meddling is appropriate and when it is not, meddling often degenerates into a resentment-producing exercise in interference in which the meddlee is neither uplifted nor chastened. Meddling, regardless of the guise in which it is posed, casts doubt on the competence and autonomy of the person with whom one is meddling. This is why even meddlers themselves preface their interventions with a series of disclaimers: "I don't mean to pry, . . . " "It may be none of my business, . . . " "I was just wondering if. . . . " Even the most flagrant meddlers seem to sense that they are on thin ice. There is also the aftermath problem. In cases where great care is not exercised, the consequences of meddling may prove to be the opposite of those claimed by the meddler, a point made nicely by Richard Klein in discussing the multitude of suggestions that people should diet and lose weight: "[D]iets don't work. Even if your fat is unhealthy, which is far from being sure, trying to lose it will increase it in the long run [95 percent of those who lose weight put it all back and more] and may well do harm, in the meantime, to body and spirit" (Klein: 1996, 107). So when we urge a friend to "lose weight," just what are we urging?

The inability to make distinctions is characteristic of meddlers and the societies that tolerate and encourage them. The pipe smoker who engages in the altogether temperate practice of enjoying two pipefuls a day—one in the morning after breakfast and one in the evening after dinner—is lumped together for the sake of public policy and interpersonal harassment in the same category as a three-pack-a-day cigarette addict: They are both "smokers." The neighbor who occasionally has one drink too many is blithely labeled an "alcoholic" by those who neither know him nor actually care. The child whose parents yell at him from time to time is too quickly assumed to be "emotionally abused." The terms fall all too easily from our lips. No one is immune from the intimidating languages of pathology. So what, then, do we make of everyday life? Is it just, as Freud claimed, a parade of illnesses? To listen to the media or read the spate of books that roll into stores daily, one would think so. But a sense of perspective immediately suggests that most of everyday life still revolves around commitments that transcend legal sources of compliance and common values such as trust and tolerance, responsibility, the giving and keeping of promises, spirituality, integrity, and authenticity. These mundane notions are not nearly as interesting as the topics discussed on *Oprah* or *Cross-Fire* (or so we think), but they constitute the ordinary lives of most Americans.

Proper distinctions and a sense of perspective may be difficult, but they are not impossible to develop. More traditional cultures, such as some native American ones, are renowned for their wisdom about when to meddle and when to leave well enough alone. But one thing seems clear: Attaining these skills is made more difficult by the living of anonymous lives. The crucial questions to be asked include Do I know and have a relationship with these people whereby meddling into their lives either is appropriate or will be understood? Is the issue I am meddling about really that important? Will it be taken well or not? Does it really matter that much? Am I right? Much contemporary meddling dissolves into exercises in futility when subjected to such questions. When we view meddling in this light, meddlers seem particularly arrogant and elitist. They know; you do not. Knowing when to meddle and when not to is, of course, not the kind of question that can be reduced to a formula—every situation is different and requires a slightly different response. Yet the art of knowing, tolerating, and treating the other with a sense of respect goes a long way toward developing these skills in a culture that is increasingly insensitive to such things. One thing is clear. We are unlikely to develop these skills within a hermetic seal containing others who are just like us—who share every prejudice and are never challenged by the good-natured response of friends and neighbors who are more like us than a narrow obsession with individualism would suggest. If it is becoming characteristic of Americans that no one really knows anybody anymore, meddling is surely one of the outcomes of this world of strangers. Of the many concerns being voiced about the rapidly developing virtual world of on-line communication, its capacity for allowing us to talk only with people whose ideas we already agree about is certainly one of the worst. Friends do not have to agree in order to respect and care for one another. But strangers seem to need this unanimity in order to establish a bond of trust.

Individual Liberty and Social Constraint

The pendulum swings that constitute the political reaction to the issues we have discussed in this book are suggestive of Americans' ongoing confusion over central issues of individual liberty and social constraint. Born in a climate of ferocious anti-meddling sentiment, the country has throughout its history hemmed and hawed over the question of the extent to which people are properly free and when they must be constrained by and for the sake of themselves and the commonweal. At times, Americans seem to have completely forgotten their anti-meddling roots. Surveys regularly show that they would reject the freedoms guaranteed in the Bill of Rights if these freedoms were put to a vote. A recent newspaper inquiry, for example, suggests that on the question of free speech Americans would scale back the First Amendment protections we have customarily enjoyed (*Chicago Tribune*, July 4, 1997). Of the more than 1,000 adults surveyed, almost half said that they favored more government restrictions of speech on the Internet. More than half said that radio personalities like Howard Stern should not be allowed to use sexual expressions or innuendo over the airwaves. And about one-quarter would not allow abortion supporters or opponents to march in communities like theirs. As new technologies have made it easier to meddle, the impulse to do so has become stronger. Moreover, as the postmodern privatization of the public proceeds apace, more and more people, fearful of the impact of images and behavior that they regard as threatening to their way of life, have called for more and more social restraints. Politicians have dutifully responded with increasingly strident forms of legal meddling, censorship, and calls for bans.[1] Whole industries have developed around the institution of law and its increasing use as a vehicle for solving human problems—often with suffocating consequences (Howard, 1994).

It is becoming sadly obvious, however, that the security of the individual cannot be accomplished merely with more legal restraint; and when a society expends huge amounts of moral energy fighting a matter like smoking at the expense of all the other problems that beset us, it becomes even more obvious that something else is going on. The recent tobacco settlement that state attorneys general struck with the cigarette companies is instructive with respect to the relationship between individual liberty and a meddling government. To listen to the attorneys general— who eagerly exploited the media attention focused on this subject to degrade and humiliate tobacco executives—one would conclude that of all the problems facing America smoking is the worst. As the society has become increasingly "indoor" (Goffman, 1959) and postwar baby boomers have focused more and more attention on health and fitness, smoking has become, as President Clinton discovered, an exploitable political issue. Indeed, his arguments for meddling into the personal choices of millions of Americans have come to be clothed in the increasingly popular "for the sake of the children" claim. But the contradictions in this conspicuously paternalistic form of government meddling are clear. As Mona Charen points out:

> If we were seriously looking to punish manufacturers of a product that kills teen-agers, we'd be locking up the guys in Detroit. Every year, 5,000 teen-agers are killed in car accidents. How many die from smoking? None. Arguably, alcohol does as much or more damage to children and teen-agers as cigarettes. Why not sue Seagrams? (Charen, 1997: 4)

Seagrams may not, indeed, be far behind. But the view of the relationship between the individual and the state acted on in the smoking controversy presages the even greater expansion of a meddling government, spurred on by an increasingly meddling constituency. When governments act to protect people from themselves, they do so for their own imperial reasons, but they are inevitably erratic and inconsistent about their targets. For example, a study published in the prestigious *New England Journal of Medicine* indicates that driving while using cellular phones leads to about the same excessive rate of deaths as drunken driving. But while studies in the same journal have been part of the governmental rationale for attacking smoking and other consumptive practices, as well as a tool of social movements that put pressure on regulatory bodies to do so, we are unlikely to see an outbreak of groups such as "Mothers Against Cellular Phones"—a point effectively driven home by a recent letter to the editor of a Southwest newspaper:

> The *New England Journal of Medicine* says our nation has a new contender for the most preventable cause of death in America: the cellular telephone. According to this report, those with telephones in their cars are four times more likely to suffer an accident. Isn't it time we recognize this despicable form of unnecessary behavior for what it is? Isn't it time we demand that those with car phones pay higher insurance premiums, both on their lives and on their automobiles? Isn't it time for those of us who may become second-hand victims of this insensitive behavior to stand up for our rights? Isn't it time the MADD mothers redirect their attention toward those who would willingly do us harm, not in a state of drunkenness but in sobriety? Isn't it time our attorney general filed suit on our behalf against the manufactures of these delivery systems of death? Isn't it time we build more prisons so we can remove these irresponsible people from our midst? After all, we should all have the right to live forever as long as we abide by the virtues of the righteous. (Cawthon, 1997: 2)

The ostensible absurdity of this argument should not put us off its point, for meddling intrusions that would have been unthinkable only a few years ago are routine today. For instance, it would have been difficult to imagine, even ten years ago, that the FDA could successfully claim that tobacco, a legal substance that has been used since the nation's beginning, should be regulated as a drug, but it has now happened—and many other substances are not far behind. (As this is being written, a call has already gone out for the government regulation of caffeine because of its alleged baleful effects on the children of America who are drinking large quantities of soda and presumably going berserk as a result.)

Individual liberty and social constraint, like many other issues we have dealt with in this book, are delicate matters that do not yield easily to the drastic remedies and coercive tactics offered by the meddlers. The frequently heard objection that we lack rules and standards is surely not the answer. If it were simply a matter of rules and rule enforcement we'd have reached utopia long ago, for there are enough rules in this society to have regulated into submission every conceivable human conflict. Attorneys and politicians prosper, but does anyone else really gain from the profusion of legal remedies sought, enacted, and imposed on every matter about which someone is distressed? As pointed out earlier, sometimes social constraint is necessary to bring about widely agreed-upon

principles, especially when the gap between what a society professes and
what it achieves is simply too wide. Such was the case in the fight to end
racial discrimination as the law of the land. But the successful tactics
used to end legally ratified forms of racism have served as a poor model
when applied to other matters about which there is considerably less
moral consensus. For those matters we need to invoke not so much a
strategy of legal constraint as the fine art of tolerance and mutual respect.
Americans have become such a condemnatory and accusatory lot, bent
on changing the world (or at least their own small piece of it) to fit their
prejudices about how things ought to be, that it sounds almost quaint to
suggest that we need to rejuvenate the gentle art of "putting up with"
and to increase our tolerance about the lives of others who are not ours to
change. But that is precisely what we need to do.

Paternalism and the Good Society

One answer to the question of the proper relationship between the individual and society is paternalism—the doctrine that individuals, weak
and irresponsible by their very nature, must be constrained in their personal conduct for their own good. Although not all forms of meddling
are paternalistic, a good number of them are. Paternalism derives its
name from the practice of a state or some other institutional or corporate
entity (the "good society"[2]) acting as a parent charged with the responsibility of caring for a child. It suggests a relationship akin to that between
parent and child—and, indeed, even in the literal case of parents and
children, as the latter grow there is always a question of how much
parental authority can (or should) be exercised.[3] Paternalism may be
summed up as doing for another person what that person would do for
himself if he were in a position to make a rational, adult choice (an increasingly difficult business as adults come to make widely differing
choices for themselves).

Even so forceful an opponent of paternalism as John Stuart Mill made
a place for paternalistic interventions that, though meddlesome, were not
only justified but, indeed, required:

> If either a public officer or anyone else saw a person attempting to cross a
> bridge which had been ascertained to be unsafe, and there were no time to
> warn him of his danger, they might seize him and turn him back, without
> any real infringement of his liberty; for liberty consists in doing what one
> desires, and he does not desire to fall into the river. (Mill, 1849/1956: 117)

Like the example of crying "fire!" in a crowded theater as a limit on free
speech, however, Mill's example must be used carefully, for it cannot be

applied to those instances in which a person's desires are in conflict. Of course, no one wants to die of lung cancer. But people may also desire to smoke, and since the outcome of smoking is not nearly so certain as that of falling in a river from a faulty bridge, one cannot apply the Millsian principle in this case.

Donald VanDeVeer, perhaps the most careful student of paternalism currently writing, suggests that paternalistic acts are "those in which one party interferes with another for the sake of the other's own good" (1986: 17). In this way of thinking, the motives of the meddler are of critical importance, for paternalistic interventions are defined in terms of their well-intentioned or benevolent purposes. VanDeVeer suggests several examples:

- motorcyclist helmet laws
- mandatory seatbelt laws
- legal prohibitions against self-medication
- the arrest of drunks to prevent them from being "rolled"
- compulsory participation in systems providing for adequate income on retirement (e.g., Social Security)
- prohibitions against gambling
- compulsory education laws
- legal prohibitions against suicide
- involuntary blood transfusions given to those who oppose them on moral/religious grounds

Although some of these examples might represent literal paternalism insofar as they involve a parent acting in the best interests of a child, all such laws and actions are commonly applied to competent adults.[4] So the term *paternalism* typically refers to someone (increasingly the state) acting *in loco parentis*, even when the object of the intervention is an otherwise competent adult. And although much meddling is paternalistic, meddling need not be paternalistic in order to qualify as meddling. One may meddle not for the benefit of others at all, not *in loco parentis*, but for profit, entertainment, or a variety of other reasons. So, whereas paternalistic interventions necessarily involve meddling, not all meddling is paternalistic.

Paternalism comes in both strong and weak versions (Feinberg, 1989). A paternalistic argument is said to be weak when it restricts the state's meddling into adults' affairs in cases where their actions are shown to be neither fully informed nor fully their own. And a paternalistic argument is said to be strong when it holds that the state can protect persons from the harmful consequences of their actions by forcing them to act or not act in certain ways, even when these actions are fully voluntary and informed.[5] The two are sometimes collapsed into a single strong version when it is claimed (as mental healthists routinely do) that in situations where people are acting in ways that the state and its agents see are clearly not in their own interests, their acts are, *by definition*, not fully voluntary or informed. Such a position recognizes the concept of free will as only an illusion, especially in cases where the terms *addiction* and *illness* are successfully attributed. Any claims of a zone of free will, in which people would choose to run risks that others would not run, are said to be fictions brought about by the claim that no one would act in certain ways if they were fully informed or in their right faculties. According to this psychomedical view of things, then, people are automatons helpless in the face of their addictions, compulsions, and phobias, and regulations against the purveyors of evil substances should be held responsible for addicting these poor victims of their mendaciousness. As suggested in Chapter 3 in the context of healthism, the health paternalist[6] claims that health is the preeminent value outweighing all others, and that there is only one correct way to live one's life and that is by acting in such a way as to maximize one's "health," one's longevity, and one's chances of contracting various illnesses. Health paternalists thus elevate *their* values about *their* lives to the level of universals that should be applied to everyone. Given its status as a moral universal, then, the state is justified in ensuring—and, indeed, can even be said to have an obligation to ensure—that its citizens conform to this rational program of health and fitness, even if they don't want to. As such, health paternalism is "thus a subtle shift away from the rarely contested right of individuals to good health to the right of the State to manipulate and coerce its citizens into conforming to a socially sanctioned definition of health" (Luik, 1993: 305). With the advent of the notion of "mental health," the water has gotten even murkier and various advantages have redounded even more decisively to the meddling paternalist. The fact that the argument is viciously circular seems to make it even more satisfying, the argument being that "no one in his right mind would smoke, so-and-so smokes, therefore he is not in his right mind." By the same token, state-sponsored intervention seemingly becomes even more justifiable.

What both the strong and the weak versions of paternalism hold in common are certain assumptions about the nature of reason, autonomy, and personhood. As articulated by John Luik (1993: 304), these include the following: (1) Autonomy is not the foundational democratic value inasmuch as considerations of happiness and welfare frequently take precedence over it; (2) individuals are frequently irrational in that they (a) often do not understand their interests, and (b) even if they do, they do not know the means best suited for the realization of those interests; and (3) individuals need the state's help in (a) discovering and realizing their "true" interests and (b) avoiding irrational courses of action that entail unhappy consequences. In other words, the state is perfectly justified in protecting competent adults from the harmful consequences of their own actions, just as a parent would be in dealing with a child before he or she has reached the age of majority.

The case of health paternalism is but one of many examples of the difficulties of paternalism in general. At best, meddling in the name of health on the grounds that people do not know their own interests is merely a nuisance; but at worst, it forms a basis for the grossest kinds of interventions into the lives of people who would never dream of being meddled with in the name of mere political or religious ideologies. Lost in the paternalist's argument is a sense of perspective about the relationship between individual liberty and social constraint. Lost, too, is the sense of trade-offs—some Faustian, to be sure—that people routinely make in their daily lives: "Consider an individual who wishes to travel to another town. The person could travel by car or by train. The risk of accident and injury is far less by train but the individual decides to go by car because of the increased convenience. Is the individual irrational?" (Luik, 1993: 306). Life is full of such trade-offs. Should we take the kids on a vacation or save the money and buy a security system for the house? When buying a car should we select the bigger engine, the luxury interior, or the optional passenger-side air bag, which, the salesman tells us, would make driving safer for everyone? Those who meddle in the name of health and safety commit the same mistake as countless others in this single issue–driven society: They look at the whole of life through the lens of just one of its prisms and are appalled by what they see. Clear a path. Call your legislator. Nothing matters but health and safety.

Alan Dershowitz offers a humorous and even more compelling example (quoted in Feinberg, 1986: 376, and cited in Luik, 1993: 307)—that of a heart patient who is confronted with a choice between sexual abstinence for the next ten years or continuing to lead a normal sex life but risking sudden death:

> *My doctor has made a prognosis*
> *That intercourse fosters thrombosis;*
> *But I'd rather expire*
> *Fulfilling desire*
> *Than abstain, and develop neurosis.*

The healthist is forced to argue that the latter alternative is irrational, as is the decision of some women to decline radical mastectomies in favor of less effective procedures that keep their breasts intact. If we do not bow to the received wisdom of the healthists, we are by definition "irrational."

And what about professional athletes who sacrifice their bodies for money and fame? Or artists who sacrifice their health for the frame of mind that they believe alcohol gives them? The list is endless and includes some of the most laudatory and widely respected activities in the panoply of human action and desire. Should we urge our children to find their fame, fortune, and key identities on the fields of athletic competition or to stay indoors where the rewards are less but the risks more acceptable? Certainly in the case of smoking, a thoughtful examination of such trade-offs is precluded by the addiction-mongering of the meddler. As in other matters, he knows what is right, whereas the meddlee does not. If the latter asserts the joys of smoking[7] and says that she is willing to give up an extra five years in a nursing home at the end of her life, she will be deemed in "denial" and become the victim of an "addiction" foisted on her by greedy tobacco companies. An overheard conversation on one of the campuses where we teach went something like this: "Don't you know smoking causes cancer? "That's O.K.—if I get sick I'll just sue the tobacco companies." A joke? Perhaps, but there also seems to be serious import in such humor.

Liberalism and Conservatism

The tiresome debates being waged between liberals and conservatives are less than helpful when it comes to the issue of meddling because neither side has addressed the proper relationship between the individual and others, which is at the heart of meddling in the first place.[8] Both contemporary "liberals" and modern "conservatives" tend to advocate various kinds of governmental meddling, differing only on the details. Libertarians at least have the virtue of consistency on their side, and yet their political poetry has led to a certain single-minded meddling in the name of civil liberties, much of which has all the earmarks of a knee-jerk reaction to the ideologies they oppose. How else can we understand the intolerant positions they take on such matters as holiday crèches, which are essentially harmless and have the added virtue of bringing communities together around the historically sacred symbols used in secular festivities? They have singularly failed to recognize the other side of individualism, which is the importance of community—an idea that their meddling interventions have done much to undermine. Meddling libertarians arose from the anarchical thinking of such visionaries as Ayn Rand, and although their thoughtful positions form the basis for many noble anti-meddling sentiments, especially with respect to drugs, tobacco, and other issues dear to the hearts of contemporary meddlers, these positions frequently dissolve into the meddling proposition that they are going to impose civil liberties on people whether they want them or not.

Non-libertarian conservatives, determined to save families and communities from the dire consequences of those who would exercise their freedoms in ways different from their righteous view of how communities deal with deviants, are, if anything, worse. A precise example of the muddled thinking of contemporary conservatives can be found in the "virtue debates" led by arch-conservative William Bennett (1995). Bennett and other virtucrats have called for a reintroduction of shame, ostracism, and humiliation as control devices to counter the increasing coarseness and incivility of American culture. In an edited collection of essays published in the Conservative *National Review,* under the title "This Will Hurt: The Restoration of Virtue and Civic Order," the nation's most prominent conservative luminaries offer such suggestions for dealing with the crisis of our time as "Administering Punishment, Morally, Publicly and Without Excuse," an article that advocates Singapore-style caning as a solution to youthful vandalism; "Uniformity, Uniforms, and the Maintenance of Adult Authority," which argues that public schools should resemble military academies in their maintenance and transmission of the values of social order; and "Ostracism and Disgrace in the Maintenance of a Precarious Social Order," which quotes approvingly from *The Scarlet Letter.* This last also makes an argument that must have been read by those conducting the recent witch hunts about alleged sexual misconduct in the military—a crusade that bagged not only Lieutenant Kelly Flynn, the Air Force's first female bomber pilot, but also a four-star general who was nominated to be chairman of the Joint Chiefs of Staff. This collection generally approves strong, repressive measures—"moral purgatives," as Gertrude Himmelfarb calls them—to counter a postmodern culture that the writers see as out of control.

Other conservatives, writing and speaking in other venues, talk approvingly of the tactics used by some of the most repressive theocratic regimes on the face of the earth—Iran, Iraq, Afghanistan. As Carl Horowitz notes in a perceptive critique of this conservatism-as-fascism, Senator Wayne Allard (R–Colo.) favors public hangings as a deterrent to street crime, and William Bennett once said that he is not "morally opposed" to the public beheading of convicted drug dealers (Horowitz, 1997: 71). These virtucrats seek to stigmatize their enemies in the culture wars as part of a general plan to restore civil decency. The particular tactic most suited to the task, they say, is shame. But, as Horowitz goes on to say, here's the rub: "Shame is an expression of collective will. It is not simple opposition, however vociferous, to someone who is objectionable" (1997: 71). In short, you cannot shame someone who, ultimately, does not share your views of proper conduct. This may be the best explanation yet for why there is so little shame in a postmodern world where every conceivable position is seriously advocated by some group or another, and where what little is left of traditional notions of community is rapidly being dissolved by the placelessness of the electronic media.

The dissolution of the historical tolerance demonstrated by political liberals on questions of lifestyle choices is a similar sign of the rampant confusion besetting contemporary political ideologies over the question of meddling. Christopher Lasch captures this paradox of political liberals:

> Upper-class liberals, with their inability to grasp the importance of class differences in shaping attitudes toward life, fail to reckon with the class dimension of their obsessions with health and moral uplift. They find it hard to understand why their hygienic conception of life fails to command universal enthusiasm. They have mounted a crusade to sanitize American society: to create a "smoke-free environment," to censor everything from pornography to "hate speech," and at the same time, incongruously, to extend the range of personal choice in matters where most people feel the need of solid moral guidelines. When confronted with resistance to these initiatives, they betray the venomous hatred that lies not far beneath the smiling face of upper-middle-class benevolence. (Lasch, 1995: 28)

Opposition to their views makes these "humanitarians" forget the liberal virtues they claim to represent, and they become, as Lasch puts it, "petulant, self-righteous, and intolerant." They find it "impossible to conceal their contempt for those who stubbornly refuse to see the light—those who 'just don't get it,' in the self-satisfied jargon of political rectitude" (Lasch, 1995: 28). So they meddle in the name of many of the ideologies analyzed in Chapter 4. They are especially fond of "for the sake of the children" arguments and of appeals to health, safety, and environmental rectitude. It is, moreover, to much of the political left that we owe the absurdities of that previously discussed meddlesome movement called "political correctness."

So neither the political left nor the right can be counted on to dampen the meddlesome impulse, for both would employ the power of the state to meddle into people's lives, differing only on what they regard as a justification for doing so. Both sides harangue, meddle, censor, and legislate. As Lewis Lapham laments: "The preferred modes of address number only three—the sermon, the euphemism, and the threat—and whether I look to the political left or the political right I'm constantly being told to think the right thoughts and confess the right sins" (Lapham, 1991: 11). These examples demonstrate that the left pursues as meddlesome a politic as the right. The left, too, is attracted to a totalitarian response and, if free to do so, would ban, censor, and control with an enthusiasm that would make Anthony Comstock proud. The impulse is the same, even as the issues differ.

Persons and Communities

Recapturing the relational basis of the self is a key ingredient in understanding the connection between persons and communities that so many postmodern theorists claim with some justification that we have lost. Fortunately, the materials with which to forge such an understanding are all around us. The increasing attempt to wrap ourselves in a hermetic seal, walled off from the intrusions of others, is neither a way to live nor a guarantee that we can escape the incursions of the meddlesome interventions of others. The self is not made out of the self. It is constructed out of relational materials rather than autonomous ones, a point made nicely by sociologist Erving Goffman:

> Universal human nature is not a very human thing. By acquiring it, the person becomes a kind of construct, built up not from inner psychic properties, but from moral rules that are impressed upon him from without. These rules, when followed, determine the evaluation he will make of himself and of his fellow participants ... the distribution of his feelings and the kind of practices he will employ to maintain a specified and obligatory kind of ritual equilibrium. ... [I]f a particular person or group or society seems to have a unique character all its own, it is because its standard set of human nature elements are pitched and combined in a particular way. (Goffman, 1967: 45)

People acquire a sense of individuality, then, only out of their relationships with others (Brissett and Edgley, 1990: 14). Individuals are something of an essential illusion related to the fact that, when we see a person expressing his or her individuality, the social sources from which such an expression was constructed are not always clear. But no one makes a self out of a vacuum, and should the materials of the human community from which they are drawn be corrupted or absent, the individual suffers such fates as well. It is in this sense that it *does* take a village to raise a child, a statement for which First Lady Hillary Clinton was widely condemned and roundly ridiculed, partly by professional meddlers for whom such a recapturing of a sense of community would ring the death knell for their professional interventions—each accompanied by an appropriate billing code.

Likewise, privacy is drawn from a human community that respects it. So does freedom. But when we meddle, we corrupt both privacy and freedom, making them less available to everyone. Human beings are delicate combinations of private and communal elements, and when nothing can be said to be private, community itself is lost. This is what Sissela Bok means when she suggests that "[w]ith no capacity for keeping secrets and for choosing when to reveal them, human beings would lose their sense of identity and every shred of autonomy"[9] (1983: 282). Likewise, Erving Goffman, in his perceptive analysis of the impact of total institutionalization, concludes that the assaults on the self associated with being confined in a mental hospital, prison, or boot camp come not from isolation but, rather, from constant exposure. To be constantly on display is to reduce a person to the status of an object—open for inspection to anyone who passes by. Most of these distinctions are lost on the meddler intent on "making a better community," or the army of chronic volunteers and board members who work for special interests masquerading as communal ones. Obviously, no one is suggesting that we could recapture the sense of community known to previous eras—nor would we want to, for it was often an excuse for the worst kind of meddling. But when we privatize the commonweal with a spate of meddling do-gooders, we only make it more difficult to relate to one another.

Being a person in the human community also involves a great deal of what is rapidly becoming the lost art of "putting up with." In an age when perfection is displayed in every media source, finishing second is synonymous with last place, fashion models are selected for their perfect looks, and every human endeavor seems to claim "excellence" as its mandate, we may forget that if perfection were really so important in every realm of life, people would have to quit their jobs, divorce their spouses, and put their children up for adoption. Perfection seems to be akin to an invitation to the everlasting orgies that decorate the movie screens and the magazine covers—meant to be understood as symbols and allegories, not as proper representations of a reality in which people could actually live. And as Lewis Lapham has observed, "[A]ny customer so foolish as to mistake the commercial intent has failed to read properly the instructions on the label. One is supposed to look, not touch; to abandon oneself to one's desire not in a cocktail lounge but in a nearby mall" (Lapham, 1997: 39).

Moreover, because persons and communities are ultimately bound in an unavoidable and largely positive dialectic, the impulse to meddle runs the risk of destroying the relationship between the two and generating the kind of Hobbesian war "of all against all" that we have sensed in the examples rampant in the present book. In James Buchanan's analysis,

[e]ach of us has a preferred pattern of behavior for others, whether they be members of our family, our neighbors, our professional peers, or our fellow citizens. I prefer that my neighbors control their children's noise making and disposal of their tricycles; I prefer that these neighbors refrain from rock music altogether, and that, if such "music" is to be played, the decibel level be kept low. I prefer that their backyard parties be arranged when I am out of town. (Buchanan, 1986: 107)

But the problem with such preferences, he goes on to say, is that if we try to enforce them, we will inevitably discover that our preferences bother our neighbors as well: "They prefer that I control the barking of my dogs and that, if dogs must bark, that this be allowed only in normal hours. The neighbors also prefer that I refrain from operating my chain saw or power mower early on Sunday mornings" (Buchanan, 1986: 108). So we largely trust our own sense of fair play, common decency, and mutual respect, for we know that if we attempt to impose our preferences on others' behavior, reciprocal attempts will be made to constrain our own. An attitude of "live and let live" is better for all of us, despite the occasional lapses and deviations from ordinary standards of decency that might occur. The citizens of a society that valued a minimum amount of meddling would not be so quick to pick up the phone and call the police about their neighbors' transgressions, would be less intolerant of preferences that were not their own, and would be skilled in the art of "putting up with."[10] Moreover, they would have a keenly developed sense of what things demanded meddling, an understanding of the limits of meddlesome interventions, and an appreciation of the diversity that meddling tries to head off in the first place.

Such a sensible attitude is not part of the mindset of meddlers. They are genuine elitists who believe that their own preferences are "superior to," "better than," or "more correct than" those of others. Their preferences about how to live are so obviously right that they must be exported to those pitiful others whose lives are not as they should be, but would be if only they would live as the meddlers do.

The Philosophy of "Anti" and the Good Society

There is always the danger in a new movement that in rejecting the aims and methods of that which it would supplant, it may develop its principles negatively rather than positively and constructively. Then it takes its cue in practice from that which is rejected instead of from the constructive development of its own philosophy.

—John Dewey

What does it mean when members of a society are more likely to define themselves in terms of what they are against than in terms of what they are for? This question strikes at the moral heart of meddling, for it seems to us that anti-philosophies bode poorly for any conception we might have of a "good society." When we define ourselves more in terms of what we aren't than what we are, we create the illusion that we can build an identity and a society out of prohibitions alone. We increasingly live in an age of deterrence, a time in which we try ever harder not to produce events but to prevent events from occurring. We try to atone for what we regard as the sins of modernity by seeking refuge in nostalgia or feverishly chasing the erasure of the latest risk factor. A wide variety of activities in American life these days are of this order. We eat not to enjoy food but to watch our weight. We exercise to ward off either physical or social death. We make love because someone has told us that it is "healthy." Foreign policy tries to deter conflict, and laws are passed to deter crime. The number of rules that try to prevent something from happening keeps proliferating at the very time that confidence in rules is waning. "No" signs keep popping up everywhere and with increasingly strident messages, but they do little to make us feel better about one another—to say nothing of halting the behavior they target.

Little wonder. A social ethic is never created simply out of opposition to things. In the last analysis, human action, as the pragmatists insist, is about doing. After we compile an exhaustive list of what people aren't supposed to do, we are still left with the nagging question of what they *are* to do. When Nancy Reagan suggested that children just say "no" to drugs, she presumably regarded this as positive advice. But it would have been more positive if it hadn't been just one more item added to an already bulging list of what adolescents are supposed to say "no" to (e.g., sex, cigarettes, alcohol, driving too fast, eating junk food, and staying out late at night). Meddlers of all sorts, even First Ladies, love saying "no" to people—denying them what they want. This simple logo sign posed on a local Wal-Mart store is instructive: "JCs against teen-smoking," it proclaims. Few who see it may know who the JCs are, but they must be good people since they are against teen-smoking. But what about saying "yes" to a few things? If *not* doing things becomes the measure of people, then the only action left is meddling—a lesson learned by the Chinese who, as we noted earlier, discovered that in dropping the retirement age to fifty-five they simply created a new burgeoning class of the retired who did nothing but sit around meddling into everyone else's lives.

We are now, at late century, living in a society where actions no longer speak louder than words. Rather, inaction speaks much louder than deeds. What one *doesn't* do becomes the measure of a man. It is in avoidance, in the shunning of the unsavory and the immoral, that our character, self-esteem, and moral worth are measured. The hallmarks of character are no longer risk-taking but caution; not excess but temperance; not play but work; not ambiguity but closure; not frivolity but seriousness—in general, not a going for things but, rather, a measured reticence.

Such reluctance to engage life—indeed, the philosophy of "anti"—conjoins with what Lance Morrow calls "the Puritan zeal to regiment others on the one hand and the victim's passion for blaming everyone else on the other." Such zealotry, says Morrow, leads to a depressing civic stupidity, for

[e]ach trait has about it the immobility of addiction. Victims become addicted to being victims: they derive identity, innocence, and a kind of devious power from sheer, defaulting helplessness. On the other side, the candlesnuffers of behavioral and political correctness enact their paradox, accomplishing intolerance in the name of tolerance, regimentation in the name of betterment. (Morrow, 1991: 22)

At least Puritanism had a sacred basis for its meddling strictures on human action. But the Puritanism of the New Temperance Movement is a decadent version or, as *The Economist* of London reports, "an odd combination of ducking responsibility and telling everyone else what to do." The contemporary meddler may not know what's right, but he is dead certain about what's wrong. Hardly a positive message for a world in disarray, and hardly a prescription for future courses of action.

The metaphor of the slippery slope so prevalent in the philosophy of "anti" lends itself to a never-ending cycle of regulation and control. As Howard Leichter argues in a book that, for all its pretensions to the contrary, surprisingly comes down on the side of defending regulation, when an activity "poses an actual, as opposed to potential, significant harm or material cost to a substantial number of others, and that harm cannot be reduced or avoided through voluntary means" (Leichter, 1991: 253), says nonetheless, there are legitimate concerns about the cumulative implications of regulation and control.

It has only been within the last decade or so that legislators, often the very same ones each time, have been asked to require the use of seat belts and motorcycle helmets, and raise the minimum drinking age, and limit the conditions of the sale and advertising of alcohol, and restrict the use of cigarettes, and support free syringes for intravenous drug users. Over and over again these legislators have asked, "Where will it all end?" (Leichter, 1991: 254)

The major concern posed by many of these legislators has to do with the interactive and precedent-producing effect of laws that meddle into people's personal lives. For example, one argument in support of adult seatbelt laws was that they were a logical extension of existing laws requiring the use of seatbelts in aircraft. Making laws is, in this sense, like eating potato chips—it is very hard to eat (make) just one. The differences in the way people use cars and the way they use airplanes becomes irrelevant to the regulators, and the compelling argument becomes "We require it in this case, so why not require it in that?" Leichter reports that during the British debate over a mandatory motorcycle helmet law, one opponent argued that the logic of the measure could just as easily be used to require people in cars to wear seatbelts—a possibility that seemed absurd at the time. But that, of course, is exactly what happened. The point at which an argument for regulating one thing because we have regulated another follows a certain cultural logic that is itself not very logical. If placing limits on the freedom of the press to run advertisements for cigarettes reduces their consumption—a proposition open to considerable debate—then restricting advertising of other harmful products such as alcohol will, to many, also make sense. But, as David Wagner has pointed out, we never ask, If it makes sense to restrict the promotion of alcohol and tobacco because their irresponsible use wrecks human lives, then why not apply this argument to advertising the sale of automobiles, the irresponsible use of which wrecks even more lives? (1997: 38–39). Wagner also points out that what he calls "claimsmakers" warn us constantly that drugs, teen pregnancy, tobacco, fat, and so on lead to *x* number of deaths each year. But they ignore the fact that automobiles cause far more rack and ruin than any of those things, and no one is calling for a ban on cars. He ticks off the statistics:

- *Auto accidents:* 43,500 deaths and 1.6 million disabling injuries in 1991 alone
- *Occupational deaths and injuries in the production of automobiles:* 1,300 of nearly 9,900 occupational deaths and 140,000 injuries
- *Household and other nonoccupation injuries as well as accidents with autos and auto-related products:* No definitive data, but clearly a goodly portion of the 38,500 deaths and 5.4 million injuries a year at home are due to automobile-related products, such as oil or other auto products swallowed by children, poisoning, fire and flames, inhalation and ingestion, hot substances, electric current, explosive gases, machinery, falling objects, and falls.
- *Cancer deaths from auto exhaust:* The EPA estimates a total of 15,000 to 30,000 excess deaths a year from vehicle exhaust. Yet no one argues in terms of a "passive driving" effect of cars or refers to "hermetic seals" in relation to other people's cars. New York City recently passed the most restrictive public smoking laws in the nation, outlawing even *outdoor* smoking. At the same time the city passed these laws, it had to be given an EPA exception for its failure to control auto and industrial pollution making the air in the Big Apple some of the most polluted in the land.
- *Noncancer deaths from auto exhaust:* The EPA doesn't even track these deaths, even though, as Wagner notes, substances bound in automobile emissions include benzene, formaldehyde, butadiene, acetaldehyde, and gas and diesel particulates, all of which have been shown in various studies to be associated with such problems as blood disorders, immune system diseases,

developmental and reproductive diseases, respiratory and lung
disease, heart disease, and genetic disorders. (Wagner, 1997: 38–39)

Moreover, if we were to tote up the entire cost of our continuing love
affair with the car (someone might surely say "addiction"), it would have
to include such intangible health risks as the increasingly sedentary
lifestyle that cars have engendered—a lifestyle that, it is continuously alleged, makes us more vulnerable to clogged arteries and heart attacks,
cancer and strokes. We would also have to add in the stresses of conges-
tion, the movement toward urban mega-centers with all of their associated problems including drive-by shootings, and the destruction of communities and a sense of place. Wagner is a careful enough scholar to note
that such an exercise in running up the bill for all automobile-related
problems hardly constitutes a call for a ban on cars; rather, he merely in-
tends to show that the same tactics used by those who call for other bans
are never applied to those who have vested interests in the continued use
of this common transportation device. He notes that the recognized problems relating to cars are all managed within the context of the assumption that cars will continue to be used, whereas tobacco, alcohol, and
drugs are discussed in the context of stamping them out. Wholesale meddling into the lives of car owners is out of the question. But meddling
into the lives of those who use drugs (both legal and illegal—the line between the two is becoming increasingly obscure as the logic of banning
consumptive practices continues apace) is seen as both possible and profitable to the interests of the meddlers.

We are also curiously selective in our use of anti-arguments. We tend to
want to ban things that we ourselves do not use, practices we ourselves
do not engage in, and people who are not like us. Hence, for example, sex
laws have historically been aimed at homosexuals but in fact outlaw
behavior in which most heterosexuals engage—such differential enforcement being counted on to ensure that the police do not arrest the wrong
people. Similarly, we argue for bans on "recreational drugs" like marijuana or cocaine, but we are not as likely to shut down the cocktail hour.
In short, our political activities mirror our interpersonal ones. We are un-
interested in anything that does not correspond to our own interests—a
trend that is not on the road to a better society.

Whatever else it may involve, meddling usually boils down to taking
something away from someone else. Whether it is a consumptive pleasure like eating, smoking, or sex, the meddler typically is pursuing an
anti-theme. People should not be doing what they are doing, and if it is
pleasurable they should especially avoid it.

There is also the nagging problem of the dialectic between those things
we despise and the contribution they make to those things we value.

Freud agonized over this issue and, at the end of his life, wondered if he had not "cured the psychotic of his disease, only to open him up to the miseries of everyday life." Every "anti" that meddlers denounce has a positive value in the life of the person with whom they are tinkering, a point made nicely by Hal Piper: "Humphrey Bogart died at 54 of throat cancer, probably by cigarettes. A pity, but maybe it was worth it to have been Bogart. I can't imagine Bogie without a cigarette in the corner of his mouth" (quoted in Wagner, 1997: 101).

Human Rights at the Cost of the
Joy of Social Obligations

The rights revolution that has effected such profound changes in America has produced a corresponding downside. For human rights, legally acquired and enforced by the power of the state, have come at the cost of the joy of social obligations. The joy that comes from helping a handicapped person is now muted by a series of rules that make such beneficence a legal requirement. In our business, college teaching, we have had many students with disabilities who requested special assistance that made it possible for them to attend class and participate as fully as possible in university life. We were always delighted to help. But with the passage of the Americans with Disabilities Act we now have an Office for Students with Disabilities, which intervenes between students with disabilities and the faculty members whose classes they are attending. The office issues lengthy letters each semester for every disabled student, reminding us that access is a legal requirement for which the university could be severely punished if we do not comply. No longer a matter of human decency and the joy of meeting social obligations, it is now one of rights and corresponding punishments for the abridgment of rights. We have also noticed that the list of students signing up for this service grows each year along with the number of letters we get. No longer is it a simple question of wheelchair access or special services for the hearing impaired or the blind. Students demanding services range all the way from those with the aforementioned and self-evident disabilities to those who suffer from a wide variety of "learning disabilities"—including attention deficit disorder, which has been called the "garbage diagnosis" of the 1990s. Furthermore, those who occupy the category called "the disabled" represent yet another instance of the postmodern problem of boundary maintenance: The center simply fails to hold. Since preferred parking for the handicapped has become a matter of rights, a certain backlash is developing. Apparently a growing number of people with handicapped-parking permits are not disabled, and there is now a black market for the permits themselves (Henderson, 1995: 50). Airport officials at the Dallas–Fort Worth Airport have begun charging for handicapped parking, a service they used to provide free of charge. They claim that the airport has lost about $900,000 in revenue from fraudulent use of the spaces (Strothers, 1995: 13–14). As Sharon Taylor laments, people are ignoring the signs posted at handicapped parking spots and rudely parking there anyway (1996: 20); when called on the matter, they question whether the people with permits are really disabled. Indeed, the anonymity afforded by the car, coupled with our increasing dependence on it, seems to make these matters worse. But it is also worth noting that the more often questions of civility are framed in the insular language of rights, the more likely we are to have these problems and the less likely we are to experience the satisfaction that comes from a civic sense of social obligation. Rights talk, says Mary Ann Glendon, is missing too many dimensions to be very helpful in working through our interpersonal and community conflicts. Among these missing dimensions, she says, are responsibility and sociality, in combination with the illusion of absoluteness and a certain insularity that is implied when people come to every situation shorn of everything but their "rights" (Glendon, 1991). This may be what the enigmatic postmodern philosopher Baudrillard means when he says that "human rights are the zero point of ideology" (1990: 87). Rights insulate and alienate—they make no sense unless the social interactions that constitute the community of man is in disarray. "If a right must be demanded," Baudrillard argues, "the battle is already lost. . . . [T]hus the very call for rights . . . indicates that they . . . are already on the way out" (1990: 87). Moreover, when people come to the table of social interaction armed with nothing but "rights," sympathy, compassion, and understanding often disappear. These age-old virtues are no longer necessary, it seems, because rights are seen as the ultimate trump cards that settle all disputes. But the playing of such cards hasn't worked, and even on short reflection it is not difficult to see why. The invocation of rights results in a kind of checkmate, a gridlock of competing claims. Because rights are abstract and social interaction is concrete, there is a fundamental disconnect between the nature of the claim and the instrument used to resolve it. The external imposition of codes of justice, rights, and the like takes away from the very virtues they seek to impose: intimacy, harmony, and goodwill. Clearly, then, the side that triumphs by hitting the other in the head with "rights" can achieve little satisfaction, for as with conflict resolution by political assassination, the winner is always waiting for the other foot to fall.

Integrity

Where are the models for the nonmeddlesome stance we advocate in this book? Although examples of perfection are hard to come by (and ultimately unnecessary to such an analysis), we do have the sense that people with integrity are not as likely to meddle and that the corresponding increase in meddling we have witnessed is in some sense a measure of the general decline in integrity. We take Stephen Carter's definition of integrity as "wholeness" to be a working definition of this concept, and find that it encompasses three ideas: (1) knowing what is right, (2) acting on what is right, and (3) being open with others about what you have done (Carter, 1996). Carter sets a very high standard—perhaps too high. For, paradoxically, people who have absolute integrity are the least trustworthy—given over, as they are, to the pursuit of ethical ideals as opposed to political expediency, personal loyalty, and the like. Nevertheless, his analysis is intriguing. The opposite of integrity, he says, is corruption. And although searching any database for the term *integrity* will yield a profusion of usages (especially by politicians), real instances of integrity are nevertheless hard to come by. So, we frequently use the term, but seldom follow its principles. Corruption, Carter says, is in many ways the opposite of integrity; but the reason we engage in so much of the former and so little of the latter may well be because of a question we have frequently addressed in this book: when to follow rules and when not to. This question of what we might call "meta-rules," or rules about following rules, is at the heart of meddling. We know that privacy is a good thing, at least for us, but also that violating privacy is both necessary and required when, say, a child's welfare in an abusive home is at stake. But having said that, we also know that we should be wary of "putting our hand between the bark and the tree." So what to do? People with integrity—a sense of wholeness—will, according to Carter, be able to sort such questions out, for they will know implicitly when to meddle and when to leave well enough alone. Given such a standard, we are now in a position to see why there is so much meddling in this society: We lack a basic sense of integrity. Absent such a standard, we meddle in an effort to give ourselves the illusion of integrity. We know that whatever wholeness people once had has been fractured by a postmodern world of competing views and multiple selves, to the point where a certain kind of schizophrenia has become the cultural climate of our times. In the *Homeless Mind*, Peter Berger and his colleagues (1974) observe that "modern man is afflicted with a permanent identity crisis, a condition conducive to considerable nervousness." Kenneth Gergen refers to the same phenomenon as "'multiphrenia'—a splitting of the self into a multitude of self-investments" (1991: 73–74). We see the problem in our children even more clearly. A cartoon shows a woman talking to a man at a cocktail party: "I know what you mean. My daughter doesn't know whether to get married or live alone or just move in with somebody or to quit smoking, except for marijuana, or to become totally drug free or to quit drinking altogether or to have a child or to adopt or just to ignore sex or become celibate and take more sedatives or. . . . " The possibilities seem endless. How can we have a sense of wholeness when so many alternative ways of living are claiming sovereignty over our lives? Where is the integrity?

Meddling and Greed: Toting and Touting

Despite howls of protest to the contrary, much of the triumph of the meddlers can be laid at the doorstep of simple greed. As we have shown throughout this book, meddlers, especially professional ones, intervene in the lives of people because doing so is lucrative business and their economic livelihood requires it. Meddlers tout their wares and tote up the costs of whatever human problems they serve. But the touting and toting are inevitably selective, and the consequences seem always to redound to the advantage of the meddlers, who come off as selfless servants working in a cesspool of diseases, disorders, and problems. An analysis of the manifestations of this greed may be organized around three key areas: economic, psychological, and social.

Economic Manifestations

As we have shown, meddlers frequently refer to the costs to society of inappropriate lifestyles as a rationale and justification for their intrusions. We are told, especially by professional and governmental meddlers, that deviant lifestyles cost money and that the requirement that we cease whatever it is the meddlers do not want us to do is justified—on these grounds alone, if for no other reason. But the problem with this position is that the costs of inappropriate lifestyles have been added up profusely whereas the benefits of inappropriate lifestyles have not. Just why do people drink, smoke, eat fatty foods, or engage in risky behavior? Obviously, there must be something in it for the person doing it. As Brissett has shown in his analysis of heavy drinking, the user achieves a wide variety of rewards from both drinking and being known as a heavy drinker (Brissett, 1979). These include such substantial gains as achieving a sense of identity (no small matter in a society where identity is difficult to achieve) and providing pauses and a sense of periodicity in lives that are already bulging at the seams from the persistent demands of work.

Breaking up the flow of work—demarcating the end of money-grubbing and the beginning of play—is one of the functions of alcohol consumption. "Happy hour" (or "attitude adjustment hour," as it is sometimes called) is that time when we make the transition from work to the many other pursuits of life. Americans in search of these "third places" (Oldenburg and Brissett, 1983) are often at a loss because the places that promote these transitions—the neighborhood tavern, the coffeehouse, the roadhouse—are under persistent pressure to conform to a world where work is the standard against which we measure everything else. Hence, "most middle-class Americans tend to worship their work, to work at their play, and to play at their worship. As a result, their meanings and values are distorted, their relationships disintegrate faster than they can keep them in repair, and their life styles resemble a cast of characters in search of a plot" (Dahl, 1972: 12). Perhaps owing to the fact that they make so much money out of this frantic confusion of "things out of place," professional meddlers frequently lose all sense of perspective in their enthusiasm for extending the net of their services even further. As Morris Chafetz has observed: "Alcohol [treatment] today is big business. It provides profits, jobs and talk-show chatter. Its practice has become an end in itself quite apart from whether its efforts significantly contribute to improved health" (Chafetz, 1987: 14).

Finally, we may note that, whereas the economic payoffs for meddling industries are obvious and easily totaled, the costs incurred by a society that allows itself to be meddled with are not so clear. Nor is this the kind of problem one could resolve with a simple computation, because, as Willard Gaylin has observed,

> [c]ost-benefit analysis is always least satisfactory when the costs must be measured in one realm and the benefits in another. The analysis is particularly skewed when the benefits are specific, material, apparent, and immediate, and the price to be paid is general, spiritual, abstract, and of the future. It is that which induces people to abandon freedom for security, pride for comfort, dignity for dollars. (Gaylin, 1988: 393)

Psychological Manifestations

Not only is the economics of greed at work in the meddling society, but it also finds alliance with the numerous psychologies that greedily appropriate the world as resources for one's "self." The "Me" generation of the 1970s had a reputation for being the era of the flowering of psychological greed, but this trend can be seen in other recent generations as well. Within this framework one finds that the "self" can never get enough. Separating themselves ontologically from others, contemporary Americans seem intent on drinking deeply from the well of life. We evaluate experiences in terms of "self," we vote for the candidate who offers the most for us, and we seem intent on living our lives to the exclusion of everyone else. What's in it for us? Happily compatible with the consumer culture of postmodern capitalism, the world in this scheme of things is a smorgasbord of provisions to be gulped down while there is still time. A new magazine called *Self* hits the newsstand with the promise that it will help the reader deal with "the most important person in the world: one's self." Others in this scheme of things are essentially secondary and are to be seen primarily in terms of what they offer *us*.

Not surprisingly, this new subjectivity of the postmodern world offers a treasure trove of possibilities for the meddler. Unable to deal with the contradictions inherent in such a kid-in-a-candy-store mentality, and frustrated by the inescapable presence of the "other," postmodern Americans have backed themselves into an impossible corner, removal from which requires constant help and attention. The greedy self is akin to Gergen's (1991) "saturated self," although it is overcome not by the demands of relating but by the cornucopia of desire. So, it is little wonder in this climate of insatiability that the meddler's counsel is both necessary and appealing. As in the case of the economic manifestations of meddling, however, we may note that the costs of inappropriate lifestyles, though not well toted, are certainly well touted. We simply don't know the psychological price to be exacted from living either a life of excess or a life of abstinent conformity; but prohibitions against these things are indeed well touted, as almost any book on the psychology of "wellness" will attest. In addition, the benefits of meddlers have been touted as psychological Rosetta stones, but they have not been toted in an effort to determine whether they are psychologically "cost-effective"—as if we could know.

Social Manifestations

An understanding of the social psychology of contemporary society also leads to the observation that much of the greed that gives meddlers so much to do arises in the context of a social life that for many people is merely an extension of their own selves. The play of vested interests make a true public life almost impossible as any attempt to appease one group inevitably runs afoul of another. Social groups, like individuals in the meddling society, cannot seem to get enough. Bonded together by their common frustration with a world that never gives them enough, various such groups vie for scarce resources with little concern for others. And others, who constitute the meaning of self and society (Mead, 1934), are increasingly seen as one set of people who are like oneself. Everyone else is an impediment to getting what one wants. Thus both pro-life and pro-choice advocates line up at election time, determined to throw out of office any politician because of his or her position on this one issue. Single-issue politics are one measure of social greed: My group, my class, my social interests override everyone else's. If politics has become a coarser and less temperate game than ever before, it is in no small measure because of this insistence that the interests of a small, and sometimes well-financed, brigade of fanatical constituents should be served above all others. The harried and hectoring mobs who bankroll lobbying offices in Washington hire their own group of interventionists, who, in turn, meddle in the political process on behalf of those who pay their salaries. This departure from any sense of a commonweal has been identified by numerous recent retiring politicians as the source of their discontent with how the country is going. In truth, we may have far fewer corrupt politicians these days than we have corrupt voters—those who look out only for themselves when they pull the lever for a candidate or an issue. The greed of social groups mirrors the greed of psychological man. Figuring out ways of turning this situation around will be one of the first orders of business for a nation sick of the role that meddlers increasingly play in our lives.[11]

When Is Meddling Necessary?

No one would argue—least of all us—that meddling is never advisable, justified, or morally and socially required. For as we have taken pains to point out, we think that there is far too much unnecessary meddling and not nearly enough of the good sort (see Box 7.1). What is the difference? Meddling may be necessary in societies that have different social arrangements than our own, where access to the lives of others is not constrained by Western notions of privacy. As our own society increasingly becomes overtly multicultural, the possibilities for conflicts over when meddling is necessary and when it isn't also increase.[12] Even within our own culture, what appears to be meddling to an outsider may be understood differently and even celebrated by social groups with alternative views about their relationship with one another. There are some families, for example, whose members tacitly understand that their relationship involves a kind of "license to meddle" and that not doing so would constitute not caring. And we are talking here not simply about the stereotype of Jewish mothers but about many other family and kinship groups as well. In some social structures, religions, and neighborhoods, then, meddling is measured and just fine. What makes it all right is a layer of understanding that implicitly authorizes specified others to meddle. It is in this sense that circumspect people who wouldn't dream of meddling into the lives of their friends and work associates may routinely meddle into the lives of close family members. Similarly, in some venues one's very presence opens up one's life to the meddling intrusions of neighbors. Regulars in neighborhood bars and taverns may consider the meddlesome questions of other regulars to be an endearing feature of these places. In such cases, nothing is sacred. The meddling is

BOX 7.1
Good Meddling: A Paradigm Case

Most of the examples of good meddling in this book have not been about relatively clear-cut, helpful, and salubrious cases. Indeed, we believe that most meddling is ill-advised and, further, that the combined weight of all the meddlers–especially professionals who make their livings fiddling with people's lives–has much to do with the woes that beset American society as we near the millennium. Having said that, however, we think it important to put in a good word for some kinds of meddling, for, as noted earlier, we believe that there is far too much bad meddling and not nearly enough of the good. A simple case will suffice to point out the dilemmas of meddling and to show why there may be precious little good meddling going on.

In a midsized town of our acquaintance there is a banker with a social conscience. Decent and honorable, Robert, as the bank's CEO, has successfully led the organization to national prominence, all the while watching its deposits sky-rocket through the use of techniques that all successful bankers employ. He is a sound marketer, keeps up with his customers' needs, and attempts to serve the community from which his bank has made so much money at the same time. Knowing that we were writing a book about meddling, he confessed recently that he had engaged in some serious meddling the week before. The story he recounted has many of the features of what constitutes "good meddling."

An elderly woman who had been a customer for some fifty years walked into the bank and wrote a check for $10,000 in cash, an amount more than one-third of her entire balance. This curious departure from the woman's usual fiduciary pattern alerted a teller, who went to her supervisor for advice. The supervisor called Robert. What to do? The immediate suspicion was that the customer had become the target of a confidence game. Robert asked if she was sure she wanted to take this money out in cash. She said "yes." They then asked if she would sleep on the matter and come back the next day. She reluctantly agreed, but said, "I'm going to give it to *him* regardless of what you say." This reply verified in their minds that she was the target of some kind of scheme. During the next twenty-four hours the banker called the police chief, who, upon being told the problem, phoned the adult children of the woman. They, too, were alarmed and could think of no legitimate reason for the unusual withdrawal. Everyone saw a confidence game in the making and yet did not know how to stop it. "We can't legally prevent a customer from withdrawing her own money, and could even get into trouble for doing what we've already done," Robert explained. The woman returned the next day, and the bank officials, not being able to figure a way out of the dilemma, cashed the check as requested.

(continues)

(continued)

This case is instructive in a variety of ways. The bank meddled because its employees cared. There was nothing to be gained from meddling into the elderly customer's life except a considerable amount of potential grief. The bankers violated their usual policies and, in the course of acting according to their consciences, brought themselves at least potentially to the brink of an untenable legal position. "Some things are more important" was the rationale. Note how this case differs from the usual scenarios that have occupied our attention throughout this book. The bankers meddled when not meddling would have been the easier course. They didn't do it for the money. Their meddling was an affair of the heart. They acted on the basis of an ethical sense that was measured and careful. Moreover, it is important to note that, whatever satisfaction the bankers may have gotten out of doing the right thing, there was nothing in it for them *but* the satisfaction of knowing they had done so—and indeed, they incurred a mountain of potential risk. Finally, the bankers recognized the limits to their meddling. When the woman came back and insisted on cashing the check, they cashed it. They did not call a psychiatrist, try to take over the conduct of her life, have her institutionalized as incompetent, or behave in any number of ways that other meddlers might have done. Their action *was* paternalistic, but it was also respectfully measured and appropriate.

Contrast this simple case with the avalanche of meddling we see all around us and it becomes apparent that there is far too much of the latter and not nearly enough of the kind just described.

---

harmless, it occurs among friends, and it may not extend beyond the boundaries of the place that defined it as acceptable. The characteristic that ties together all these cases of good meddling is that the parties know one another intimately, especially in situations that do not involve meddling, and thus understand that what would seem notorious meddling interventions to an outsider are in actuality a matter of good friends caring about one another's lives and problems.

But even when we know each other well, it is difficult to determine when to meddle and when not to. Even those close to us who ask for advice often don't really want it. What they want is the close interpersonal connection afforded by affirmation and support. Although situations differ, the Hippocratic rule might be seen as the overarching one: Do no harm. This of course presumes that one knows what the consequences of the meddling will be. Since such prescience is rarely available, one has to rely on caution, wisdom, and good sense. Since these qualities, too, are in short supply in this society, one can safely conclude that less meddling is, in the main, better than more.

Humility and the Common Good

Finally, it may be worth considering that the common good is advanced by a certain measure of humility—the sense that even as the information age explodes upon us, knowledge is less certain than ever, if only because there is so much of it and so much of that, in turn, is contradictory. As a doctor has observed about heart attacks:

> It may help the patient to realize that we are not really sure what causes cardiovascular disease—or any chronic disease. . . . [A] risk factor is not a cause. . . . Rather than embarking on a philosophical discussion regarding whether information sufficient for a truly deterministic causal schema is unknown or unknowable, let us agree that from a utilitarian point of view, it makes no difference which view is correct. Either way, there is always something inexplicable in the fact that some people do things right and die young, while others break all the rules and get away with it. . . . Let us help [patients] understand that there is no life-style, no matter how hedonistic, which assures disease; just as there is no life-style, no matter how austere, which assures longevity. (Charlton, 1993: 32)

Even more important, humility is an attitude that bodes well for our relationships with one another because it ties together the interpersonal with the social. Members of cultures less meddlesome than our own, such as certain Native American ones, have traditionally gained their sense of self from spiritual sources that impress upon them the necessity of approaching others with a sense of grace. Contemporary Americans, by contrast, increasingly seem to be getting their sense of identity from self-promotion: the self-centered, felt necessity of blowing their own horns and sending their logos and marquees higher than those of the next person. The dismal status of the "other" seen in the rudeness of public space, the coarseness in which discourse is now framed, the wholesale lack of respect for anything or anybody, and the Darwinian environment that highways seem to have become are all suggestive of a society whose members have lost the simple ethic of respect and humility (Morris, 1996). The quaint tradition of teaching manners—which Judith Martin claims is the "first virtue," since nothing else matters if people don't have them (Martin and Stent, 1990)— seems to have been relegated to a previous century. Those who come to this country from more humble countries are often shocked at the extent to which Americans push, shove, and race against each other for everything from theater seats to parking spots. They are appalled at the coarseness of political discourse here and stunned by the verbal aggressions that Americans heap on each other daily. Others are spoken of as if they were foreign and despised. The perception of the quickening tempo of modern life is partially due to the shameless lack of humility that people exercise in their relationships with one another. To the benefit of the meddlers, we seem to believe that we must always present ourselves as correct, in control, and self-confident. Obviously, such presentational stances exact much from us emotionally—a circumstance that creates a market for additional meddlers who treat the "emotionally ill."

There is an even more troubling aspect of this "me first" ethic, and that is the inevitable realization that self-promotion necessarily involves others' *de*motion. We seem to reward those who are best at it. Those humble others who by nature, culture, or personal disposition are less inclined to push themselves to the front are often left behind. This is why American society has increasingly taken on a zero-sum flavor, even under circumstances in which very little is at stake. In a world of self-promotion, it is dialectically impossible to raise ourselves up without pushing someone else down (Kohn, 1986). Talk of the commonweal aside, much meddling is merely an attempt to reshuffle the deck in an effort to obtain an advantage for the interests of the meddler—hardly a purpose that ennobles us as human beings. So humility is the key to the development of a less meddlesome society, and we are urged to keep it in mind as we complete our examination of the meddling impulse in the final chapter.

Notes

1. Politicians are of little help when it comes to decreasing the sum total of meddling in the world, for their enterprise, by its very nature, has a vested interest in engaging this reigning tendency. Politicians are in the business of answering grievances, so they are likely to react positively to the whining of constituents who encourage them to meddle more into the lives of others while meddling less into their own. Likewise, politicians do best when times are bad, when a sense of chaos and doom is imminent, or when people are sufficiently distanced from one another that they cannot work out grievances on their own.

2. We take the term from Charles Murray, whose conception of the importance of a "good society" we agree with, though not necessarily his definition of one.

3. No matter what the "rights" of parties may be construed as being, many parental interventions are purely meddlesome (though perhaps not as many as children believe). Meddling into the lives of one's children, though absolutely obligatory in some situations, is meddling nonetheless, and most parents know that the situation is fraught with difficulties even when the mandate to do so is clear and obvious.

4. The term *competent*—meaning "making choices of which others approve"—is increasingly void of content.

5. Given this paternalistic bent, it is doubtful that anyone has ever truly given "informed consent." If things don't work out, an argument can always be made that a person's consent was not completely informed. The arguments of coerced and uninformed choices are rampant in the nation of meddlers, which is aided and abetted by a nation of lawyers who seek to exploit every conceivable situation in which things don't work out.

6. Of course, very few people admit to being paternalists. For most Americans, the term has a nasty, dictatorial ring to it. Nevertheless, many people act out paternalistic ideologies even while insisting that they are doing nothing of the sort.

7. For an elaboration of the joys of smoking, even against the increased odds of dying sooner, see Klein (1993).

8. We use the terms *liberal* and *conservative* advisedly, for what passes as liberal and conservative political theory in contemporary America is wildly inconsistent and bears little resemblance to the historical uses of these terms. Neither Jeffersonian Democrats nor John Adams Republicans would recognize what has happened to their respective parties: Both meddle in ways that are anathema to their historical roots.

9. And the problem promises to worsen. With the advent of new technologies such as cellular phones and personal paging devices, as well as the introduction of the computer into arenas far removed from the need to "compute," we are now so thoroughly saturated with the flow of technology that getting away from people in any sense—either physically or informationally—can be a significant achievement.

10. Constance Perin, in her study of relationships between neighbors, found that meddling is actually a form of aggression in which each side tries to "get back" at the other for some alleged wrong. But she also discovered how people of good will handle such problems. In a chapter titled "Tattling on Neighbors," she reports that "[n]either anger nor complaints, but 'learning to live with,' is a common axiom. Our neighbor's dog pees on our lawn, but we'd rather continue to have coffee with them than mention it. We've learned to live with it. They put up with our several cars, and we've mentioned how appreciative we are of that. . . . They're nice people, and I like them, so we just put up with it" (Perin, 1988: 71).

11. The cyber-revolution will make the challenge all that greater, for as we increasingly isolate ourselves from one another in front of electronic monitors, we will have fewer and fewer uninvited guests. As Ted Gup suggests in a piece about the end of serendipity brought about by hyper-linked on-line newspapers as opposed to real ones that you hold in your hand: "[N]othing will come unless summoned. Unless the mouse clicks on the story, the account will not materialize. And who will click on the story headlined 'Rwandans Flee,' 'Inner-City Children Struggle,' or even 'Endangered Butterflies Fight for Survival'? If the mouse is a key, it is also a padlock to keep the world out" (Gup, 1998: 18).

12. Eve Browning Cole, writing about the new scourge of "political correctness," offers an answer to the question of when to meddle and when not to: "Where do we draw the line between reasonable accommodation and unreasonable micromanagement? . . . [T]his is a profound and difficult question that we must answer

with our behavior every day. But perhaps a good working rule would be this: When presented with any proposed bit of PC rule-making, we can ask whether it will make human interactions smoother, more pleasant and more harmonious—or rougher, more painful and more problematic. Such a rule might aid us in distinguishing, and discouraging, the bullies on *both* sides of our social dilemmas" (Cole: 1993: A-5).

8

Conclusion:
Toward a Less Meddlesome Society

The reason we have to do so much good in public, to pass so many laws and make so many public speeches, is always, in the last resort, that somebody is not minding his own business.

—L. P. Jacks

The Social Psychology of Helping

How do we move toward a less meddlesome society? The reader who expects to find a formula or a general panacea to the questions we have set forth in this book will surely be disappointed, as we urge no meddling programs in the name of eliminating meddling. What we do urge is a general reassessment of the nature of helping relationships and, more generally, a greater degree of understanding and humility in our dealings with one another. A less meddlesome society would certainly be one that was more honest about its methods of helping others. There is nothing, for example, in our critical analysis of the professional meddlers who delve so readily into people's alcohol use (discussed in Chapter 3) that should in any way be construed to suggest that people with a drinking or any other kind of problem should not be helped. Nor should any of us be discouraged by the arguments and observations in this book from assisting people to acknowledge their possible need for help. Rather, the implication is that we should play it straight with them and not use various subterfuges such as "denial" as a justification for meddling into their lives. As we argued earlier, appealing to the psychological reality of denial is simply another way in which we can force unwilling people to do something that we wish them to do while at the same time feeling good about it. At the very least, we should recognize that it is often for our *own* good and not theirs that we meddle in the lives others. To be sure, we sometimes help others when we intervene in their lives. But it is the recognition by the helpers that they are primarily helping themselves that is so easily obscured in this society where mindless meddling has been routinely confused with altruistic helping.

Politeness and Manners

We also urge a reconsideration of the art of politeness, a social virtue that Judith Martin defines as "the respectful pretense of interest in each other" (1990: 243). We believe that this underappreciated form of interpersonal morality is under considerable pressure when people indulge their enthusiasm for saying what they think, no matter what the circumstances. When fashion designer Gianni Versace was murdered in front of his Miami Beach estate, CNN interviewed people on the street regarding their feelings about his death. "I don't care," said one. "I didn't buy his clothes." No pretense there. Yet honorable pretenses are not only the defining moment of politeness; they define other important things as well:

> Manners have only superficially to do with the right fork and the timely acknowledgment. Observing the old formal rules of etiquette . . . has always been less important than instilling a sensibility of concern and regard. And that more valuable interior sensibility is showing signs of erosion. There exists an uncertainty about critical norms of conduct and aesthetic judgment, and a reluctance to define or invoke them. One consequence has been a widespread, and usually unwitting, coarsening of behavior. (Morris, 1996: 25)

If our society is becoming coarser and more Darwinian, it is at least in part because we do not respect other people enough to engage even in a modest pretense about their lives, their wishes, or their choices. The uplifted middle finger seems to be emerging as the primary semiological vehicle for getting along in public, especially along the public highways. What do we do about people who disagree with us? "F— 'em" is coming to be the routine response.

Tolerance

"Toleration of difference in moral judgment," said John Dewey, "is a duty which those most insistent upon duty find it hardest to learn" (1908/1932: 252). The postmodern condition has made it all the more important that we develop a stance of tolerance when faced with questions of moral judgments. Beset as we are with a cafeteria of choices—each backed by its own developed rationale—easy judgments about others' lifestyle choices are fraught with peril. According to Dewey: "Tolerance is not just an attitude of good-humored indifference. It is a positive willingness to permit reflection and inquiry to go on in the faith that the truly right will be rendered more secure through questioning and discussion, while things which have endured merely from custom will be amended or done away with" (1908/1932: 252). Indeed, we need to exercise more discretion when we call on the government to meddle in the lives of others, especially groups with whom we disagree. People are of two minds when it comes to this question. On the one hand, we are quick to applaud meddling in cases where those being meddled with represent interests that are not our own. The existence of obvious and clear-cut cases where meddling is imminently justifiable spurs these efforts on. On the other, we don't want the government to meddle into our own affairs, and equally clear-cut cases suggesting that meddling is out of control reinforce these sentiments. For example, *Advertising Age* reports that anti-smoking groups are putting pressure on publishers who print tobacco advertisements. Among the magazines being targeted are *Glamour* and *People Weekly*. At the same time, however, the FDA's office has been flooded with letters protesting the agency's plan to regulate tobacco advertising (*Advertising Age*, 1995: 54). People want it both ways. But we cannot create a world in which freedom of speech and the press flourish at the same time that, in recognition of the power of the press, we slap restrictions on content of which we disapprove.

A Moratorium on Rights Talk

Our conclusions about meddling also concur with those of Mary Ann Glendon, who calls for a moratorium on "rights talk" (Glendon, 1991). There is simply too much meddling into the lives of others in the name of "rights." From a handful of cases that now seem as straightforward and justifiable an instance of meddling into the affairs of others as the Civil Rights Movement of the 1960s, the legacy of that salutary endeavor has deteriorated into a babble of rights claims and rights talk on every conceivable matter. In the face of such babble, the contemporary American has little room to negotiate. Even the family has been reduced to the status of a loose collection of rights-bearing individuals, each wrapped in a hermetic seal of legally secured claims. Prenuptial agreements increasingly begin marriages.[1] Relationships based on trust are thus set on their way with a blatant act of distrust. In the name of rights, people become more and more involved with things that do not involve them. And as they become less and less connected, their meddling gives them a false sense of connection. "Surely I must care or I wouldn't bother" is the most common implied rationale of contemporary meddlers. Rights are typically viewed as laws, and the explosion of claimed rights is at least partially responsible for the morass of regulations out of which much meddling is consummated.

The Wages of Virtue and the Place of Pleasure

We need not go so far as Samuel Butler, who once suggested that "there should be some schools called deformatories to which people are sent if they are too good," to understand that the unrestrained pursuit of virtue often creates the opposite of virtue and goodness. In meddling with our neighbor in the name of health and fitness, for example, we are "too good," confusing our certain sense of what is right with a righteousness unworthy even of spiritual paragons. Although we certainly would not wish to quarrel these days with the faith and moral rectitude of the person seeking healthy "oneness," the secular uses of such a holistic program, imposed by totalitarian political assumptions and justified in the name of health, not only raise questions of freedom *from* health but incur other dilemmas as well. It may turn out that the pursuit of health is just as costly as the pursuit of hedonics. If one takes Freud even half seriously, to live in a society where every physical pleasure is severely regulated is to pay a very high social and individual cost. The repressed life, the Freudian argument goes, may pop out in all kinds of unforeseen deviance. For example, Bible Belt fundamentalism, with its grim view of sex before marriage, unquestionably seems to be correlated with high rates of teen pregnancy, to say nothing of a host of other forms of deviance. Socially, the cost of unrestrained virtue may be much higher than we thought.

One need not go even that far. Only a moment of reflection is required to imagine what life would look like if lived according to the .05 statistical-significance levels of the research published in the *New England Journal of Medicine*. What should one eat? What should one drink? No more morning coffee because, after all, it has been linked to pancreatic cancer. Although that link now appears to be tenuous, the anxiety has been established, and that is exactly the point: Under the sway of healthists who meddle in the name of the Holy Grail of inner and outer fitness, everything one eats, breathes, and does is potentially suspect and may be only a study away from disapproval, stigma, and total banishment. A ravenous media system sounds the alarm: no decaffeinated coffee because the solvents used in the extraction process have been shown to be carcinogenic. Herb teas may not be a healthy substitute because who knows what kinds of pesticides were sprayed on the leaves? Fat isn't good for you, but Olestra is worse. No artificial sweeteners to help with weight control, for what right-thinking, *Prevention Magazine*–reading American doesn't know about the dangers of that stuff? And we haven't even gotten to the entrée yet. Forgive most Americans for their bewilderment. One wonders just what people are supposed to eat and drink, to say nothing of the other pleasures that make life worth living. If people can't drink coffee with a clear conscience, image how they might feel about drinking a beer or smoking a cigar. Furthermore, ridding the world of tobacco, coffee, alcohol, and other consumptive enjoyments has had the effect of purifying, sterilizing, and discouraging the use of those few enclaves of pure sociability that represent what little is left of the public domain. For where would the *kaffeehaus* be without coffee, or the pub without ale? Say what you wish about the pariah smokers, who, even in their outcast status, huddle around the entrances to buildings—killing themselves, as the healthists would have it, a cigarette at a time: At least they are absorbed in a lively sociability with their fellow human beings. They are doing what few of the rest of us have time for: engaging one another in face-to-face conversations about matters of common interest. They pause to enjoy the simple pleasure of each other's company. Couldn't they do it without taking part in such an unhealthy practice? Of course, but we must observe, as Oliver Wendell Holmes once did, that "[f]resh air and innocence are good if you don't take too much of them—but I always remember that most of the achievements and pleasures of life are in bad air." It is hard to imagine devotees of health standing around idly for even a few moments of talk with their fellow human beings. It is apparent that for many people the thoroughly conformed life is much like the unexamined one was to the Greeks: not worth living. The larger question is this: Must some people make these choice for others? Is it really any of their business? The meddlers think so; we don't.

In raising questions about the place of pleasure in a rounded conception of life, we do not for a moment mean to suggest that disease and debility are not real. There are plentiful data indicating that persons can get sick or even die from the wide assortment of pernicious afflictions that plague the planet. Indeed, scientists have shown themselves quite adept at measuring the relative risks incurred in various habits of living. They can tell you statistically, to the day or minute, what this food or that behavior cuts off your life span. Epidemiologists, in particular, have demonstrated far beyond a reasonable doubt that a decision to live a certain way, work in a particular field, and follow certain consumptive practices and ways of the flesh constitute decisions, at least statistically, to get sick or even die from the pathogens most likely to pile up in those pursuits. Their computers work overtime cranking out the data. But few scientific studies have the good sense to accompany their Cassandras with a sense of perspective—with a gentle reminder that there is a difference between statistical risk and actual risk, and that living one's life in an effort to avoid the dreaded sequela posed by medical studies carries its own peril, namely the danger of leaving out of the equation those pleasurable elements of a "healthy" life not easily reducible to a science of bodies alone. All the talk is of security. "The depressive power of good intentions," as Jean-Paul Baudrillard writes, "is a power that can dream of nothing except rectitude in the world" (1990: 66). Perhaps we talk of risks because the language of crisis and imminent doom seems in a mass society to be the only way to get anyone's attention. Perhaps we do it for other, less defensible reasons. But whatever the reason, human beings might be well-advised to consider *all* the evidence, and not simply that part most easily rendered by scientific techniques of investigation. For science to be right is one thing; for it to be righteous is quite another.

It is all but amusing to observe that even as we rediscover the pleasure of drinking a glass of wine with dinner or the nuanced delight of splashing a splendid varietal olive oil on our salad, people seem compelled to justify their gratifications in the name of health. "The flavonoids in red wine actually protect you from heart disease," the latest study reports. "Olive oil is a monounsaturated fat," we cheerfully remind our guests. It's a fat, but a "good" one. Pleasure, tradition, and self-fulfillment seem to have been removed from the lexicon of proper motives for human behavior, health having replaced them as the only acceptable reason for engaging in this activity or that. This medicalization of pleasure hasn't yet hit Europe and Asia, older civilizations whose inhabitants seem to understand what the meddling Puritans on our shores have thoroughly obscured—that the ritual act of enjoying these substances in the company of others may even have something to do with their physiological effects. Instead, Americans want to isolate the specific flavonoids and put them in pills.[2] Nutritionists have gotten their message across with uncharacteristic effectiveness: Read the labels and take note—fat and sugar are bad, carbohydrates are good. Ask any health-food store to describe the effects of a newspaper report on the latest scientific findings about victims, minerals, or herb supplements and they will tell you: a run on the product. A month later it sits on the shelves—the masses are chasing the next report. But like many other alarm-sounding Savonarolas, they have focused only on the bodily side of the question and left out the human and social side. Eating is perhaps *the* basic social bond, and when it becomes associated with disease and death, that bond is torn apart.[3]

It may not be insignificant that our obsession with health as a moral issue is occurring during a time that, if not one of the most politically corrupt of our national life, is at least one of the most investigated. This obsession, which inevitably entails meddling, insulates us from larger problems that we may feel we cannot do anything about. But chasing health while avoiding pleasure is a fool's errand that, even if it does add any time to our lives (and that is far from certain), surely does so at the cost of reducing the pleasurable moments that make that time worth living. The use of medical science as a guide to life is itself misguided because, as Jean-François Lyotard (1993) points out, it keeps revising itself.

Failing to restrict itself to the study of what he calls "useful regularities" and instead pontificating about the truth, this activity becomes just another game one plays with words—a game with its own rules whereby adherents prove their fidelity to the camp (Lyotard, 1993: xxiii). And given an age in which certainty is not possible and tomorrow's latest finding threatens to sweep away today's medical dogma, it fails to offer what people seem to need the most: a stable set of guidelines for living one's life.

Professionals who engage in the meddling trades for money are the worst of all, for their sense of their own importance is underscored by a culture that often obfuscates their professional rhetoric of expertise with the conflicts of interest inevitably posed by their money-grubbing. Maintaining a sense of perspective when one's livelihood depends, for example, on diagnosing illness with medical markers and scientific tests may be too much to ask, yet that is precisely what is demanded. It can be done. Robert Dingwall recounts a story about a young physician who, upon joining the laboratory of an older and wiser physician (Dingwall himself), wondered what the normal hemoglobin level of the blood was:

> When I answered, "Twelve to sixteen grams, more or less," he was very puzzled. Most labs, he pointed out, called 15 grams normal, or perhaps 14.5. He wanted to know, if my norm was so broad and vague, how he could possibly tell whether a patient suffered from anemia, or how much anemia. I agreed that this is a very difficult thing to tell. So difficult, in fact, that trying to be too precise is actually misleading, inaccurate, stultifying to thought, and philosophically very unsound. He wanted to know why I didn't take one hundred or so normal individuals, determine their hemoglobin by our method, and use the resulting figure as the normal value for our method. This, I agreed, was a splendid idea. But how were we to pick out the normals? The obvious answer is, just take one or two hundred healthy people, free of disease . . . but that is exactly the difficulty. We think of health as freedom from disease, and disease an aberration of health. This is traveling in circles, getting us nowhere. (Dingwall, 1976: 46–47)

When we try to resolve such inherent ambiguities through an act of faith posing as a truth that also agreeably coincides with our financial interests, we run the risk of surrendering all our credibility—a circumstance that is surely responsible for the cynicism that is so widespread these days.

Caring Without Meddling: The Gift of Sociability

The matters we have discussed in this book continue to be couched in a language of extremes: "privacy and connection," "individual and society," "self and other." In a nation of meddlers we talk about one pole as though it has to be eliminated in order to achieve the other. We either recognize an absolute privacy à la Ayn Rand or turn our culture into a 250 million–person commune. Our talk is like Glendon's complaint about the language of rights: "The winner takes all and the loser has to get out of town. The conversation is over" (1991). But whatever binary language we select to talk about the relationship between ourselves and other people, in the end the dualism dissolves. No such language will hold the complexities of human interaction or what Alan Wolfe (1989) calls "the gift of sociability." Privacy and connection are not mutually exclusive categories. They are mutually interdependent ones. Our fate depends on one another, and if meddling becomes the normative mode of human association, there will be little left for such a dialectic to practice upon. This notion of mutual interdependence seems to be a difficult point for Americans to accept. Wedded to a nineteenth-century conception of individualism, we think that the self must dominate the discourse or be overwhelmed by an equally primitive conception of a leviathan social order out to do people in. So privacy and connection are seen as opposites.

Such talk frequently surfaces in discussions of the problems that beset us. Joseph Califano, for example, in discussing the crisis of health care, rails against what he calls "the petticoats of privacy" (Califano, 1994: 141). Privacy is "misguided," he says. We must stick our noses into other people's business if we want to stop the epidemic of chronic and acute diseases that plagues us. A health-care system that is sensitive to privacy will not, he believes, unravel the personal behaviors that are at the root of our bad health. Smoking, drug use, nutritional promiscuity, and other sins of the flesh currently hide under a petticoat of privacy that shields people from the kind of "aggressive health promotion and disease prevention efforts" that are the only solution to the health-care crisis. Denial is endemic, he says, and since others pay the bill, sacred conceptions of privacy must go. At the other end of the continuum is the primitive conception of individualism that Lyotard chastises for its hollowness: "Each individual is referred to himself. And each of us knows that our self does not amount to very much" (Lyotard, 1993: 15).

In between these examples of extreme talk is the notion of sociability. We are social creatures, even if not always fully socialized ones or fully comfortable with the others with whom we share space on this planet. We live and die in social relationships that, for all their totalitarian possibilities, ordinarily exist in a definitional context that recognizes, defines, and supports individuality. We are, at the same time, individual and social, self and other. We are connected in our own definitional disconnections.[4] We are like performers in the eighteenth-century tradition of *commedia dell'arte*. Social relationships are ways in which people discover their possibilities *and* their limits. We are seldom at peace in this process but, instead, hover in a state of limbo, always finding out who and what we are by measuring ourselves against what others are and how they react to us. We may prod, push, cajole, suggest, or even ultimately reject the choices of others, and we have special obligations to do so when it comes to our children, but none of this adds up to the kind of meddlesomeness with which this book has been concerned; in fact, it militates against it. No hermetic seals will suffice in this relational dance. To be a human being is to be connected to other similarly situated human beings. But like other gifts, that of sociability can be lost through abuse or neglect. When we meddle into the lives of others in order to promote our own narrow conceptions of ourselves, we short-circuit the feelings, choices, and even those very lives. We deny their differing conceptions of what it means to live a life, and we do so to serve our own narrow interests, blithely oblivious to our ultimate mutuality. Indeed, meddling casts us into a situation that is collectively akin to Wolfe's sensitive caution raised in the context of his discussion of our obligations toward the poor, but which applies here also:

> [H]ere is society; you have given it to yourself as a gift; if you do not take care of it, you should not be surprised when you can no longer find it. That message by itself cannot tell people how to satisfy their obligations to intimate and distant others simultaneously, but it at least makes it clear that if people themselves do not continue to try to meet those obligations, no one else will do it for them. (Wolfe, 1991: 261)

A civil society is not one whose citizens meddle unduly. So, if we sense the decline of sociability, see the rising tide of rudeness, and decry the feeling of our fellow human beings as impediments, alien and despised—whose life choices must be countered in order for us to secure the blessings of life—then we will be compelled to work out other ways of dealing with our conflicts.

Toward a Less Meddlesome Society

We have become so accustomed to the emotionally cramped life of an indoor society, where sheer access to one another increases the possibilities of meddling, that it may be difficult to envision our society as becoming less meddlesome than it is. But there are signposts that suggest that Americans may be fed up with the increasing number of intrusions into their everyday lives. Public-opinion polls show a dramatic increase, from 6 percent in 1983 to 19 percent in 1989, in the number of Americans who agree that we are already there when asked how close our country is to an Orwellian type of "Big Brother society." The *New York Times* reports that privacy issues abound and that new groups such as the United States Privacy Council are seeking ways to keep "my business from becoming yours." And as of 1991, at least nineteen states had regulated against employer discrimination of workers on the basis of lifestyle. (On the other hand, if your "lifestyle" includes smoking or drinking, you're increasingly fair game.) The price of meddling could finally become higher than we are willing to pay. To move toward a less meddlesome society, though, will require that we think differently about our relationships with one another. We might begin the process by contrasting our society, and its penchant for meddling, with other cultures that have shown a remarkable aversion to this practiced bit of Americana. Such an exercise will show by example that there are social ethics less meddlesome than our own that could and do prevail. Americans put up with a level of meddling that most European countries wouldn't abide for a moment. For instance, the brash lengths to which anti-smokers in this country are willing to go to repress the enjoyment of their fellow citizens are receiving considerable resistance in the older civilized countries. Native American societies, too, have historically objected to meddling into neighbors' lives. Moreover, we might recall our own history in light of modern meddling and notice just how far we've come. In the process, we could begin to understand the changes that shaped our movement from a nation attempting to keep the meddling inclination in check to one that in many ways now embraces that impulse wholesale. We could also become more alert to the growing number of meddlesome intrusions in our lives and begin to sort those that are genuinely helpful from those that are decidedly not. In this process we could create a whole new series of cultural heroes who remind us that baring our souls, meddling into other people's lives, and playing the role of victim are not among the more ennobling ways to get through life. J. D. Salinger's Holden Caulfield remains one of ours: "If you really want to hear about it, the first thing you'll probably want to know is where I was born and what my lousy childhood was like, and how my parents were occupied and all before they had me, and all that David Copperfield kind of crap, but I don't feel like going into it" (Salinger, 1951: 3).

We might also try to practice a good deal more forbearance in our dealings with one another. Americans have always been wary of strangers, but we seem to be increasingly suspicious of our friends, neighbors, and acquaintances as well. The postmodern indiscriminate sensitivity to the foibles, mistakes, and offenses of others has occasioned a pandemic of fault-finding. When things go wrong, as they so often do, our overriding concern has become one of finding what, or more often who, is at fault. Although this mechanistic logic may be suitable to the high-tech investigation of plane crashes, it seems pathetically misguided when applied to the age-old conundrums of life. But goaded as we are by the scientific persuasion whereby whatever bad things happen are a consequence of the preventable conditions that preceded them, Americans have become a mercilessly accusatory lot. Our belief in the promise of a trouble-free life seems preserved and rationalized by the persistent identification of those persons who would make trouble for the rest of us. Nirvana is within our grasp, we seem to be saying, if only we could educate, rehabilitate, or treat these trouble-makers. So we meddle, seemingly oblivious to the possibility that life may just be that proverbial "vale of tears" or, at the very least, an imperfect juxtaposition of human frailty and power. If we must meddle, we might consider appreciating and acting upon such old-fashioned sentiments as "putting up with" and "learning to live with"—hallmarks of minding one's own business. We might even become reacquainted with that central communal gift of sometimes ignoring those things with which we disagree or find offensive. For it seems to us that in the long run, reasonable tolerance—not reasoned intolerance—is the far more essential component in sustaining both human relationships and communities.

We might also recognize that meddling, no matter what else it might be or do, involves a too-facile control over the options of others. Caring for, helping, supporting, treating, and even protecting others are too often expressed through minimizing their choices while maximizing our own. Few meddlers would tolerate for a moment the kind of reductions in choice they routinely foist on others. By obscuring or disguising this element of control, the cornerstone of meddling, we too readily overlook the protestations of the meddlee, firm in our conviction that meddling is obviously in the best interest of those fortunate enough to be meddled with. Meddling is then easily viewed as the granting of a favor, meddlers being individuals who goes out of their way to make things right. A more critical and balanced perspective is that meddling can't help but involve assuming command over another person's life. Whether such control is favorable or not, necessary or not, humane or inhumane, depends entirely on the circumstances and focus of, and coercive means available to, the meddler. But it is precisely this inattention to the context and outcomes involved in meddling that makes the promiscuous poking of one's nose into other people's business such an attractive venue for so many meddlers. If meddlers could somehow be held personally responsible for the outcomes of their directives and advice, they might see at once that other people's lives are not theirs to control and that they shouldn't want it any other way.

Reflections such as these might force us to reexamine the entire concept of the "good society" in the light of new questions concerning the proper relationship between self and others and between private behavior and public obligations. Some of what people do in their everyday lives can surely have nasty public consequences. But in scrutinizing and distinguishing that elusive boundary between the private and the public sectors of our existence, we would ultimately embrace Alan Wolfe's (1991) suggestion for a politics of tolerance and accommodation rather than one of absolutism. As a society we seem increasingly, albeit grudgingly, accommodative of political diversity—an accommodation premised on the actual or potential power of certain organized cultural groups such as gays, feminists, and other minorities. However, meeting the demands of these groups does not extend to accommodating the differing views and behavior of individuals unaffiliated with such powerful collective interests. Of course, arguments like this sometimes seem to imply a kind of cranky individualism—more appropriate to another age—that is resentful of others and seeks solace in being left alone. But we believe that such an interpretation is needlessly dualistic, and it strikes us as sad that in this polarized age the alternative to isolation and loneliness for so many people seems to lie either in meddling into the lives of others or in spreading out their own lives for meddlers to see and fix. For surely it is possible for a person to be intimately tied to all manner of social networks, to appreciate and enjoy the company and participation of others, and still resent meddling.

The righteous attitude that so often attends an absolutist stance toward other people's lives seems to occasion not only an insensitivity but also a rudeness in human affairs. As Judith Martin observes, "[T]he moral virtue of devotion to the well-being of others supposedly obliterates the rule of etiquette against minding other people's business" (1990: 15). Indeed, she notes, in a society where moral rectitude is valued over common courtesy, nosiness is justified as curiosity: "In those rare instances nowadays, when someone who asks personal questions is taxed with invasion of privacy, the offender points out he was simply wondering or 'interested in' what another paid for his house, why he uses a wheelchair, or whether he is planning to get a divorce" (Martin, 1990: 16). When meddlers armed with righteousness become not only curious but also proactive, any sense of mannerly interaction is subordinated to their cause, whether they are proponents of clean air, clean talk, clean sex, or clean breath. We agree with Martin that it is time to reexamine the social cost exacted by a society of moral and legal absolutists who have forgotten, if they ever knew, that the oldest virtues of communal harmony, cultural coherence, and dignity of the person derive far more from our practiced civility with one another than from our attempts to frighten, harass, and coerce each other into not doing whatever it is we don't like.

The reader might recall the historically obscure fact that witnesses in courts of law could once be sued for meddling if they testified voluntarily, but not if they were forced to appear. So the subpoena was created to provide court-sponsored protection for those who offered testimony. Now we find ourselves in need of a new scheme to protect ourselves from the unsolicited testimony, prying, and intrusions of those who would meddle in our everyday lives. Perhaps instead it is time that we seriously consider ways to live together in a manner that discourages such meddling intrusions, lest we become a nation where "every fool will be meddling" and where nothing whatsoever is allowed save the minding of our neighbors' business.

Notes

1. Some of these agreements are so detailed as to be hilariously ludicrous. In a prenuptial agreement filed in Albuquerque, New Mexico, a new couple legally pledged to honor such itemized responsibilities as the amount of money to be spent on Christmas presents and birthday cards for all family members, the names by which they would refer to their stepchildren, the number of times per week they would have sex, the time they would get up and go to bed, and, further, their intention to "only purchase Chevron unleaded fuel" ("Conditional Love," 1996: 24–25).

2. After the results of this latest research on the positive effects of drinking were announced, companies began to market "Wine in a Pill" concoctions that promised all the benefits of red wine without the alcohol. Similarly, when studies recently suggested that the flavonoids in green tea seemed to protect Asians against heart disease, "Green Tea Pills" began to appear in pharmacies. It never occurred to anyone that maybe the ritual act of drinking these substances with others, not simply the presence of flavonoids, might be part of the equation.

3. A sense of perspective about these matters can be gotten by the simple act of reading. See, for example, *Drinking, Smoking, and Screwing: Great Writers on Good Times* (Nickles, 1994), a delightful compendium on the lost art of living well through simple pleasures.

4. A difficult but thorough rendering of the ethical imperatives of such a stance can be found in the work of Emmanuel Levinas, especially his *Ethics and Infinity* (1985).

References

ABC News. 1996. "Are We Scaring Ourselves to Death?" (March 13).

Advertising Age. 1995. "Letters Tell FDA to Butt Out" (October 23), p. 54.

Aharoni, Yair. 1981. *The No-Risk Society.* Chatham, N.J.: Chatham House Publishers.

American Psychiatric Association. 1994. *Diagnostic and Statistical Manual of Mental Disorders,* 4th ed. American Psychiatric Association.

"America's Decadent Puritans." 1990. *The Economist* (London). (July 28, 1990), pp. 11–12.

Anderson, D. J. 1981. *The Psychopathology of Denial.* Center City, Minn.: Hazelden Professional Education Series.

Anderson, Digby. 1995. *This Will Hurt: The Restoration of Virtue and Civic Order.* London: Social Affairs Unit.

Angell, Marcia. 1996. *Science on Trial: The Clash of Medical Evidence and the Law in the Breast Implant Case.* New York: W. W. Norton.

Baker, Russell. 1994. "The Joy of Being Earnest." *New York Times* (Current Events Edition, July 12), p. A-19.

Barsky, Arthur J. 1988a. "The Paradox of Health." *New England Journal of Medicine,* Vol. 318, No. 7, pp. 414–418.

_____. 1988b. *Worried Sick: Our Troubled Search for Wellness.* Boston: Little, Brown.

Baudrillard, Jean-Paul. 1990. *The Transparency of Evil.* New York: Verso.

Bayer, Ronald. 1987. *Homosexuality and American Psychiatry: The Politics of Diagnosis.* Princeton: Princeton University Press.

Bear, Greg. 1997. *Slant.* New York: Tor Books.

Becker, Howard S. 1963. *Outsiders: Studies in the Sociology of Deviance.* New York: Free Press of Glencoe.

_____. 1994."Foi por Acaso': Conceptualizing Coincidence." *Sociological Quarterly* (May).

Bellah, Robert. 1985. *Habits of the Heart: Individualism and Commitment in American Life.* Berkeley: University of California Press.

Bennettt, William J. (Ed.). 1996. *The Book of Virtues : A Treasury of Great Moral Stories.* New York: Touchstone Books.

Berger, Peter L. 1963. *Invitation to Sociology.* New York: Doubleday and Company.

_____. 1974. *The Homeless Mind: Modernization and Consciousness.* New York: Random House.

_____. 1988. "Environmental Tobacco Smoke: Ideological Issue and Cultural Syndrome." In Robert D. Tollison (Ed.), *Clearing the Air.* Lexington, Mass.: Lexington Books.

_____. 1994. "Furtive Smokers–and What They Tell Us About America." *Commentary* (June), pp. 21–28.

Berger, Peter, and Thomas Luckmann. 1966. *The Social Construction of Reality*. New York: Doubleday and Company.

Bergmann, Jorg R., and John Bednarz, Jr. 1993. *Discreet Indiscretions: The Social Organization of Gossip*. Hawthorne, N.Y.: Aldine DeGruyter.

Berkowitz, Marvin. 1990. "Marketing Self-Help Groups." In Seymour H. Fine (Ed.), *Social Marketing*. Boston: Allyn and Bacon.

Bernstein, Richard. 1994. *Dictatorship of Virtue: Multiculturalism and the Battle for America's Future*. New York: Alfred A. Knopf.

Best, Joel. 1987. "Rhetoric in Claims-Making: Constructing the Missing-Children Problem." *Social Problems*, Vol. 34.

Blocker, Jack S. 1989. *American Temperance Movements: Cycles of Reform*, Boston: Twayne Publishers.

Bloodstock Research and Information Service. 1997. Lexington, KY.

Boeffeta, Paolo, and Lawrence Garfinkel, 1990. "Alcohol Drinking and Mortality Among Men Enrolled in an American Cancer Society Prospective Study." *Epidemiology*, Vol. 1, No. 5 (September), pp. 342–348.

Bok, Sissela. 1983. *Secrets: On the Ethics of Concealment and Revelation*. New York: Vintage Books.

Boorstin, Daniel. 1964. *The Image: A Guide to Pseudo-Events in America*. New York: Harper Colophon.

Boyle, T. Coraghessan. 1984. *The Road to Wellville*. New York: Penguin USA.

_____. 1994. *The Road to Wellville*. New York: Signet Books.

Briffault, Robert. 1931. *The Mothers: The Matriarchal Theory of Social Origins*. New York: Macmillan.

Brill, Alida. 1990. *Nobody's Business: The Paradoxes of Privacy*. Springfield, Ill.: Addison-Wesley.

Brissett, Dennis. 1979. "Toward an Interactionist Understanding of Heavy Drinking." *Pacific Sociological Review*, Vol. 21, No. 1, pp. 3–20.

_____. 1988. "Denial in Alcoholism: A Sociological Interpretation." *Journal of Drug Issues* (Summer), pp. 385–402.

Brissett, Dennis, and Charles Edgley. 1990. *Life as Theater: A Dramaturgical Sourcebook*. Hawthorne, N.Y.: Aldine/DeGruyter.

Brissett, Dennis, and Lionel Lewis. 1978. "The Natural Health Food Movement: A Study of Revitalization and Conversion." *Journal of American Culture* (Spring), pp. 61–76.

_____. 1981. "Paradise on Demand." *Society* (July/August), pp. 85–90.

Brissett, Dennis, and Ray Oldenberg. 1982. "Friendship: An Exploration of Ambiguity." *Psychiatry*, Vol. 45, No. 4, pp. 329–335.

Brissett, Dennis, and Robert P. Snow. 1993. "Boredom: Where the Future Isn't." *Symbolic Interaction*, Vol. 16, No. 3, pp. 237–256.

Brookner, Anita. 1995. *Hotel du Lac*. New York: Vintage Paperbacks.

Brooks, Peter. 1976. *The Melodramatic Imagination*. New Haven: Yale University Press.

Bruce-Briggs, B. 1988. "The Health Police Are Blowing Smoke." *Fortune*, Vol. 117, No. 9 (April 25), pp. 349–352.

Brumberg, Joan Jacobs. 1989. *Fasting Girls: The Emergence of Anorexia Nervosa as a Modern Disease*. Cambridge, Mass.: Plume Publishing Co.

Brzeczek, Richard. 1989. *Addicted to Adultery: How We Saved Our Marriage, How You Can Save Yours*. New York: Bantam Books.

Buchanan, James M. 1986. "Politics and Meddlesome Preferences." In Robert D. Tollison (Ed.), *Smoking and Society*. Lexington, Mass: Lexington Books.

Bunton, Robin, Sarah Nettleton, and Roger Burrow. 1995. *The Sociology of Health Promotion*. London: Routledge.

Burke, Kenneth. 1965. *Permanence and Change*. Indianapolis, Ind.: Bobbs-Merrill.

Burner, David, Robert Marcus, and Jorj Tilson. 1974. *America Through the Looking Glass*. Englewood Cliffs, N.J.: Prentice-Hall.

Burnham, John. 1993. *Bad Habits: Drinking, Smoking, Taking Drugs, Gambling, Sexual Misbehavior, and Swearing in American Society*. New York: New York University Press.

Califano, Joseph, Jr. 1994. *Radical Surgery*. New York: Times Books.

Callahan, Daniel. 1990. *What Kind of Life? The Limits of Medical Progress*. New York: Simon and Schuster.

Caputi, Jane, and Diana Russell. 1990. "Femicide: Speaking the Unspeakable." *Ms.* (October/November), pp. 34–37.

Carson, Gerald. 1957. *Cornflake Crusade*. New York: Rinehart.

Carter, Stephen. 1996. *Integrity*. New York: Basic Books.

Cawthon, David L. 1997. "Phone Hang-Ups." *Daily Oklahoman* (February 24), p. 2.

Chafetz, Morris E. 1987. "The Third Wave of Prohibition Is Upon Us," *Wall Street Journal* (July 21).

_____. 1996. *The Tyranny of Experts*. New York: Madison Books.

Chapkis, Wendy. 1986. *Beauty Secrets: Women and the Politics of Appearance*. Boston: South End Press.

Charen, Mona. 1997. "Tobacco Settlement Assumes Smokers Are Automatons." *Daily Oklahoman* (July 23), p. 4.

Charles, Murray. 1994. *In Pursuit of Happiness and Good Government*. New York: Simon and Schuster.

Charlton, Bruce. 1993. "The Health Obsession." *Salisbury Review* (March), pp. 31–35.

Chesterton, G. K. 1906. *Twelve Types*. London: Arthur L. Humphreys.

Cole, Eve Browning. 1993. "PC Movement Puts Barriers Between People." *Duluth News Tribune* (October 3), p. A-5.

"Conditional Love." 1996. *Harper's* (February), pp. 24–25.

Conrad, Peter, and Joseph W. Schneider. 1992. *Deviance and Medicalization: From Badness to Sickness*. Philadelphia: Temple University Press.

Cox, Brian. 1992. "Meddling with the Mechanics." *Times Educational Supplement* (March 13), p. S-9.

Crawford, Robert. 1980. "Healthism and the Medicalization of Everyday Life." *International Journal of Social Services*, Vol. 10, No. 3.

_____. 1984. "A Cultural Account of 'Health': Control, Release, and the Social Body." In J. B. McKay (Ed.), *Contemporary Issues in Health, Medicine, and the Social Policy*. New York: Travisstock Publications.

Crawford, Will. 1997. "Taxing for Health?" *Consumer's Research Magazine* (October), p. 34.

Curry, Richard O. (Ed.). 1988. *Freedom at Risk: Secrecy, Censorship, and Repression in the 1980's.* Philadelphia, Temple University Press.

Curti, Merle. 1940. *The Growth of American Thought.* New York: Harper.

Cyr, Diane. 1995. "Double-Click on Privacy." *Catalog Age.* September 1, 1995.

D'Souza, Dinesh. 1992. *Illiberal Education: The Politics of Race and Sex on Campus.* New York: Vintage Books.

Dahl, Robert Alan. 1972. *Democracy in the United States: Promise and Performance,* 2nd ed. Chicago: Rand McNally.

Davis, L. J. 1997. "The Encyclopedia of Insanity." *Harper's* (February), pp. 61–66.

Davis, Murray S. 1983. *Smut: Erotic Reality/Obscene Ideology.* Chicago: University of Chicago Press.

Denfeld, Rene. 1995. *The New Victorians.* New York: Warner Books.

Denzin, Norman K. 1991. *Images of Postmodern Society.* Newbury Park: Sage Publications.

Dershowitz, Alan M. 1995. *The Abuse Excuse: And Other Cop-Outs, Sob Stories and Evasions of Responsibility.* Boston: Little, Brown.

Dewey, John, and James H. Tufts. 1908/1932. *Ethics.* New York: Henry Holt and Co., Inc.

Dingwall, Robert. 1976. *Aspects of Illness.* New York: St. Martin's Press.

Douglas, Mary. 1966. *Purity and Danger: An Analysis of Concepts of Pollution and Taboo.* New York: Praeger.

Douglas, Mary, and Aaron Wildavsky. 1982. *Risk and Culture.* Berkeley: University of California Press.

Dowd, Maureen. 1997. "Death and the Maiden." *New York Times* (September 3), p. 23.

Dworkin, Andrea. 1987. *Intercourse.* New York: Free Press.

Edelman, Murray. 1984. "The Political Language of the Helping Professions." In Michael J. Shapiro (Ed.), *Language and Politics.* New York: New York University Press.

Edgley, Charles, and Dennis Brissett. 1990. "Health Nazis and the Cult of the Perfect Body: Some Polemical Observations." *Symbolic Interaction* Vol. 13, No. 2, pp. 257–279.

_____. 1995. "A Nation of Meddlers." *Society* (May/June), pp. 44–54.

Ehrenreich, Barbara. 1995. *The Snarling Citizen: Essays.* New York: Farrar, Straus, and Giroux.

Ellis, John M. 1997. *Literature Lost: Social Agendas and the Corruption of the Humanities.* New Haven, Conn.: Yale University Press.

Epstein, Joseph. "Smoke Gets in Your Eyes. *American Scholar* (Winter), pp. 7–17.

Erikson, Kai T. 1968. *Wayward Puritans: A Study in the Sociology of Deviance.* New York: Macmillan.

Fairlie, Henry. 1987. "Huffing and Puffing," *New Republic,* (April 27), pp. 22–24.

_____. 1989a. "Fear of Living." *New Republic,* (January 23), pp. 14–19.

_____. 1989b. "Hushed Puppies." *New Republic* (April 24), p. 43.

Faludi, Susan. 1991. *Backlash: The Undeclared War Against American Women.* New York: Crown Publishing Co.

Farb, Peter, and George Armelagos. 1980. *Consuming Passions: The Anthropology of Eating.* Boston: Little, Brown.

Featherstone, Michael (Ed.). 1988. *Postmodernism: Special Issue of Theory Culture and Society.* London: Sage Publications.

Featherstone, Michael, Mike Hepworth, and Bryan S. Turner (Eds.). 1991. *The Body: Social Process and Cultural Theory.* London: Sage Publications.

Feinberg, Joel. 1986. *The Moral Limits of the Criminal Law: Harm to Self.* New York: Oxford University Press.

_____. 1989. "Legal Paternalism." *Canadian Journal of Philosophy,* Vol. 1, No. 1, pp. 106–124.

Ferris, Jan. 1994. "Butt Out." *Columbia Journalism Review,* Vol. 32, No. 5, p. 16.

Fineman, Howard. 1993. "The Power of Talk." *Newsweek* (Feb. 8, 1993), pp. 24–29.

Foucault, Michel. 1961. *Madness and Civilization.* London: Tavistock.

_____. 1963. *The Birth of the Clinic.* New York: Vintage.

_____. 1975. *Discipline and Punish.* New York: Vintage.

Fox, Norman, and T. J. Jackson Lears. 1983. *The Culture of Consumption: Critical Essays in American History, 1880–1980.* New York: Pantheon Books.

Frankel, Glenn. 1997. "The Issue Is Freedom, Not Health." *Washington Post Weekly* (January 13), p. 8.

Freud, Sigmund. 1938. The Basic Writings of Sigmund Freud. New York: Modern library.

Friedson, Eliot. 1970. *Profession of Medicine.* New York: Dodd-Mead Publishing Co.

Fuller, Thomas. 1732. *Gnomologia.* Noted in H. L. Mencken, *A New Dictionary of Quotations* (1942). New York: Knopf.

Garner, Roberta. 1996. *Contemporary Movements and Ideologies.* New York: Mc-Graw-Hill.

Gaylin, Willard. 1988. "Harvesting the Dead." *Harper's* (September), pp. 23–44.

Geis, Gilbert. 1979. *Not the Law's Business: An Examination of Homosexuality, Abortion, Prostitution, Narcotics, and Gambling in the United States.* New York: Schocken Books.

Gergen, Kenneth J. 1991. *The Saturated Self: Dilemmas of Identity in Contemporary Life.* New York: Basic Books.

Glass, Stephen. 1996. "Hazardous to Your Mental Health." *New Republic* (December 30), pp. 17–20.

Glasser, William. 1972. *The Identity Society.* New York: Harper and Row.

Glassner, Barry. 1988. *Bodies.* New York. G. P. Putnam's Sons.

Glendon, Mary Ann. 1991. *Rights Talk: The Impoverishment of Political Discourse.* New York: Free Press.

_____. 1996. *A Nation Under Lawyers: How the Crisis in the Legal Profession Is Transforming American Society.* Cambridge, Mass: Harvard University Press.

Glick, Paul C. 1984. "How American Families Are Changing." *American Demographics* (January), pp. 21–25.

Goffman, Erving. 1959. *The Presentation of Self in Everyday Life.* New York: Anchor Books.

_____. 1961. *Asylums: Essays on the Social Situation of Mental Patients and Other Inmates.* New York: Doubleday Anchor.

_____. 1967. *Interaction Ritual.* New York: Doubleday and Sons.

_____. 1971. *Relations in Public: Microstudies of the Public Order.* New York: Basic Books.

_____. 1975. "Ordinary Troubles." In Goffman, *Frame Analysis: An Essay on the Organization of Experience.* Cambridge, Mass.: Harvard University Press.

_____. 1981. *Forms of Talk.* Oxford: Basil Blackwell.

Goldstein, Richard. 1986. "The New Sobriety." *Village Voice.* (December 30), pp. 23–28.

Goleman, D. 1990. "New Paths to Mental Health Put Strains on Some Healers." *New York Times* (May 17), pp. A-1, B-12.

Goodman, Robert, and Aaron Ben-Ze'ev (Eds.). 1994. *Good Gossip.* Lawrence: University of Kansas Press.

Goodman, Walter. 1991. "Decreasing Our Word Power: The New Newspeak." *New York Times Book Review* (January 27).

Goodwin, Robert E. 1989. *No Smoking: The Ethical Issues.* Chicago: University of Chicago Press.

Gouldner, Alvin. 1980. *The Coming Crisis of Western Sociology.* New York: Basic Books.

Green, Harvey. 1986. *Fit for America: Health, Fitness, Sport, and American Society.* New York: Pantheon Books.

Green, Jonathan. 1984. *The Cynic's Lexicon.* New York: St. Martin's Press.

Griffin, Clifford Stephen. 1960. *Their Brothers' Keepers: Moral Stewardship in the United States, 1800–1865.* New Brunswick, NJ: Rutgers University Press.

Grube, G.M.A. 1988. Translation of *Plato's Republic.* Indianapolis, Ind.: Hackett Publishing Co.

Gup, Ted. 1998. "The End of Serendipity." *Reading Today* (February/March), pp. 17–19.

Gusfield, Joseph R. 1963. *Symbolic Crusade: Status Politics and the American Temperance Movement.* Urbana: University of Illinois Press.

_____. 1991. "Risky Roads." *Society,* Vol. 28, No. 3 (March/April), pp. 10–16.

Hamill, Pete. 1991. "A Confederacy of Complainers." *Esquire* (July), pp. 26–30.

Hanson, Richard R., and Julius A. Roth. 1971. "Health Nuts and Hippies: Old and New Movements Meet." Paper presented at the meeting of the American Sociological Association, Denver (August), p. 8.

"Harmful Habit." 1987. *Wall Street Journal* (April 23), p. 1.

Harris, Marvin. 1990. *The Sacred Cow and the Abominable Pig: Riddles of Food and Culture.* New York: Touchstone Books.

Henderson, André. 1995. "Handicapped Parking: Triumph of the Cheats." *Governing* (May), p. 50.

Higdon, Hal. "Is Running a Religious Experience?" *Runner's World Magazine* (March), pp. 75–78.

Hochschild, Arlie. 1983. *The Managed Heart: The Commercialization of Human Feeling.* Berkeley: University of California Press.

Hoffer, Eric. 1966. *The True Believer.* New York: Harper and Row.

Hofstadter, Richard. 1955. *The Age of Reform: From Bryan to F.D.R.* New York: Knopf.

Holland, Barbara. 1995. *Endangered Pleasures: In Defense of Naps, Bacon, Martinis, Profanity, and Other Indulgences.* Boston: Little, Brown.

Horowitz, Carl F. 1997. "The Shaming Sham." *The American Prospect* (March/April), pp. 70–75.

Howard, Phillip K. 1994. *The Death of Common Sense: How Law is Suffocating America*. New York: Random House.

Huber, Peter W. 1990. *Liability: The Legal Revolution and Its Consequences*. New York: Basic Books.

Hughes, Robert. 1993. *The Culture of Complaint*. New York: Oxford University Press.

Illich, Ivan. 1986. "Body History. *Lancet* (October), pp. 1325–1327.

Illich, Ivan, Jonathan Caplan, and Harley Shaiken. 1998. *Disabling Professions*. London and New York: Marion Boyars.

Jacks, L. P. 1924. *Realities and Shams*. New York: George H. Doran Company.

Jacobson, Michael F., and Laurie Ann Mazur. 1995. *Marketing Madness*. Boulder: Westview Press.

Jacoby, Jeff. 1997. "Deficit Being Erased, Along with Our Rights." *Tulsa World* (November 4), p. A-13.

Jacoby, Russell. 1975. *Social Amnesia: A Critique of Contemporary Psychology from Adler to Laing*. Boston: Beacon Press.

Jameson, Frederic. 1991. *Postmodernism, or The Cultural Logic of Late Capitalism*. Durham, N.C.: Duke University Press.

Janov, Arthur. 1970. *The Primal Scream*. New York: Putnam.

Joffee, Carole E. 1977. *Friendly Intruders: Childcare Professionals and Family Life*. Berkeley: University of California Press.

Jones, Tim. 1996. "Cable's Lament: 57 Channels . . . And It's Just Not Enough." *Chicago Tribune* (October 7), p. 41.

Judd, Fran. 1993. "A Tonic for the Troops." *Times Educational Supplement* (December 24), p. 13.

Kaminer, Wendy. 1992. *I'm Dysfunctional, You're Dysfunctional: The Recovery Movement and Other Self-Help Fashions*. Reading, Mass.: Addison-Wesley.

Kantor, Donald L. 1989. *The Cynical Americans: Living and Working in an Age of Discontent and Disillusion*. San Francisco: Jossey-Bass.

Kantor, Leslie. 1994. "Many Abstinence-Based Programs Are Harmful." In Karin Swisher, *Teenage Sexuality: Opposing Viewpoints*. San Diego: Greenhaven Press.

Kaufman, Walter. 1973. *Without Guilt and Justice: From Decidophobia to Autonomy*. New York: Peter H. Wyden.

Kellogg, John Harvey. 1918. *Autointoxication or Intestinal Toxemia*. New York: Modern Medicine.

Kirk, Stuart A., and Herb Kutchins. 1992. *The Selling of DSM: The Rhetoric of Science in Psychiatry*. New York: Aldine/DeGruyter.

Klein, Richard. 1993. *Cigarettes Are Sublime*. Durham, N.C.: Duke University Press.

_____. 1996. *Eat Fat*. New York: Pantheon Books.

Kleinig, John, 1984. *Paternalism*. Totowa, N.J.: Littlefield, Adams and Co.

Kohn, Alfie. 1986. *No Contest: The Case Against Competition*. Boston: Houghton Mifflin Company.

Kurtz, C. Brooks. 1997. "Health Issues, Stop-Smoking Fest on the Mind of Columnist." *Daily O'Collegian* (November 20), p. 4.

Kurtz, Howard. 1996. *Hot Air: All Talk, All the Time*. New York: Random House.

Landeen, R. H. 1978. "Willpower and Denial: Clinical Findings About These Pervasive Concepts. *Currents in Alcoholism,* Vol. 5, pp. 301–307.

Lapham, Lewis. 1991. "Notebook: Sense and Sensibility." *Harper's* (October), p. 11.

_____. 1997. "In the Garden of Tabloid Delight: Notes on Sex, Americans, Scandal, and Morality." *Harper's* (August), pp. 35–43.

Larana, Enrique, Hank Johnston, and Joseph R. Gusfield (Eds.). 1997. *New Social Movements: From Ideology to Identity.* Philadelphia: Temple University Press.

Lasch, Christopher. 1979. *The Culture of Narcissism: American Life in an Age of Diminishing Expectations.* New York: Norton.

_____. 1995. *The Revolt of the Elites.* New York: W. W. Norton.

Leaffer, T. 1982. "Denial in Substance Abuse and Sexual Dysfunction." *Journal of Psychoactive Drugs,* Vol. 14, pp. 143–151.

Leichter, Howard M. 1991. *Free to Be Foolish: Politics and Health Promotion in the United States and Great Britain.* Princeton: Princeton University Press.

Leo, John. 1997. "Rights Spring Up Like Crabgrass." *Daily Oklahoman* (July 30).

Leonard, John. 1997. "The New Puritanism: Who's Afraid of Lolita? (We Are)." *The Nation* (November 24), pp. 11–15.

Lerner, Michael. 1997. *The Politics of Meaning: Restoring Hope and Possibility in an Age of Cynicism.* Boulder: Perseus Books.

Levenstein, Harvey A. 1988. *Revolution at the Table: The Transformation of the American Diet.* New York: Oxford University Press.

Levinas, Emmanuel. 1985. *Ethics and Infinity.* Pittsburgh: Duquesne University Press.

Levine, H. G. 1984. "What Is an Alcohol-Related Problem? *Journal of Drug Issues* (Winter), pp. 45–60.

Lincoln, Abraham. 1850/1957. "Notes for a Law Lecture." In *Selected Speeches, Messages, and Letters,* edited by T. Harry Williams. New York: Holt, Rinehart.

Luik, John C. 1993. "Tobacco Advertising Bans and the Dark Face of Government Paternalism." *International Journal of Advertising,* Vol. 12, pp. 303–324.

Lyman, Stanford M. 1978. *The Seven Deadly Sins: Society and Evil.* New York: St. Martin's Press.

Lynd, Helen Merrell. 1965. *On Shame and the Search for Identity.* New York: Science Editions.

Lyotard, Jean-François. 1993. *The Postmodern Condition.* Minneapolis: University of Minnesota Press.

MacAndrew, Craig. 1969. "On the Notion That Certain Persons Who Are Given to Frequent Drunkenness Suffer from a Disease Called Alcoholism. In S. C. Plog and R. B. Edgerton (Eds.), *Changing Perspectives on Mental Illness.* New York: Holt, Rinehart and Winston.

Madigan, Charles M., and Bob Secter. 1997. "Second Thoughts on Free Speech." *Chicago Tribune* (July 4), section 1, pp. 1–3.

Marantz, Paul R. 1990. "Blaming the Victim: The Negative Consequences of Preventive Medicine." *American Journal of Public Health,* Vol. 80, No. 10 (October), pp. 1186–1187.

Maratos, Telemaque. 1996. "No Smoke Without a Greek." *Spectator* (December 16), p. 46.

Marin, Peter. 1996. "An American Yearning: Seeking Cures for Freedom's Terrors." *Harper's* (December), pp. 35–43.

Martin, Daniel. 1995. "The Politics of Appearance: Managing Meanings of the Body Organizationally." Ph.D. dissertation, University of Minnesota.

Martin, Judith, and Gunther S. Stent. 1990. "I Think; Therefore I Thank." *American Scholar*, Vol. 59, No. 2 (Spring), pp. 237–254.

Matheny, Dave. 1989. "As Decades Go, It Was Not the Best, Nor the Worst; It Was Just the Silliest." *Minneapolis Star-Tribune* (December 28).

McClary, Susan. 1987. "Getting Down Off the Beanstalk: The Presence of Women's Voice in Janika Vandervelde's *Genesis II: Minnesota Composers Forum* (January).

McWilliams, Peter. 1993. *Ain't Nobody's Business If You Do: The Absurdity of Consensual Crime in a Free Society*. Los Angeles: Prelude Press.

Mead, George Herbert. 1934. *Mind, Self and Society*. Chicago: University of Chicago Press.

Mechanic, David. 1978. "Persuasion and Coercion for Health: Ethical Issues in Government Efforts to Change Life-Styles." *Milbank Memorial Fund Quarterly*, Vol. 56, No. 3, p. 14.

Mencken, H. L. 1916. *Sententiae*. New York: Alfred Knopf.

_____. 1921. *A Book of Burlesques*. New York: Alfred A. Knopf.

Meyerwitz, Joshua. 1986. *No Sense of Place: The Impact of Electronic Media on Social Behavior*. New York: Oxford Publishing Co.

Mill, John Stuart. 1849/1956. *On Liberty*. New York: Liberal Arts Press.

Mills, C. Wright. 1940. "Situated Actions and Vocabularies of Motive." *American Sociological Review*, Vol. 5, pp. 904–913.

_____. 1956. *The Power Elite*. New York: Oxford University Press.

Money, John. 1984. "Food, Fitness, and Vital Fluids: Sexual Pleasure from Graham Crackers to Kellogg's Cornflakes." In Mary Ann Watson (Ed.), *Readings in Sexology*. Dubuque, Iowa: Kendall Hunt Publishing.

Morgan, Robin. 1978. *Going Too Far: The Personal Chronicle of a Feminist*. New York: Vintage Books.

Morison, Samuel Eliot. 1965. *The Oxford History of the American People*. New York: Oxford University Press.

Morris, James. 1996. "Democracy Beguiled." *Wilson Quarterly*, Vol. 20, No. 4 (Autumn), pp. 24–35.

Morrow, Lance. 1991. "A Nation of Finger Pointers." *Time* (August 12), pp. 14–18.

Murray, Charles. 1994. *In Pursuit of Happiness and Good Government*. Institute for Contemporary Studies.

Nelson, Jill. 1995. "Talk Is Cheap." *The Nation* (June 5).

Newman, Judith. 1997. "At Your Disposal: The Funeral Industry Prepares for Boom Times." *Harper's* (November), pp. 61–71.

Nickles, Sara (Ed.). 1994. *Drinking, Smoking, and Screwing: Great Writers on Good Times*. New York: Chronicle Books.

Nissenbaum, Stephen. 1980. *Sex, Diet, and Debility in Jacksonian America: Sylvester Graham and Health Reform*. Westport, Conn.: Greenwood Press.

Nock, Steven L. 1993. *The Costs of Privacy: Surveillance and Reputation in America.* Hawthorne, N.Y.: Aldine/DeGruyter.

Nye, Russel Blaine. 1974. *Society and Culture in America, 1830–1860.* New York, Harper & Row.

Oldenburg, Ray. 1989. *The Great Good Place.* New York: Paragon House.

Oldenburg, Ray, and Dennis Brissett. 1983. "The Third Place." *Qualitative Sociology*, pp. 265–294.

Olson, Walter. 1988. "When Safety Becomes Dangerous." *Reason*, Vol. 20, No. 6 (November), pp. 52–53.

_____. 1992. *The Litigation Explosion.* New York: Plume Publishing Company.

Ornstein, Robert, and David Sobel. 1989. *Healthy Pleasures.* Reading, Mass: Addison-Wesley.

Owen, P. L. 1984. "The Measurement of the Concept of Denial Among Alcoholics." Ph.D. dissertation, University of Minnesota.

Perin, Constance. 1988. *Belonging in America: Reading Between the Lines.* Madison: University of Wisconsin Press.

Perinbanayagam, Robert S. 1985. *Signifying Acts.* Carbondale: Southern Illiniois University Press.

Plyman, Jeffrey S., and Lyndon D. Perkins. 1983. "Fitness Monitoring." *Public Management* (August), p. 7.

Polsky, Andrew. 1991. *The Rise of the Therapeutic State.* Princeton: Princeton University Press.

Postman, Neil. 1985. *Amusing Ourselves to Death: Public Discourse in the Age of Show Business.* New York: Viking Press.

"The Princess and the Press." 1997. *Frontline* documentary, aired by the Public Broadcasting Company (November).

Rafferty, Frances. 1997. "Nonsense Diet Leaves No Room for Respect." *London Times*, Educational Supplement (January 31).

Ranulf, Svend. 1937. *Moral Indignation and Middle-Class Psychology.* New York: Schocken.

Reiland, Ralph R. 1998. "Today Joe Camel, Tomorrow the Pillsbury Doughboy." *The American Enterprise* (September/October), pp. 12–13.

Rich, Adrienne. 1980. "Compulsory Heterosexuality and Lesbian Experience." *Signs*, Vol. 5, pp. 631–660.

Rieff, David. 1991. "Victims, All? Recovery, Co-Dependency, and the Art of Blaming Somebody Else." *Harper's* (October), pp. 49–56.

Rieff, Philip. 1987. *The Triumph of the Therapeutic: The Uses of Faith After Freud*, 2nd ed. Chicago: University of Chicago Press.

Riesman, David. 1950. *The Lonely Crowd: A Study of the Changing American Character.* New Haven: Yale University Press.

Ritzer, George. 1993. *The McDonaldization of American Society.* Thousand Oaks, Calif.: Pine Forge Press.

Robbe-Grille, Alain. 1972. "For a Voluptuous Tomorrow." *Saturday Review* (May 20), pp. 44–46.

Rodale, J. I. 1966. *Rodale's System for Mental Power and Natural Health.* Englewood Cliffs, N.J.: Prentice-Hall.

Rogers, Will. 1975. *The Cowboy Philosopher on Prohibition*. Stillwater, Okla.: Will Rogers Memorial Commission.

Roiphe, Katie. 1994. *The Morning After: Sex, Fear, and Feminism*. Boston: Little, Brown.

Room, Robert. 1984. "Alcohol and Ethnography: A Case of Problem Deflation?" *Current Anthropology*, Vol. 25, pp. 169–191.

Rosenau, Pauline Marie. 1992. *Postmodernism and the Social Sciences*. Princeton: Princeton University Press.

Rossi, Alice (Ed.). 1993. *The Feminist Papers: From Adams to de Beauvoir*. New York: Columbia University Press.

Rudy, D. R. 1986. *Becoming Alcoholic*. Carbondale: Southern Illinois University Press.

Sacks, Peter. 1996. *Generation X Goes to College*. LaSalle, Ill.: Open Court Press.

Safire, William. 1997. Commentary in *New York Times News Service* (November 18).

Saletan, William. 1989. "If Fetuses Are People. . . . " *New Republic* (September 18), p. 23.

Salinger, J. D. 1951/1991. *The Catcher in the Rye*. Boston: Little, Brown.

Samuel, Peter, and Peter Spencer. 1993. "Facts Catch Up with 'Political' Science." *Consumers' Research* (May), pp. 10–15.

Scheer, Robert. 1994. "Butt Out." *Playboy*, Vol. 41, No. 8 (August), p. 41.

Scheff, Thomas. 1966. *Being Mentally Ill: A Sociological Theory*. Chicago: Aldine Publishing Co.

Schofield, William. 1973. *Psychotherapy: The Purchase of Friendship*. Englewood Cliffs, N.J.: Prentice-Hall.

Schulberg, H. C., and R. W. Manderscheid. 1989. "The Changing Network of Mental Health Service Delivery." In C. A Taube and D. Mechanic (Eds.), *The Future of Mental Health Services Research*. Washington, D.C: U.S. Department of Human Services.

Schuman, Joseph. 1998. "Soda Pop Called Danger to Teens." *Tulsa World* (October 22), p. 2.

Schur, Edwin. 1976. *The Awareness Trap*. New York: McGraw-Hill.

Schwartz, Hillel. 1986. *Never Satisfied: A Cultural History of Diets, Fantasies, and Fat*. New York: Free Press.

_____. 1996. "Introduction to the Question of Illness and Fitness." In Micki McGee and Hillel Schwartz (Eds.), *The Body in Question*. New York: YMCA of America.

Scott, Marvin, and Stanford Lyman. 1968. "Accounts." *American Sociological Review*, Vol. 33, No. 1, pp. 46–62.

Scott, Robert A. 1979. *The Making of Blind Men: A Study of Adult Socialization*. New Brunswick, N.J.: Transaction Books.

Seely, David. 1987. "The No Decade." *Texas Monthly* (June), pp. 104–109, 156–158.

Sennett, Richard. 1975. *The Fall of Public Man*. New York: Doubleday.

Shapiro, Michael. J. (Ed.). 1984. *Language and Politics*. New York: New York University Press.

Shattuc, Jane M. 1997. *The Talking Cure: T.V. Talk Shows and Women*. New York: Routledge.

Shaw, David. 1996. *The Pleasure Police: How Bluenose Busybodies and Lily-Livered Alarmists Are Taking All the Fun Out of Life.* New York: Doubleday.

Shields, Rob. 1992. *Lifestyle Shopping: The Subject of Consumption.* London: Routledge.

Sinclair, A. 1962. *The Era of Excess.* Boston: Little, Brown.

Slaughter, James B. 1985. *Settlers, Southerners, Americans: The History of Essex County, Virginia, 1608–1984.* Tappahannock, Va.: Essex County Board of Supervisors.

Smith, Dinitia. 1984. "The New Puritanism." *New York Magazine* (June 11), p. 27.

Smith, Timothy Lawrence. 1965. *Revivalism and Social Reform: American Protestantism on the Eve of the Civil War.* New York: Harper & Row.

Sommers, Christina Hoff. 1994. *Who Stole Feminism?* New York: Simon and Schuster.

Sowell, Thomas. 1996. "California Leads the Battle Against Ideological Bullies." *Daily Oklahoman* (December 2), p. 2.

Spaceapan, Shirlynn, and Stuart Oskamp. 1992. *Helping and Being Helped: Naturalistic Studies.* Newbury Park, Calif.: Sage Publications.

Spacks, Patricia. 1985. *Gossip.* New York: Knopf.

Staples, William G. 1997. *The Culture of Surveillance: Discipline and Social Control in the United States.* New York: St. Martin's Press.

Stein, Howard F. 1982a. "'Health' and 'Wellness' and Euphemism: The Cultural Context of Insidious Draconian Health Policy." *Continuing Education* (March), pp. 33–44.

———. 1982b. "Wellness as Illusion." *Delaware Medical Journal,* Vol. 54, No. 11 (November), pp. 637–641.

———. 1985. "Alcoholism as Metaphor in American Culture: Ritual Desecration as Social Integration." *Ethos,* Vol. 13, pp. 195–235.

Stockwell, H.G. et. al. 1992. "Environmental Tobacco Smoke and Lung Cancer Risk in Nonsmoking Women. *Journal of the National Cancer Institute* (September 16, 1992), pp. 1417–1422.

Straus, Murray. 1980. *Behind Closed Doors: Violence in the American Family.* Garden City, N.Y.: Anchor/Doubleday.

Strong, P. M. 1983. "The Importance of Being Erving: Erving Goffman, 1922–1982. *Sociology of Health and Illness,* Vol. 5, No. 3, pp. 345–355.

Strothers, William G. 1995. "Parking Abuse." *Mainstream* (February), pp. 13–14.

Sullum, Jacob. 1991. "Smoke and Mirrors." *Reason* (February), pp. 28–33.

Sykes, Charles J. 1992. *A Nation of Victims.* New York: St. Martin's Press.

Szasz, Thomas S. 1961. *The Myth of Mental Illness.* New York: Dell Publishing Co.

———. 1977. *The Theology of Medicine.* New York: Harper Colophon Books.

———. 1984. *The Therapeutic State.* Buffalo, N.Y.: Prometheus Books.

———. 1985. *Ceremonial Chemistry.* Holmes Beach, Fl.: Learning Editions.

———. 1994. "Mental Illness Is Still a Myth." *Society,* Vol. 31 (May 1994), pp. 34–37.

Tabori, Paul. 1959. *The Natural Science of Stupidity.* Philadelphia: Childton Publishing Co.

Taylor, Jane. 1801/1976. *Original Poems for Infant Minds, and Rhymes for the Nursery.* New York: Garland Publishing Co.

Taylor, Sharon. 1996. "You're in My Spot." *Newsweek* (February 19), p. 20.

Telemaque, Maratos. 1995. "No Smoke Without a Greek." *Spectator*, Vol. 275, No. 8736 (December 16), p. 46.

Tenner, Edward. 1996. *Why Things Bite Back: Technology and the Revenge of Unintended Consequences*. New York: Alfred Knopf.

Thomas, Laurence. 1994. "The Logic of Gossip." In Robert Goodman and Aaron Ben-Ze'ev (Eds.), *Good Gossip*. Lawrence: University of Kansas Press.

Tiger, Lionel. 1992. *The Pursuit of Pleasure*. Boston: Little, Brown.

Tisdale, Sally. 1994. *Talk Dirty to Me*. New York: Doubleday.

Todd, Terry. 1994. "Muscle Behind Bars." *Muscle & Fitness*, Vol. 55, No. 10 (October), pp. 160–163.

Tollison, Robert D. (Ed.). 1986. *Smoking and Society: Toward a More Balanced Assessment*. Lexington, Mass.: Lexington Press.

Tribe, Lawrence. 1992. *Abortion: The Clash of Opposites*. New York: W. W. Norton.

Trujillo, René. 1996. "Human Rights in the 'Age of Discovery.'" In Rita C. Manning and René Trujillo (Eds.), *Social Justice in a Diverse Society*. Mountain View, Calif.: Mayfield Publishing Co.

Turner, Ralph, and Lewis Killian. 1987. *Collective Behavior*. Englewood Cliffs, N.J.: Prentice-Hall.

VanDeVeer, Donald. 1986. *Paternalistic Intervention: The Moral Bounds of Benevolence*. Princeton: Princeton University Press.

Vatz, R., and L. Weinberg. 1983. *Thomas Szasz: Primary Values and Major Contentions*. Buffalo, N.Y.: Prometheus Books.

Vidal, Gore. 1992. "Monotheism and its Discontents." *The Nation*, 255 (July 13, 1992), pp. 37, 54–57.

Viscusi, W. Kip. 1992. *Smoking: Making the Risky Decision*. New York: Oxford University Press.

Viscusi, W. Kip. 1994. "Cigarette Taxation and the Social Consequences of Smoking." Cambridge, Mass.: National Bureau of Economic Research, Working Paper No. 4891.

Wagner, David. 1997. *The New Temperance: The American Obsession with Sin and Vice*. Boulder: Westview Press.

Wallace, J. 1985. "Critical Issues in Alcoholism Therapy." In S. Zimberg, J. Wallace, and S. B. Blume (Eds.), *Practical Approaches to Alcoholism Psychotherapy*. New York: Plenum Press.

Watney, Simon. 1989. *Policing Desire: Pornography, AIDS and the Media*. Minneapolis: University of Minnesota Press.

Watts, Alan. 1970. *Does It Matter? Essays on Man's Relation to Materiality*. New York: Pantheon Books.

Weber, Max. 1930. *The Protestant Ethic and the Spirit of Capitalism*. London: G. Allen and Unwin.

Whitehead, Barbara. 1997. *The Divorce Culture*. New York: Alfred Knopf.

Whorton, James C. 1984. *Crusaders for Fitness: The History of American Health Reformers*. Princeton: Princeton University Press.

Wildavsky, Aaron. 1988. *Searching for Safety*. Rutgers, N.J.: Transaction Publishing Co.

Winokur, Jon. 1992. *The Portable Curmudgeon Redux*. New York: Dutton.

Wolf, Naomi. 1992. *The Beauty Myth: How Images of Beauty Are Used Against Women*. New York: Doubleday.

Wolfe, Alan. 1989. *Whose Keeper? Social Science and Moral Obligation*. Berkeley: University of California Press.

Wuthnow, Robert. 1994. *Sharing the Journey: Support Groups and America's New Quest for Community*. New York: Free Press.

Yardley, Jonathan. 1996. "You Can Have Your Cake, But Don't Eat It." *Washington Post* (January 8), p. B-2.

Zilbergeld, Bernard. 1983. *The Shrinking of America*. Boston: Little, Brown.

Zimmerman, Dennis, and Jane G. Gravelle. 1994. "Cigarette Taxes to Fund Health Care Reform: An Economic Analysis." *Congressional Research Service Report* (March 8, 1994), pp. 94–214.

Zola, Irving K. 1977. "Healthism and Disabling Medicalization." In Illich et al., *Disabling Profession*. London: Marion Boyars.

Zuboff, Shoshana. 1988. *In the Age of the Smart Machine*. New York: Basic Books.

Index

V-chips, 127